Bhabha
and his
Magnificent Obsessions

Vignettes in Physics

A series by **G Venkataraman**

The Many Phases of Matter

Why Are Things the Way They Are?

Bose and His Statistics

Chandrasekhar and His Limit

A Hot Story

At the Speed of Light

The Quantum Revolution (3 volumes)

1. The Breakthrough
2. QED: The Jewel of Physics
3. What is Reality?

Raman and His Effect

Bhabha and His Magnificent Obsessions

Saha and His Formula

The Big and the Small (2 volumes)

1. Journey into the Microcosm: The Story of Elementary Particles
2. From the Microcosm to the Macrocosm: The Fascinating Link Between Particle Physics and Cosmology

Prime Minister of India launches the birth centenary of Dr Homi Jehangir Bhabha

Extract from Dr Manmohan Singh's address on 30 October 2008

It gives me very great pleasure to launch the celebrations to commemorate the birth centenary of Dr Homi Bhabha. Over the next one year, we will celebrate the far-sighted vision and scientific and intellectual legacy of Dr Homi Bhabha whose vision was shared and supported by Pandit Jawaharlal Nehru. These two great sons and intellectual giants of our country were the fathers of our atomic energy programme.

Dr Bhabha's leadership of the atomic energy programme spanned 22 years. It began in 1944 with a letter he wrote to the Sir Dorabji Trust proposing the establishment of an institute devoted to fundamental research. He continued his work with passion and commitment right till his untimely death in an air accident in 1966.

Since the setting up of the Tata Institute of Fundamental Research in December 1945 we have come a long way. This has been possible because of the strong foundations laid by Dr Bhabha during his lifetime.

The three-stage nuclear programme, based on a closed nuclear fuel cycle, was first outlined by Dr Bhabha in a conference on Development of Atomic Energy for Peaceful Purposes in India held as early as 1954 in New Delhi. It was based on self-reliance and sought to exploit our plentiful thorium reserves and our existing industrial capability.

Dr Bhabha sought to achieve a balance between indigenous development and international cooperation. He negotiated the setting up of reactors at Tarapur on a turnkey basis to demonstrate our willingness to take recourse to international trade in commercial nuclear power. But he also went ahead with the opening of uranium mines at Jadugoda in Singbhum despite its seemingly unviable ore grade. That was at a time when uranium was available in the international market.

Thus we got a head start in nuclear power as well as our self-reliant three-stage development with a robust and commercially successful first stage consisting of PHWRs that operated on natural uranium produced at Jadugoda.

The speed with which we can develop nuclear power is constrained by the availability of uranium. The initiative to open civil nuclear trade with the international community is a step towards accelerating the development of nuclear energy in the service of our country. This initiative will have far reaching effects on the growth of nuclear energy in India and I can say that this is a period of transition in our programme.

As we develop and expand the nuclear power programme, I believe that we should redouble our efforts in promoting indigenous R&D and manufacturing capabilities and in the autonomous pursuit of the three-stage nuclear programme and the strategic programme.

India has contributed successfully towards the construction of the Large Hadron Collidor built by CERN in Geneva. We are a party to the most advanced global project in the area of fusion science—ITER. India is also part of the advanced research reactor project being built in France, the Jules Horowitz Reactor. Clearly our capabilities, particularly in nuclear science and engineering, are being recognised the world over.

In August 1955, Dr Homi Bhabha said 'For the full industrialisation of the underdeveloped countries, for the continuation of our civilisation and its further development, atomic energy is not merely an aid, it is an absolute necessity. The acquisition by man of the knowledge of how to release and use atomic energy must be recognised as the third epoch of human history.'

Dr Homi Bhabha spent his whole life in pursuit of this grand vision. He inspired a generation of scientists with his bold dreams and ambitions for the nation and his selfless service. He was a great scientific pioneer and a great builder of modern India.

If we show the same wisdom, pragmatism and foresight that Dr Homi Bhabha did, I have no doubt that we will move ahead purposefully and substantially to realise his grand vision.

PMO: Press Information Bureau, Government of India

Vignettes in Physics

Bhabha

and his

Magnificent Obsessions

G VENKATARAMAN

Universities Press

BHABHA AND HIS MAGNIFICENT OBSESSIONS

Universities Press (India) Private Limited

Registered Office
3-6-747/1/A & 3-6-754/1, Himayatnagar, Hyderabad 500 029, Telangana, India
info@universitiespress.com; www.universitiespress.com

Distributed by
Orient Blackswan Private Limited

Registered Office
3-6-752, Himayatnagar, Hyderabad 500 029, Telangana, India

Other Offices
Bengaluru, Chennai, Guwahati, Hyderabad, Kolkata,
Mumbai, New Delhi, Noida, Patna, Visakhapatnam

First Published 1994
Reprinted 1997, 2004, 2005, 2008, 2009 (thrice), 2013, 2016, 2018, 2019, 2022, 2023

ISBN: 978 81 7371 007 0

Typeset by
Access Centre, Hyderabad 500 003

Printed at
B.B. Press
Noida 201 301

Published by
Universities Press (India) Private Limited
3-6-747/1/A & 3-6-754/1, Himayatnagar
Hyderabad 500 029, Telangana, India

Contents

Preface

To the adult reader

This book and others in this series written by me are inspired by the memory of my son Suresh who left this world soon after completing school. Suresh and I often used to discuss physics. It was then that I introduced him to the celebrated *Feynman Lectures*.

Hans Bethe has described Feynman as the most original scientist of this century. To that perhaps may be added the statement that Feynman was also the most scintillating teacher of physics in this century.

The Feynman Lectures are great but they are at the textbook level and meant for serious reading. Moreover, they are a bit expensive, at least for the average Indian student. It seemed to me that there was scope for small books on diverse topics in physics which would stimulate interest, making at least some of our young students take up later a serious study of physics and reach for the Feynman as well as the Landau classics.

Small books inevitably remind me of Gamow's famous volumes. They were wonderful, and stimulated me to no small extent. Times have changed, physics has grown and we clearly need other books, though written in the same spirit.

In attempting these volumes, I have chosen a style of my own. I have come across many books on popular science where elaborate sentences often tend to obscure the scientific essence. I have therefore opted for simple English, and I don't make any apologies for it. If a simple style was good enough for the great Enrico Fermi, it is also good enough for me. I have also employed at times a chatty style. This is deliberate. Feynman uses this with consummate skill, and I have decided to follow in his footsteps (whether I have succeeded or not, is for readers to say). This book is meant to be read for fun and excitement. It is a book you can even lie down in bed and read. Without going to sleep I hope!

Naturally I have some basic objectives, the most important of which is to stimulate the curiosity of the reader. Here and there the reader may fail to grasp some details, and in fact I have deliberately pitched things a bit high on occasions. But if the reader is able to experience at least in some small measure the *excitement* of science, then my purpose would have been achieved. Apart from excitement, I have also tried to convey that although we might draw boundaries and try to compartmentalise Nature into different subjects, she herself knows no such boundaries. So we can always start anywhere, take a random walk and catch a good glimpse of Nature's glory. Where she is concerned, all topics are "fashionable". There is today an unnecessary polarisation of the young towards subjects that are supposed to be fashionable. To my mind this is unhealthy, and I have tried to counter it.

This series is essentially meant for the curious. With humility, I would like to regard it as some sort of a "Junior Feynman Series", if one might call it that. With much love, and sadness, it is dedicated to the memory of Suresh who inspired it.

To the young reader

This book is about a remarkable man, Homi Jehangir Bhabha. He went to Cambridge in the late twenties at the young age of eighteen, studied physics, and started his research career there. In 1939, he came to India on what was supposed to be a short vacation. But the Second World War intervened and Bhabha was forced to stay on. For all of us, it was a tremendous blessing because later he steered the country's scientific destiny.

Great scientists are remembered for their outstanding achievements. Almost invariably, they are purely scientific. But Bhabha's contributions were in many dimensions. What exactly were they? Read on and find out!

Acknowledgements

Writing this book has been a totally different experience since it is about a man who directly enabled me (and hundreds like me) to pursue a satisfying scientific career here in this country. In preparing this volume, I have had to lean for help on many sources which I wish to acknowledge. Firstly, I would like to express my gratitude to Dr.V.K. Balasubramaniam for lengthy and most valuable conversations about Homi Bhabha and the early days of the Tata Institute of Fundamental Research (TIFR). Professor Virendra Singh and Professor R. Vijayaraghavan were kind enough to provide me with much original material concerning the activities of TIFR.

To Professor B.M. Udgaonkar, I am indebted for access to the Bhabha–Chandrasekhar correspondence reproduced in Chapter 5. I have also derived useful material from (i) *Nuclear India* (published by the Department of Atomic Energy, Vol.26/1/1989), (ii) *Collected Scientific Papers of Homi Bhabha* (published by TIFR), (iii) *Homi Bhabha as an Artist* (Marg Publication, edited by Jamshed Bhabha), (iv) *The Heartbeat of a Trust* by R.M. Lala (published by Tata McGraw-Hill) and (v) *Science Today* (Times of India Publication, October 1984 issue). Special thanks are due to Dr. M.R. Balakrishnan of the Bhabha Atomic Research Centre (BARC) for helping me with archival material as well as several photographs. Mr. A. Ratnakar as usual was a pillar of strength. I am particularly grateful to Mr. Jamshed Bhabha for his kind and sympathetic interest in my effort and for making several useful suggestions. Mrs. G. Naga Nirmala provided, as usual, valuable assistance in preparing the manuscript. Friendly cooperation from the Publisher is also acknowledged.

G. VENKATARAMAN

1 *Homi Bhabha—A Thumbnail Sketch*

These days, young people often dream of going abroad even before they have completed their studies. They are eager to go out, not merely to pursue higher studies or even research but to settle there permanently. Half a century ago, a young man made the journey in the reverse direction. He was then about twenty-nine years of age and had spent thirteen impressionable years in England. He had studied and worked in Cambridge, then the Mecca of physics, and had an excellent track record in research. True he came to India for a short holiday but he stayed on, not merely to show that he could do equally well in research in India but, more importantly, to change the course of science and technology in the country. This book is about that man – Homi Jehangir Bhabha.

Homi Bhabha was a Parsi. The Parsis are originally from Iran or rather Persia as it was called in those days. Their religion is Zoroastrianism which is probably as old as the Hindu religion. Indeed, ancient Parsis and the Vedic Aryans had much in common. When Islam spread from Arabia to Persia, some of the Parsis fled seeking religious asylum and a group of them landed in Surat in the eighth century. The story goes that when they made a representation to Rama Jadhav the local ruler to let them stay in India, the ruler indicated that there was no room for an outside group. This he did by offering to the leader of the refugees, a pot filled to the brim with milk. The reply was symbolic. This was done by dropping some unrefined sugar (*gur*) into the milk. By so doing, the immigrants were saying that they would mix easily with the locals, add sweetness and not be a burden. Accepting the assurance, the ruler granted them permission to stay.

The Parsis have remained mainly on the west coast, in and around Gujarat and Bombay. True to the promise they gave at the time they were granted asylum, they mingled freely with the native population and also adopted the local language (Gujarati) besides many other customs. In return, the Parsis were allowed the freedom to follow their own religion and their ancient traditions. They are very energetic and have done particularly well in trade and commerce. Above all, they are peace loving. They are community conscious and always lend a helping hand through charities and trusts, especially to fellow Parsis in need.

When the British came, the Parsis eagerly took to English education. So did the people in South India and in Bengal. But the impact of English education was totally different in the three cases. For the Bengalis, Western education was a window to Western thought. The writings of Voltaire, Rousseau, Marx and others kindled a revolutionary fervour and we saw towards the end of the last century, a mini renaissance which spilled over into this century. Professor Chandrasekhar (see the companion volume *Chandrasekhar and His Limit*) believes that the spark we saw in Indian physics in the twenties (I am referring here to the epoch-making work of Raman, Bose and Saha) was but an echo of this revolutionary fervour and spirit.

In contrast to the Bengalis, the South Indians looked upon English education as a passport to jobs. While a few rose to high positions, most were content with clerical jobs. There was therefore nothing like the renaissance witnessed in Bengal.

The impact of Western education on the Parsis was totally different. They not only welcomed the opportunity to learn English but also took to Western music, art and culture in a big way. And unlike the Bengalis or the South Indians, they mixed freely with the British and took to their life style.

The Parsi community was always rather small – it remains so even today. Nevertheless, the community has produced distinguished men and women, far out of proportion to its size. To name just a few, there was the visionary Jamshedji Tata after whom the city of Jamshedpur is named, Bharat Ratna J.R.D. Tata known for his numerous contributions, the eminent jurist Nani Palkhivala, Field Marshal Maneckshaw, and the internationally famous musician Zubin Mehta. Homi Bhabha belongs to this distinguished set.

Bhabha was born on 30 October 1909. His grandfather – with the same name as his, i.e., Dr. H.J. Bhabha – was the Inspector General of Education in the state of Mysore. Bhabha's father was named Jehangir Hormusji Bhabha. He was born in Bombay in 1876 but was brought up and educated at Bangalore. Bhabha's mother Meheren (nee Meheren Panday) was the grand daughter of Sir Dinshaw Maneckji Petit. Hormusji's sister, i.e., Homi Bhabha's aunt Meherbai married Sir Dorab Tata, son of Jamshedji Tata. Homi Bhabha was thus well connected; the Tata connection in particular, was to prove useful later on.

Bhabha's father J.H. Bhabha was educated at Oxford and later qualified as a lawyer. He started his career by working in the judicial service in the state of Mysore. But when he got married he moved to Bombay which is where young Homi grew up. In Bombay, J.H. Bhabha was associated with many enterprises of the Tata industrial empire.

When he was a child, Homi used to sleep very little compared to children of his age. His parents were naturally worried and consulted many doctors but none of them could say what the problem was. Finally, a European doctor said that there was really no problem with the child; he slept little simply because he had a hyperactive brain!

Young Homi was educated at the Cathedral and John Connon High School in Bombay. He was not much interested in sports but was absolutely brilliant in studies, and the many prizes he won made him a celebrity. He was also gifted with a musical ear. Once during his childhood he began to cry loudly. His mother tried to soothe and console him in various ways but Homi would not stop crying. In the meantime, from another room strains of music on the gramophone were heard. The moment this happened, the child stopped crying and began to listen attentively. The mother thus discovered the musical interest of her child and thereafter always used it to her advantage to stop the child from crying!

As a boy Homi was attracted to playing with meccano as it challenged his abilities. He was also a voracious reader and his reading was helped by his father's wonderful collection of books on various subjects, particularly art and music. And of course, Bhabha showed his strong liking for science from a young age. His parents encouraged his interests by acquiring many books on science. It is said that by the age of sixteen, Homi Bhabha had already studied the special theory of relativity.

As a boy, Bhabha often used to go to the house of his aunt Meherbai Tata, especially for lunch. Many national leaders including Mahatma Gandhi used to call on the Tatas, and as a result Homi was exposed to discussion on national affairs. Homi's father was a nationalist in spirit and so were the Tatas. Thus young Homi grew up in a nationalistic environment; later this moulded his attitude on many matters.

At the age of 15, Homi Bhabha passed the Senior Cambridge examination. He then entered the Elphinstone College in Bombay and later the Royal Institute of Science, also in Bombay. At the age of eighteen, his parents decided to send him to England for higher studies; they could easily afford it.

Bhabha joined the Gonville and Caius College in Cambridge in 1927. His uncle Sir Dorab Tata had studied in the same college and had made a donation of 25,000 pounds to it in 1920. It is interesting that while the father went to Oxford, the son went to Cambridge. In the case of the Nehru family, it was the other way about; the father, i.e., Jawaharlal Nehru went to Cambridge while his daughter, Indira Gandhi, went to Oxford.

The intention of Bhabha's parents in sending their son to Cambridge was very clear. They knew he was brilliant and they felt that if he was trained in engineering, he could build a great career in the Tata industries. However, Homi's heart was not in engineering but in science. Nevertheless, in order to please his parents he enrolled for the B.A. degree in mechanical engineering. Even as he was studying engineering, young Bhabha conveyed strongly to his father his passion for science. In a letter written in 1928 he said:

> I seriously say to you that business or job as an engineer is not the thing for me. It is totally foreign to my nature and radically opposed to my temperament and opinions. Physics is my line. I know I shall do great things here. For, each man can do best and excel in only that thing of which he is passionately fond, in which he believes, as I do, that he has the ability to do it, that he is in fact born and destined to do it. My success will not depend on what A or B thinks of me. My success will be what I make of my work. Besides, India is not a land where science cannot be carried on.

Mark those last words in the above quotation. Bhabha continued:

> I am burning with a desire to do physics. I will and must do it some time. It is my only ambition. I have no desire to be a 'successful' man or the head of a big firm. There are intelligent people who like that and let them do it. I hear you saying 'But you are not Socrates or Einstein'. No — and that is what Berlioz's father said to Berlioz. He called him a useless musician when he was young — Hector Berlioz who is now accepted as one of the world's greatest geniuses and France's greatest musician. How can anybody else know at what time what one will do, if there is nothing to show. ... It is no use saying to Beethoven 'You must be a scientist for it is a great thing', when he did not care two hoots for science; or to Socrates 'Be an engineer; it is the work of an intelligent man'. It is not in the nature of things. I therefore earnestly implore you to let me do physics.

Bhabha's yearning for physics was perfectly understandable. Not only did he have the intrinsic mathematical ability so necessary for a successful physicist, but more important, this was also the period when physics was going through a major revolution – see the companion volume *The Quantum Revolution*: *Part* I. Added to all this, Rutherford's lab in Cambridge was regularly churning out sensational discoveries. And to cap it all, there was Dirac there in Cambridge, adding poetry to physics. Is it any wonder that Bhabha's attention turned where it did?

Bhabha's father saw his son's point and yielded. But he made a deal. He said that he would finance his [Homi's] stay in Cambridge for two more years to enable him to take the Mathematics Tripos, provided he completed his studies in mechanical engineering and came out successful. Just before the Mechanical Tripos exam, Bhabha wrote to his father: "No exam was ever a test of original or creative ability in anybody. However, don't let that disturb you; you shall get the results you want."

Bhabha came through the Mechanical Tripos with a first class. True to his promise, his father now allowed Homi to study mathematics. Two years later, Bhabha cleared the Mathematics Tripos, once again with a first.

Unlike in India, Bhabha seems to have developed a liking for athletics and sports in Cambridge. W.B. Lewis, a fellow student at Cambridge and who later headed the Atomic energy programme in Canada (and in that capacity came into close contact with Bhabha) has this to say:

> We first met as freshmen at Cambridge in the same college, Gonville and Caius, in 1927, and in its boat club ... Being at first light in weight, Homi Bhabha was appreciated as a coxswain in the rowing eights; he was, however, growing and putting on weight so he transferred his athletic activities to track running at "Fenners" [playground in Cambridge] and to tennis.

After completing the Maths Tripos, Bhabha won the Rouse Ball Travelling Fellowship in 1932 which enabled him to travel to other places and work there. Thus he went to Zurich to work with Pauli and later to Rome to work with Fermi. By now he was well into research and in 1934 he was awarded the Isaac Newton Studentship. He held this studentship for three years, working mainly in Cambridge with a short spell in Bohr's Institute in Copenhagen. In between, Bhabha completed the requirements for the Ph.D. degree. His thesis supervisor was R.H. Fowler, who was also the supervisor for Chandrasekhar (see the volume, *Chandrasekhar and His Limit*).

In 1937, he was awarded the 1851 Exhibition Scholarship which enabled him to continue his research work at Cambridge.

In September 1939, the Second World War broke out. At that time, Bhabha was in India on what he intended to be a short holiday but the war changed his plans. Most of the scientists in England went over to the war effort and basic research everywhere in Western Europe came more or less to a grinding halt. Going back to England to continue research did not seem a practical idea, especially as Hitler was rapidly running over Europe and an attack on England seemed imminent. The question naturally arose as to what he should do in India. A few universities made an offer – I believe Allahabad and Calcutta were among these. Finally Bhabha accepted the offer of Readership from the Indian Institute of Science in the Physics Department. This was a turning point in his life – see also Box 1.1.

The Indian Institute of Science (I.I.Sc.) in Bangalore was founded by Jamshedji Tata way back in 1911. Even today, among the locals, the Institute is popularly known as Tata Institute. Because a Tata founded it, the Tatas always had a representative of theirs on the Institute Council, and both Bhabha's grandfather and his father had served there. An important attraction of the Institute in those days was the presence of C.V. Raman as head of the Physics Department – see the volume, *Raman and His Effect.* Raman had built up a lively school of physics, and this in many ways influenced Bhabha's decision.

To help Homi Bhabha in his work, the Sir Dorab Tata Trust (remember, Bhabha's aunt was married to Sir Dorab) gave him a small grant. With this, Bhabha established the Cosmic Ray Research Unit. In passing I should also mention that on the recommendation of Jawaharlal Nehru, Mr. J.R.D. Tata who was closely connected with the Sir Dorab Tata Trust suggested to the Trust that a grant be made to Meghnad Saha in Calcutta for building a cyclotron. Even before Bhabha arrived, Raman was seeking to start research in nuclear physics at I.I.Sc., and had approached the Tata Trust for a grant, which was refused. Perhaps the Trust felt that having supported Saha, there was no need to fund nuclear physics again in another institute, even though it had been founded by none other than Jamshedji Tata.

For Homi Bhabha, there was an ocean of difference between Bangalore and Cambridge, especially considering that in Cambridge he could make frequent contacts with peers. But Homi took it all in his stride. Years later when facilities in India had improved, most

Box 1.1 Prior to Bhabha, there was another distinguished Indian who went through a similar experience. He was P.C. Mahalanobis. Prasantha Chandra Mahalanobis was born in a well-to-do family in Calcutta in the year 1893. After receiving the B.Sc. degree in physics in 1912, he left for England for further studies. As the result of a chance encounter with a friend in Cambridge, he decided to study mathematics. Later, finding mathematics too abstract, he again switched over to physics.

In Cambridge, Mahalanobis came in contact with the mathematics genius Ramanujan. One day Ramanujan invited Mahalanobis for lunch and while he was cooking, Mahalanobis kept himself busy with a small mathematics puzzle. After working out the solution, Mahalanobis read out the problem to Ramanujan. From the kitchen the latter dictated a continued fraction, and said the first term of that was the solution to the problem Mahalanobis was solving!

After completing the Cambridge Tripos examination in physics, Mahalanobis went to the Cavendish Laboratory of which Rutherford was the head. It was decided that Mahalanobis would work under C.T.R. Wilson (famous for his invention of the cloud chamber). Mahalanobis then returned to India on what he thought was a short vacation. Meanwhile, the First World War broke out and Mahalanobis was grounded in India. This was a turning point because thereafter Mahalanobis stayed in the country, in the process making great contributions to it.

A vacancy for the post of physics lecturer arose in the Presidency College because the Englishman holding the job had gone off to fight in the war. Mahalanobis was appointed to that post. Although he was teaching physics (and planned to pursue physics research under Wilson after the war), Mahalanobis became increasingly interested in mathematical statistics and its applications. This led to the founding of the Indian Statistical Institute which has now grown very big and has several branches throughout India. Of course, all this was possible because of the excellent research work done by Mahalanobis himself, for which he received international recognition. Like Bhabha, Mahalanobis, also a favourite of Nehru, was invited to join the Planning Commission. The Second Five Year Plan was largely his brain child.

Mahalanobis received many honours, including that of being elected a Fellow of the Royal Society. He died in 1972.

scientists came back only to complain and immediately leave. Bhabha was made of sterner stuff. He not only continued with research but began to collaborate with Indian colleagues. In Cambridge his work was influenced by experimental research in cosmic rays but here in India, cut off as he was (in any case, physics research, including experiments, had drastically slowed down due to the war), he began to take on problems which were more mathematical in nature. In a way this suited him, bringing forth the mathematician lurking inside. I shall tell you more about this in later chapters.

To get on with the story, Raman took an instant liking for Bhabha and promptly got him elected a Fellow of the Indian Academy of Sciences. He also proposed Bhabha's name for election as a Fellow of the Royal Society (FRS) and wrote to Dirac to second the proposal. Bhabha was duly elected FRS. In 1943 he was awarded the Adams Prize by the University of Cambridge for his work on cosmic rays. Professor Ramaseshan recalls Raman introducing Bhabha at the Annual Meeting of the Indian Academy in 1941. That year, the Meeting was held in Nagpur. Ramaseshan says:

> Bhabha gave two lectures – an honour which Raman usually reserved for himself. In introducing Bhabha, Raman said, "Bhabha is a great lover of music, a gifted artist, a brilliant engineer and an outstanding scientist ... He is the modern equivalent of Leonardo da Vinci."

We shall come back to Bhabha's multi-faceted personality in the last chapter, after discussing his scientific and technical achievements.

The Bangalore period of Bhabha is interesting for another very important reason because it was here that Bhabha had a go at experiments. Very rare are those physicists who work both in theory as well as with experiments. Fermi was an outstanding example in this category. Theorists generally like to stay away from experiments – they think it involves mundane work – and exceptionally rare is the case of a physicist hardened by years of theory having a crack at experiment. In India, experiments have their own added difficulty, and Bhabha's turning to experiments might be either a sign of rashness or extreme self-confidence. I don't know about that but this brief fling was to produce a tremendous fallout. Note once again Bhabha's *extremely positive attitude*, in marked contrast to the tendency among Indian scientists today to avoid hardware and experiments, despite the fact that conditions are undoubtedly much better.

At Bangalore, Bhabha initiated experiments to study the so-called hard component of the cosmic rays. I shall tell you more about cosmic rays in the next chapter; here I shall merely describe what Bhabha did. Basically, he was trying to test aspects of his cascade

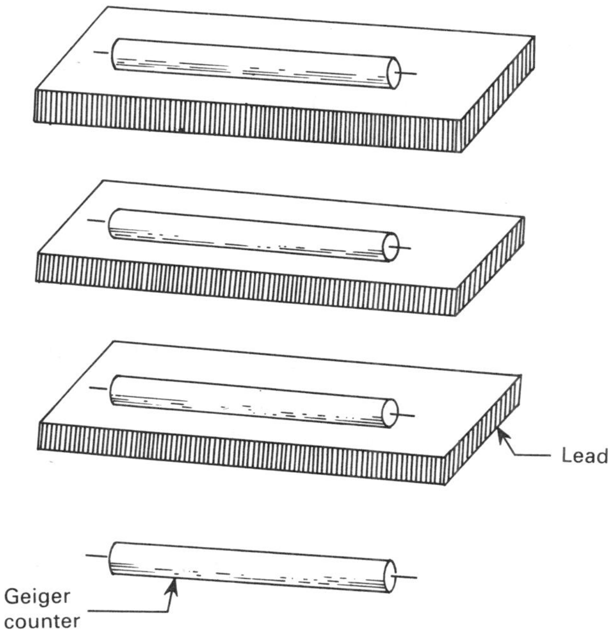

Fig.1.1 This is one of the counter telescopes used by Bhabha. It is made up of four Geiger counters with lead shields in between. The counters can detect radiation if it passes through them. The counters are so connected that unless the particle traverses all of them, it is not counted. This is why the arrangement is called a telescope – it is sensitive only to particles travelling vertically. The lead pieces are for cutting out the so-called soft component.

theory (see Chapter 3). For this purpose, he designed a Geiger-counter telescope which is sketched in Fig.1.1. A second telescope was also designed by him. These were fabricated in the workshop of the Institute. The year was 1944, and the war was still in progress. The American Air Force had a presence in India and Bhabha was able to make some contact with them. With their help he arranged for the counter telescopes to be flown in a B-29 bomber to reasonably high altitudes. On 26 December 1944, two flights were made upto about 5 km. Two days later another flight was made, this time upto 11 km. Yet another flight was made on 21 July 1945, this time going upto about 13 km. Being the monsoon period, the weather conditions were a bit rough. Bhabha also got built a cloud chamber identical to the one that was being used by Prof. Blackett at Manchester University. These experiences were to prove vital in launching various experimental programmes later.

In 1944, Bhabha was promoted from a Reader to a full Professor. The Institute was fine but already it was beginning to look a bit small for his plans. So Bhabha approached the Sir Dorab Tata Trust again, this time with a proposal to start an institute of his own which would be fully devoted to the nuclear sciences. This was not only a turning point for Bhabha but indeed for the country itself. The full story is reserved for a later chapter. The Tata Trust responded favourably to Bhabha's request and as a result the Tata Institute of Fundamental Research (TIFR) came into being. The Bangalore period was over and Bhabha now moved to Bombay. Reflecting on his stay in Bangalore, Bhabha later said, "I have great pleasure in recording that they were six very happy and fruitful years in my life".

The year was 1945. The war was over and physicists the world over were itching to resume their interrupted research. Here in India Bhabha geared up for the competition. Organisation came easily to Bhabha unlike to many others, and as an organiser of massive programmes, only Oppenheimer, popularly known as the Father of the Atomic Bomb, stands comparison.

Organisation was exciting but it also began to take its toll, and Bhabha found it increasingly difficult to devote time to his personal research. So his own scientific publications began to peter out and disappeared altogether after 1954 or so. But his loss was the gain of a new generation of young homegrown physicists who later went on to write a new chapter in the history of science in India.

Meanwhile, in 1947, India achieved Independence. True, the country had been rudely torn apart into two pieces and was drenched in the blood of the riots that followed, but even so expectations were high everywhere. Elsewhere in the world, atomic energy was being spoken of as an unlimited source of electric power and not merely as a source for weapons of mass destruction.

Bhabha saw his chance and swung into action. He was keen to launch an atomic energy programme in India for a variety of reasons, which I shall explain later. All I would like to say here is that atomic energy work not only propelled Bhabha into a much bigger orbit of activity but also brought him close to Jawaharlal Nehru, the Prime Minister. Together they worked wonders, and the

Nation owes a deep debt of gratitude to both for dragging India from the bullock cart to the modern age.

In 1964 Nehru died and the question on everybody's mind was whether Bhabha would continue to enjoy the same access to the PM as before and whether he would have the same equation as well. Before the answers could come, though, Nehru's successor, Lal Bahadur Shastri, died suddenly of a heart attack. On 22 January 1966 Bhabha addressed a huge condolence meeting at the Atomic Energy Establishment, Trombay, the premier laboratory he had founded. I was present in the audience. On the following day, Bhabha took off from Bombay for Geneva by an Air India flight. He was on his way to Vienna to attend a meeting. The plane never made it to Geneva. Just as it was about to land, it hit the Alps near the famous Mont Blanc peak. There were no survivors. Indeed for nearly fifteen years or so, no one could go near that spot – so inaccessible it was. Only later was a party able to visit the site and pick up some of the debris.

The Nation was shocked by Bhabha's sudden death when he was still so full of promise. Indira Gandhi, the new Prime Minister, while mourning Bhabha's death said that she was hoping to induct Bhabha into her Cabinet as a Minister. She spoke for the country when she observed:

> India will long cherish Homi Bhabha's memory, for he was deeply involved in her destiny and in the process of changing the texture and the quality of her society.

Usually, when a leading personality passes away, public establishments are closed as a mark of respect (at least in India). When Bhabha died, all the different units of the Department of Atomic Energy throughout the country – there are a large number of these units – observed a working day to honour a man who drove himself no end to give all that he could to science and to the country.

Bhabha is no more but his work lives. The outside world knows him largely for his scientific contributions whereas in India he is remembered more as an institution builder. These are but two sides of Homi Bhabha. There are many more, as you will discover later. In the following chapters, I shall describe the various achievements of Homi Bhabha and his multi-faceted personality.

2 *Cosmic Rays*

Bhabha's early work revolved around cosmic rays. The reason why this was so would be explained later. In this chapter, I shall offer a brief overview on cosmic rays so that we can appreciate better Bhabha's contributions.

Cosmic rays are extremely penetrating radiations coming from outer space. Over ninety years have passed since their discovery but even today we know little about their origin; only guesses are available.

The discovery of cosmic rays may be said to have occurred in 1900 when C.T.R. Wilson (the inventor of the cloud chamber) noticed that electroscopes exhibited leaks despite very careful insulation – see Box 2.1. Clearly radiation was coming from somewhere and

Box 2.1 The electroscope is one of the oldest instruments used for detecting charge. It consists of two gold "leaves" as in (a). When a charge is deposited as shown in (b), the leaves move apart on account of electrostatic repulsion. As long as the electroscope retains charge the leaves remain opened out. Wilson discovered that despite care, electroscopes lost the charge stored in them. Eventually this led to the discovery of cosmic rays.

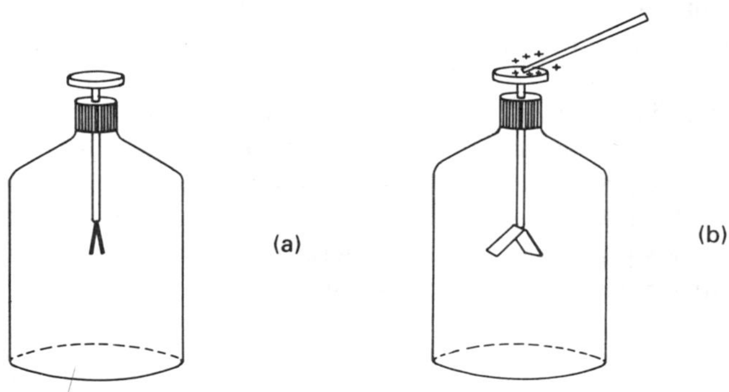

discharging the electroscope. Was it from the materials out of which the electroscope itself was constructed? In 1903 Rutherford and Cooke ruled this out. They surrounded the electroscope with lead and iron shields and found that the discharge rate went down considerably. The radiation was evidently coming from outside the apparatus but from where? Perhaps it was coming from the Earth, possibly originating in the radioactive materials there. If so, the intensity of the radiation should decrease as one goes up into the atmosphere. To check this out, one Father Wulf (a Jesuit priest) went up the Eiffel Tower in 1910. This was then the tallest man-made structure. Wulf spent three days on top of the tower and made observations using a sensitive electroscope designed by him (now called the Wulf electroscope). The electroscope continued to discharge as on the ground. If the radiations were coming from the ground, they should have been absorbed by the air between the ground and the tower top. But this did not seem to be the case. Wulf therefore suspected that there was "another source (of radiation) in the upper portions of the atmosphere". To verify this, in August 1912, Victor Hess of Austria climbed into a balloon, taking with him instruments to measure the intensity of this unknown radiation. He went up to about 5500 metres and to his great surprise observed that the intensity of the radiation actually increased. Clearly the radiation was coming from somewhere outside the atmosphere. Millikan in America who was also interested in this radiation contested this view but eventually yielded when the evidence was overwhelming and convincing. For a while this radiation was called *ultrasstrahlung*, the German word for radiation coming from beyond the atmosphere. The term *cosmic rays* was suggested in the early twenties by Millikan and continues to be used even today.

Research on cosmic rays during the last eight decades or so has centred around the following questions:

1. Where do these rays come from?
2. How are they produced in the first place?
3. What is their composition as they arrive at the top of the atmosphere?
4. What happens to them when they enter the atmosphere?

As of now, one has a reasonably good idea of the answers to questions 3 and 4. But about the first two, speculation continues.

Let us start with question 3. The radiation reaching the top of the atmosphere from outer space is referred to as *primary cosmic rays*. It consists of various types of nuclei but predominantly protons. The composition at the top of the atmospheres at two different latitudes is as in Table 2.1.

Table 2.1 Composition of the primary at two latitudes. All energies are included. Only relative values are shown. Z is the nuclear charge.

	Lat 55°N	Lat 30°N
Protons (Z=1)	1	1
Alphas (Z=2)	0.3	0.15
$6 < Z < 9$	0.007	0.005
$10 < Z$	0.003	0.002

The numbers are different at the two latitudes because the particles are charged and get deflected by the magnetic field of the Earth. More about this soon.

Now take a look at Box 2.2. This should prepare you for a discussion of the energies of the primaries, which is the next item of interest. The primaries are very energetic, energies in the GeV range being common. Particles with energies as high as 10^{17}eV are

Box 2.2 Suppose an electron is moved up against an electric potential as shown in figure (a). Work has to be done for this purpose, just as work has to be done to lift a stone against the force of gravity. The work done in moving an electron against a potential of 1 volt is referred to as an *electron volt* (eV). One eV = 1.602×10^{-12}ergs. In atomic physics, the eV is a convenient energy unit. In nuclear physics one uses MeV (million electron volt) and in elementary particle physics the unit GeV (giga electron volt). Cosmic-ray energies are expressed in GeV and upwards.

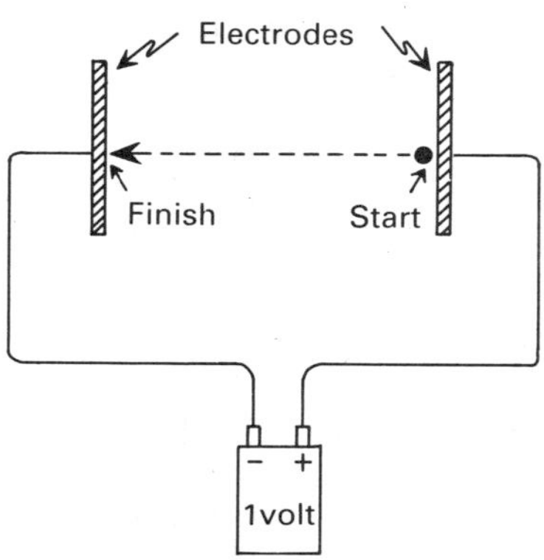

known. In fact, until giant accelerators came to be built, cosmic radiation was regarded as a high-energy physics laboratory (for a brief story on accelerators, see *Why Are Things the Way They Are?*).

The primaries are charged particles. Since the Earth acts like a big bar magnet (see Fig. 2.1), the particles get deflected as they approach the Earth. Naturally, the deflection would depend on (i) the particle energy, and (ii) distance of closest approach, also known

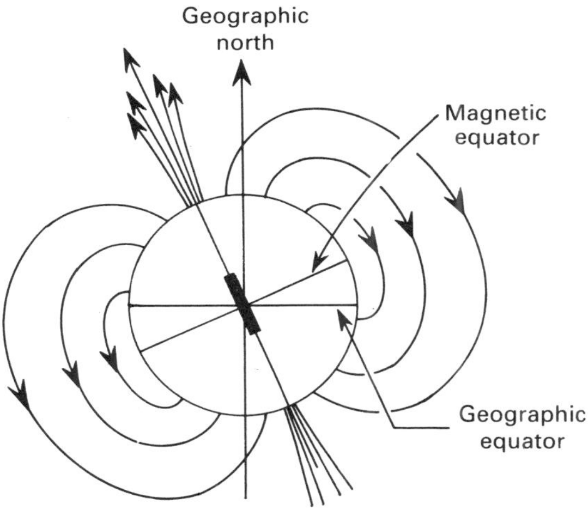

Fig.2.1 Schematic of the magnetic field around the Earth.

as the *impact parameter* – see Fig. 2.2(a). Suppose we consider protons (say) of fixed energy but with different impact parameters. As you can see from Fig. 2.2(b), their deflection varies considerably. The final message is the following: (i) Depending on the impact parameter and the incident energy, the particle could completely miss the Earth. (ii) No matter what the impact parameter, there is a minimum energy such that particles with energies less than this minimum will not reach the Earth. (iii) The minimum energy varies with the latitude and only at the (magnetic) poles is the cutoff zero. Remark (iii) is important because it is connected with the *latitude effect* which I shall discuss shortly. The reason why all particles travelling "vertically" are able to reach the Earth's surface at the poles should be clear from Fig. 2.1; here the field is parallel to the direction of travel and in this case the magnetic field produces no force.

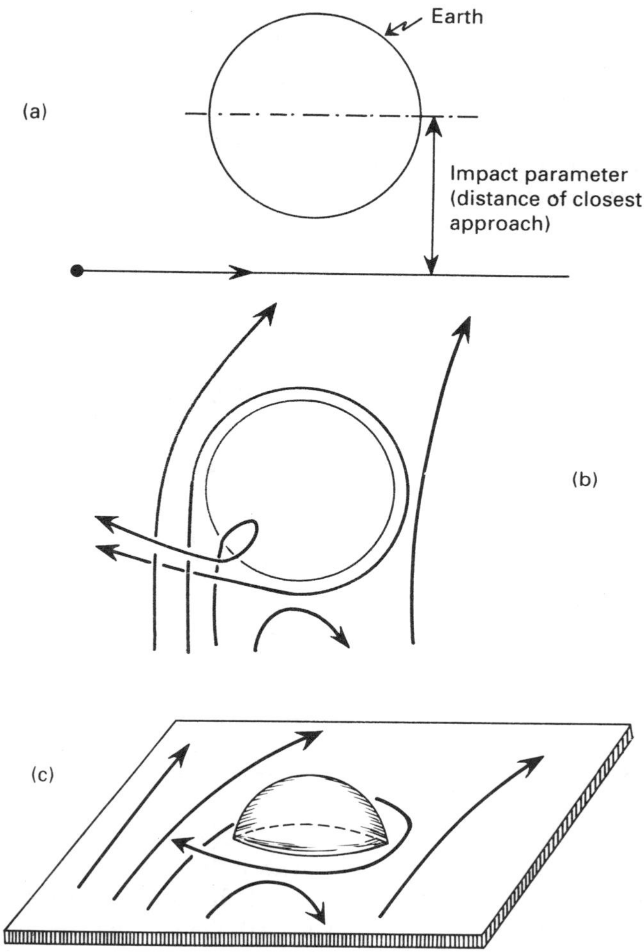

Fig.2.2 (a) shows the meaning of the impact parameter. (b) shows the paths of protons of fixed energy but having different impact parameters. The circle represents the equator. The magnetic field direction is out of the paper in (b). (c) shows a 3-D perspective of the trajectories of (b).

Keeping all this in mind, let us now go back to the question of the energy of the primaries, as they arrive at the top of the atmosphere. We shall consider only protons since they alone dominate. We now ask for the energy or rather the momentum distribution. As a preparation, first take a look at Box 2.3.

Box 2.3 According to special relativity, the total energy E of a particle of mass m and momentum p is given by

$$E = \sqrt{m^2c^4 + p^2c^2}$$

where c is the velocity of light. The kinetic energy is given by

$$\text{K.E} = pc.$$

Thus

$$p = (\text{K.E}/c).$$

Therefore, momentum of cosmic ray particles is measured in units of GeV/c or MeV/c as the case may be.

Figure 2.3(a) shows the spectrum of primary protons arriving at the pole. At lower latitudes, there is a cutoff on the lower side as (b) and (c) show.

This brings us to the latitude effect mentioned earlier. Here I must point out that the geographic and magnetic poles do not coincide (see Fig.2.1). Consequently, the magnetic equator is different from the geographic equator. In fact, unlike the geographic equator, the magnetic equator passes very close to Thiruvananthapuram. Taking advantage of this, scientists at the Vikram Sarabhai Space Centre, Thiruvananthapuram, carry out many experiments related to geomagnetic effects.

The latitude effect was discovered by the Dutch scientist Clay in 1927–1928. In those days, Indonesia was a Dutch colony known as the Dutch East Indies. Not surprisingly, there was a lot of traffic of ships between Holland and the East Indies. Clay went on one of these ships from Holland to the island of Java and back. He carried with him instruments and recorded the cosmic-ray intensity (at sea level of course) as the ship sailed leisurely across the oceans. From his measurements he found that the intensity was consistently lower at the equator. Based on Fig. 2.2, this should be no surprise to us but at that time, people did not have the benefit of this analysis.

I draw your attention to the fact that whereas earlier I was talking about primaries at the top of the atmosphere, Clay made his measurements at the sea level. His observation would therefore include particles produced by the primaries in the atmosphere. More about that kind of complication soon.

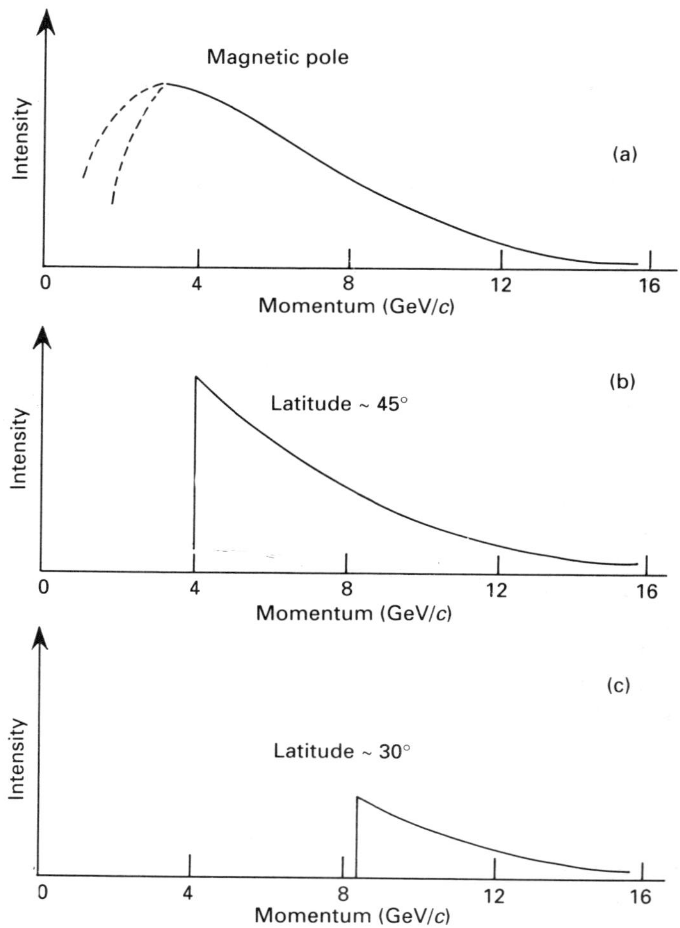

Fig.2.3 (a) Schematic of the energy spectrum of primary protons arriving at the magnetic pole. The dotted lines are speculations about the lower energy end, about which the available information is less certain. Figures (b) and (c) show the spectrum at smaller latitudes. Due to the Earth's field, there is a lower energy cutoff.

Soon after Clay's discovery, Störmer in Sweden worked out the theory of the motion of charged particles in Earth's magnetic field.

Bhabha himself has summarised Störmer's work and I cannot do better than to quote him. He says:

> It has been shown by him [Störmer] that in order to reach a given point on the Earth's surface of geomagnetic latitude Λ in a vertical direction and not be bent away by the Earth's magnetic field, a particle must have a minimum momentum p given by the formula
>
> $$cp = 1.54 \times 10^{10} \cos^4(\Lambda) \text{ eV.}$$
>
> This formula is exact, and shows that it is only the relativistic momentum that matters quite irrespective of the mass of the particle. The theory also shows that at any given place the number of particles coming in different directions may be different, and indeed, if the primary particles were all positively charged there would be preponderance of particles coming from a westerly direction; if they were negatively charged, the excess would be from an easterly direction.

This effect is known as the *East–West effect* – see Box 2.4.

Box 2.4 In Fig. 2.2(b) we considered particles approaching the Earth parallel to a particular direction. Consider now a certain latitude Λ – see (a) – and consider particles approaching the Earth at various angles – see (b).

Let θ be the angle between the vector pointing west and the velocity vector of the particle when it strikes the Earth – see (c).

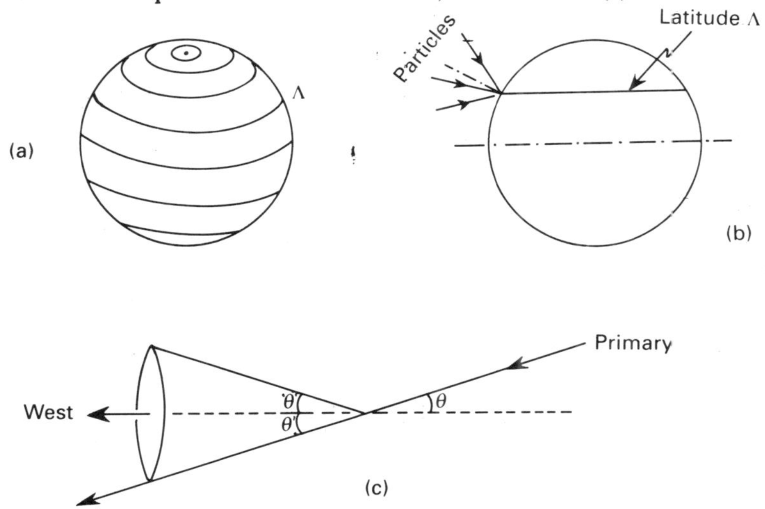

Stormer's theory shows that in order to reach the Earth at latitude Λ, at angle θ with momentum p, the momentum must *exceed* a certain minimum value $p_{\min}$.

Table below gives the limiting momenta $p_{\min}$ for protons incident from the east ($\theta = 0$), zenith ($\theta = \pi/2$) and the west ($\theta = \pi$). Limiting momenta $p_{\min}$ in (GeV/c).

	$\Lambda = 0$	$\Lambda = 45°$	$\Lambda = 90°$
From east	60	4.6	0
From zenith	15	3.7	0
From west	10	3.1	0

The table shows that if the primaries are predominantly positive, more particles are expected to arrive from the west than from the east because $p_{\min}$ for westward incidence is lower. This is the East–West asymmetry, and it has been confirmed by experiments.

Going back to Clay, although he found a latitude effect, many others did not (e.g., Kennedy, Bothe and Kolhorster, Hoffmann). Millikan too did not believe in it because according to him, cosmic radiation was nothing but high-energy gamma rays. And gamma rays being electromagnetic in nature, cannot be deflected by the Earth's magnetic field. And so in 1930, A.H. Compton, famous for the effect named after him, together with R.D. Bennett and J.C. Stearns organised "a worldwide study of the geographical distribution of cosmic rays". In a paper published in 1933, Compton gives a comprehensive account of this global study. A message which comes through is that good science is not always brilliance (brilliance is welcome but somewhat rare!); rather, more often than not, it involves careful study and measurements, *backed by thorough planning and meticulous attention to details.*

Compton arranged eight expeditions which recorded data in different parts of the world. In all, over sixty physicists took part. All expeditions used identical recording instruments. These were very carefully designed. They not only had to be simple to assemble and operate but also light since many expeditions went to remote areas accessible only on foot.

Figure 2.4 shows a map of the world and the location of the observation sites. Notice that data was recorded in upper India also. In the acknowledgements, Compton thanks, among others, Professors Ross Wilson of Lahore and Sharma of Allahabad "who helped with the Himalayan measurements".

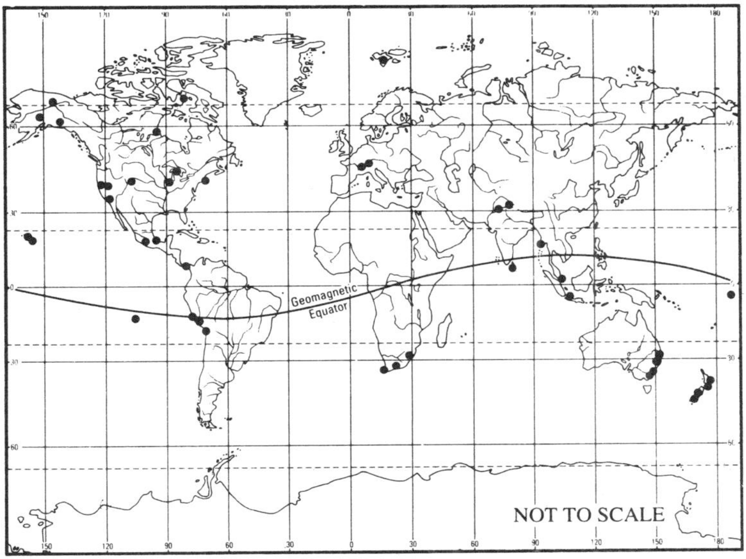

Fig.2.4 Map of the world showing the location of the stations where observations were made as a part of the expedition organised by Compton.

Let us now jump to the important results pertaining to geomagnetic effects. Figure 2.5 shows the total cosmic-ray intensity as a function of latitude. The variation arises due to the effect of the

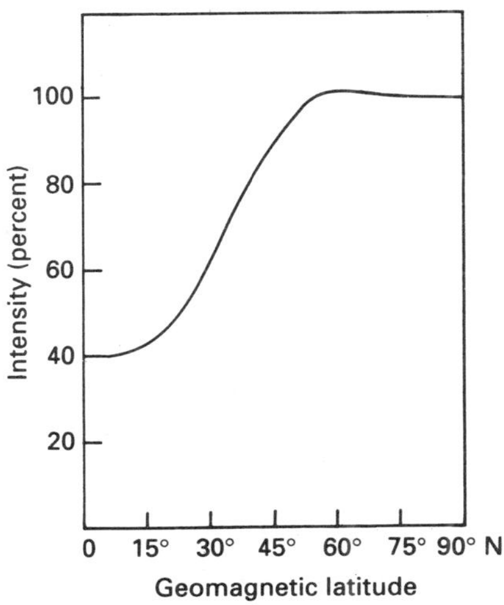

Fig.2.5 Intensity vs geomagnetic latitude at sea level.

Earth's field. Of greater interest are the results shown in Fig. 2.6. Bhabha often cited this figure and discussed its implications. Notice that the figure features data recorded at Madras. Millikan came to India (in 1937) for this purpose. During this trip, he visited Raman at Bangalore. This was probably to return the visit Raman had made in 1924 to the California Institute of Technology (as Millikan's guest).

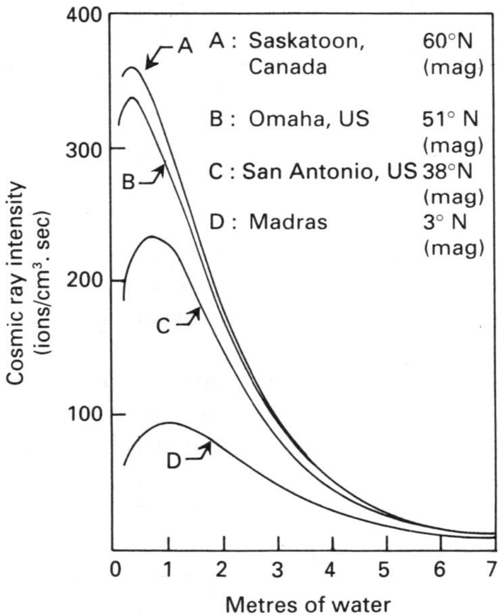

Fig.2.6 Cosmic-ray intensity as a function of atmospheric depth in four latitudes. Zero along the abscissa corresponds to the top of the atmosphere.

A few other comments about Fig. 2.6. Firstly, these curves show that at all latitudes, the cosmic-ray intensity increases as one goes up in the atmosphere, exactly as Hess first discovered. Secondly, beyond a certain height, the intensity decreases. Thirdly, the intensity increases as one goes to higher latitudes; this of course we expect from the previous figure. Perhaps you are worried by the abscissa being labelled in terms of metres of water. Box 2.5 should clear your difficulty.

Box 2.5 Pressure is force per unit area. Consider a prism of material of uniform density as in figure (a). If M is the mass of the prism, then

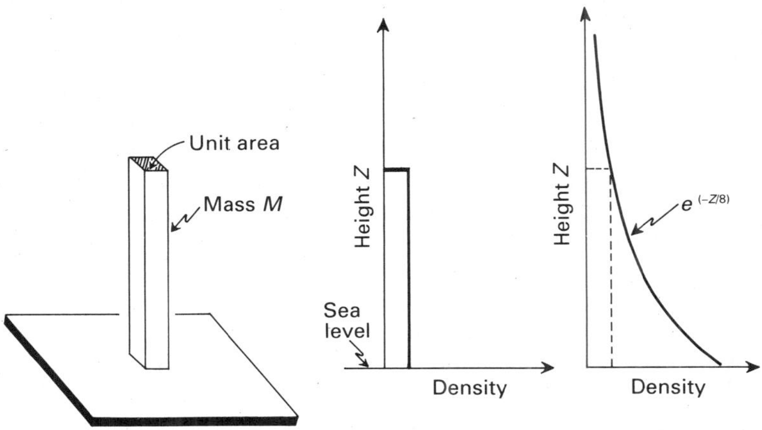

pressure P exerted by the prism on the sheet below is Mg, where g is the acceleration due to gravity. Let us express pressure in the units gm/cm^2. If we express atmospheric pressure at sea level in these units, it has the value 1030 gm/cm^2. Assume the density of the atmosphere is uniform as in (b) (not true of course!). In this case, the height of the atmosphere works out to be 8 km. In practice, the density varies with height as sketched in (c), and 8 km can be taken as the mean height of the atmosphere. With this interpretation, the pressure at altitude z km is given by

$$P(z) = 1030e^{-z/8} \text{ gm/cm}^2. \tag{1}$$

Now water has density 1 gm/cm^3 . Therefore, a water column of height P cm would exert a pressure of P gm/cm^2. In the early days of cosmic-ray physics, atmospheric height sometimes used to be expressed in terms of equivalent height (in metres) of a water column, i.e.,

$$\begin{aligned} \text{atmospheric height } z \text{ km} &= \text{pressure } P(z) \text{ gm/cm}^2 \\ &= \frac{P(z)}{100} \text{meters of water equivalent} \quad (2) \end{aligned}$$

In cosmic-ray studies, one not only examines passage through atmosphere but through other materials as well, like lead and iron. Thus thickness of absorber is nowadays given in gm/cm^2. Using these units absorber thickness of 150 gm/cm^2 translates roughly to 13 cm of lead.

The peak in the intensity curves of Fig. 2.6 clearly indicates that things happen in the atmosphere when the primaries enter it. One probability is that primaries upon entry are absorbed. But this would decrease the intensity.The observed increase suggests that primaries produce other particles, namely *secondaries*, which would account for the peaking.

To cut a long story short, it was discovered that cosmic rays consist of two components, a *hard* one and a *soft* one. The later gets easily absorbed in a few millimetres to a few centimeters of lead whereas the former can penetrate several metres of lead. The soft component occasionally occurs as a shower of particles spread out in space, rather like a spray of bullets.

The existence of these components and of the shower phenomenon was discovered in the early thirties. The only particles known then were the electron, the proton, the neutron and the photon. With these, one could not explain the shower phenomenon but the discovery of the positron provided an opening. How Bhabha seized it will be described in the next chapter.

The variation in the vertical intensities of these two components is shown in Fig. 2.7. By way of preparing you for Bhabha's work on

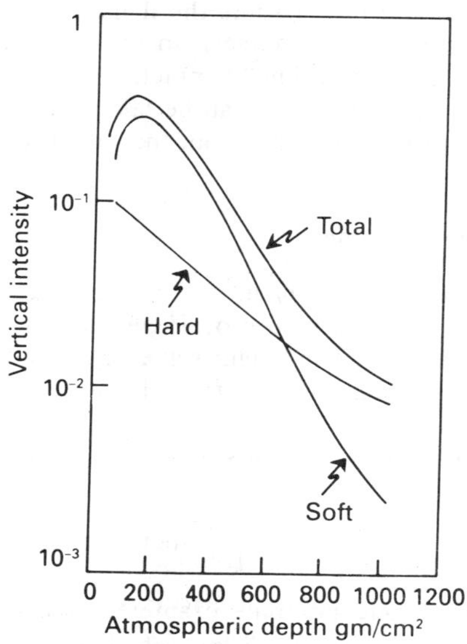

Fig.2.7 Schematic of the variation of the intensity of the hard and soft components as a function of atmospheric depth.

showers, I give in Fig. 2.8 a simplified schematic of the origin of the two components. This figure needs some explanation. I must first introduce you to the participants in the various processes illustrated. When a high-energy primary interacts with an atomic nucleus, many particles are born. The particles so produced are quite energetic themselves and in turn cause reactions in other nuclei. This process goes on and a cascade develops. The process of multiplication continues till the energy of the reaction products becomes insufficient for causing further breakups. The above is a thumbnail sketch of the generation of secondaries in the atmosphere.

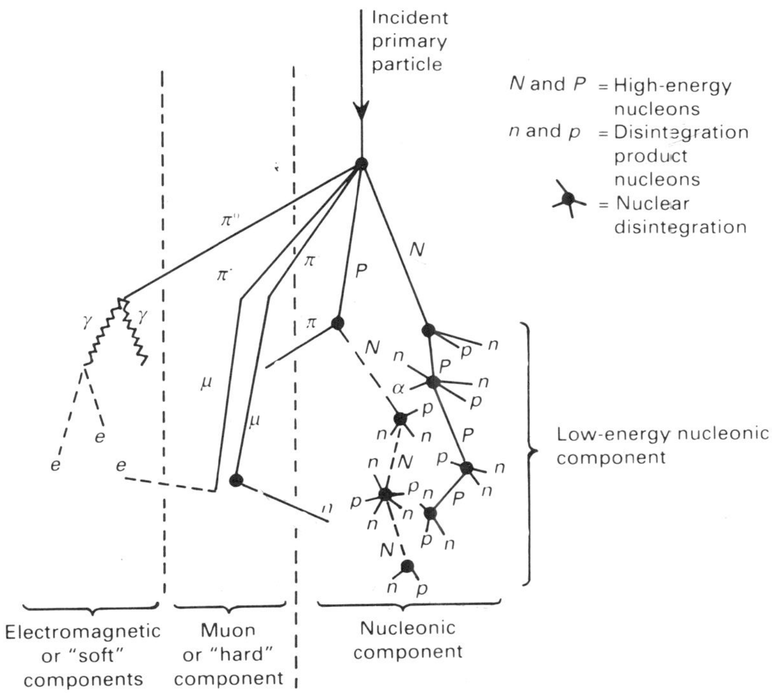

Fig.2.8 Production of secondary cosmic-ray particles in terrestrial atmosphere.

Now for a closer look at the players. When a nucleus like say oxygen, breaks up, many neutrons (n) and protons (p) are ejected. As can be seen from Fig. 2.8, these in turn can cause reactions of their own. Sometimes, photons (γ) are also produced. And when photons of high energy are created, they can transform into an electron–positron pair via the pair-creation process. Some particles in Fig. 2.8 have been labelled as π^+ or π^- or π^0. These are *π-mesons* called *pions* for short. They come in three varieties – π^0 which is neutral, π^+ which is positively charged and π^- which is negatively charged. The story of the discovery of these mesons will come up later, but I might mention that here again Bhabha played a role, including in suggesting the name meson. For the present let us note the following: Charged pions decay in about 2.5×10^{-8}s into what are called *μ-mesons*. Thus,

$$\pi^{\pm} \xrightarrow{2.5 \times 10^{-8}\text{s}} \mu^{\pm} \pm \text{ neutrino } (\nu)$$

What about the π^0? It decays into two photons. The decay is so rapid ($\sim 10^{-16}$s) that π^0s are not directly observed in the atmosphere. However, there is good experimental evidence to believe in their existence, besides sound theoretical reasons. The π-meson has a mass of about $273m_e$, where m_e is the rest mass of the electron. The μ-meson is lighter, having a mass of $207m_e$.

You might wonder: Where do the π-mesons come from? Are they in the nucleus? If so, how come we are told that the nucleus consists just of protons and neutrons? Good question. The pion business is complicated.

Let me give a simplified picture here. You must be aware that charged particles interact with each other by exchanging photons (see the volume on *QED*). This photon exchange is the basis of electromagnetic interactions. Likewise, *nucleons* (this is the comprehensive name for neutrons and protons) interact with each other by exchanging pions. In other words, pions provide the basis for strong interaction or nuclear forces – see Box 2.6.

Box 2.6 Charged particles interact via the Coulomb force, the potential energy of interaction between two particles of charges Z_1e and Z_2e being given by

$$U = \frac{Z_1 Z_2 e^2}{r}. \tag{1}$$

In 1935, Yukawa suggested that nucleons, i.e., neutrons and protons interact with each other via a potential somewhat like (1), i.e.,

$$U_{\text{nucleon}} = -g^2 \frac{e^{-\kappa r}}{r}. \tag{2}$$

Here g^2 plays a role similar to e^2 in (1). Unlike the electrostatic potential, the Yukawa potential decreases much faster with the distance r. The constant κ in (2) is related to the "range" of nuclear forces by

$$\text{range} \sim (1/\kappa). \tag{3}$$

From QED we know that electrical forces are mediated by the exchange of photons (see *The Quantum Revolution*: *Part* II). Analogously, Yukawa postulated that this field should be accompanied "by a new sort of quantum". This was called the U-particle and was believed to have either positive or negative charge. After the discovery of the π-meson in the late forties, U^+ was identified with π^+ and U^- with π^-. The following rough picture was then proposed: A neutron spends part of its time as a "mixture" of a proton and a π^-, i.e., $n \rightarrow p^+ + \pi^-$. Similarly $p \rightarrow n + \pi^+$. Just as photons are emitted when an atom is ripped apart, pions are emitted from the nucleus when the primary disintegrates it.

Like photons, pions also are Bosons, i.e., they obey Bose statistics (see *Bose and His Statistics*). Inside a nucleus, the neutrons and protons are busy exchanging pions amongst each other. When the nucleus is ripped apart by a primary, some of these pions get away. Later, the pions (i.e.,the charged ones) decay into μ-mesons which in turn decay (in around 2.2×10^{-6}s) into electrons. I hope all these (handwaving!) remarks would enable you to understand better what is shown in Fig.2.8.

Let us go back briefly to the history of cosmic rays; to the mid-thirties. Yukawa in Japan developed a theory of the forces acting between the particles in the nucleus. Yukawa modelled the nucleon force by analogy to the electromagnetic force and in the process postulated a new particle which he named as the U-particle. This U-particle was supposed to be similar to the photon but was charged (it could have positive or negative charge) and also had mass. Yukawa further argued that the U-particle was also responsible for radioactivity; in other words, the Yukawa particle participated both in strong as well as weak interactions. Meanwhile, Anderson and Neddermeyer found evidence for a new particle which Yukawa promptly identified as his U-particle. People then interpreted the soft component of the cosmic rays with electrons and the hard component with the U-particle. It was only in the late forties that it was realised that the hard component was actually made up of μ-mesons and that it was the pion which was really the Yukawa particle.

The background on cosmic rays needed to appreciate Bhabha's early contributions is now more or less complete. Essentially we have to keep in mind the following facts:

- Cosmic rays are charged particles coming from outer space.
- They are very, energetic.
- Primaries produce secondaries by interaction in the atmosphere.
- In effect, there are two components – the hard and the soft.
- The hard component is today identified with μ-mesons.
- In the thirties, the distinction between π-mesons and μ-mesons was not known and the hard component was erroneously identified with the Yukawa particle. Actually the Yukawa particle is better identified with the π-meson.

I have not told you the full story of cosmic rays, because this is not the place for it. However, I should mention that till the early sixties, cosmic rays were the only way of obtaining very high-energy particles. One then studied the rays both for their own sake as well as for the reactions they could produce. And from such studies, many elementary particles were discovered. After the sixties, high-energy accelerators took over. Even so, if one is looking for particles of extremely high energies like 10^6GeV, then one still has to go to cosmic rays. Table 2.2 shows a list of the elementary particles discovered in cosmic-ray interactions.

Table 2.2 Particles discovered in cosmic rays

Particle		Mass (m_e)	Charge (e)
Positron		1	+1
μ-meson	(μ^-)	207	−1
	(μ^+)	207	+1
π-meson	(π^-)	273	−1
	(π^+)	273	+1
	(π^0)	266	0
K-meson	(K^-)	966	−1
	(K^+)	966	+1
	(K^0)	974	0

Table 2.2 Particles discovered in cosmic rays *contd.*

Particle		Mass (m_e)	Charge (e)
Hyperons (Λ^0)		2183	0
	(Σ^0)	2332	0
	(Σ^+)	2328	+1
	(Σ^-)	2341	−1
	(Ξ^0)	2566	0
	(Ξ^-)	2580	−1

At the present time cosmic rays are regarded primarily as tools for exploring aspects of astrophysics, although some consider them as a "poor-man's" high-energy physics laboratory. There are also others for whom cosmic rays are the source of radioactive isotopes (produced in the atmosphere) which facilitate various geophysical and geochemical explorations. Some of these topics will come up for discussion in later chapters.

3 *Bhabha At Cambridge*

3.1 Introduction

Bhabha's scientific career extended from 1933 when he published his first paper (in German) to 1953 when he presented some reports to the International Conference on Theoretical Physics held in Tokyo. Of these two decades, the European period constituted only six years; the Indian period on the other hand was more than twice the European one. Thus Bhabha not only did his work in two different places but also under totally different circumstances. Many interesting facts emerge when one looks at his work in totality.

In a series of lectures delivered in Calcutta in December 1940 (at the invitation of Meghnad Saha), Bhabha started off by dividing the energy scale into three regions based on physical processes (as then known) – (i) $E < 0.5$ MeV, (ii) $0.5 < E < 100$ MeV and (iii) $E >$ 100 MeV, the reasons for such a division being as follows: The rest mass of the electron in energy units is 0.5 MeV. Therefore, for $E <$ 0.5 MeV, particle creation involving even the lightest of particles, i.e., the electron, is not possible. In energy region (ii) the creation of electrons and positrons is allowed but not of mesons as that requires an energy of $\sim$ 100 MeV, this being roughly the rest mass of the meson. Obviously then, $E > 100$ MeV becomes a different category. Bhabha's work dealt almost exclusively with regions (ii) and (iii).

The twenties and the early thirties were the Golden era of the Cavendish laboratory in Cambridge. Lord Rutherford was the presiding deity and there was a veritable flood of momentous discoveries in nuclear physics. In short, Cavendish was the Mecca and nuclear physics the subject to work in; and Bhabha was right there – close to where the action was. Yet, he rejected the idea of pursuing nuclear physics. Commenting on this, Heitler, a collaborator of Bhabha (about the famous Bhabha–Heitler theory you will hear shortly) says:

> In 1936, theoretical physics was still the occupation of a relatively few. The fashion of the day was nuclear physics. Bhabha was one of the

few who saw the promise that the high-energy region had for the future of physics.

We have already noted in Chapter 1 that Bhabha was attracted greatly towards mathematical physics since it combined the best of both worlds namely, mathematics and physics. As a student he was deeply influenced by Dirac's far reaching contributions. Besides, he had enjoyed the benefit of discussing physics with Dirac. Not much was known about cosmic rays in those days but Bhabha clearly saw in them an opportunity to test Dirac's quantum electrodynamics (QED) and indeed other possible theories of elementary particles as well. It is not surprising then that almost all his scientific papers revolved around cosmic rays and elementary particles. Before I start describing his contributions, a few introductory remarks about the passage of radiation through matter are desirable.

3.2 Passage of radiation through matter

The word radiation is used here in a comprehensive sense and includes both charged particles (electrons, protons, alphas, etc.,) as well as photons (gamma rays). Imagine a radiation-beam incident normally on a slab of say, lead. What happens to it?

To make matters specific, say we have a beam of charged particles. As the beam passes through the slab, the incident particles would excite the atoms in the host material meaning that the electrons of the lead atoms would be excited to higher energy levels. In some cases the electron might even be pulled apart, leaving the atom in an ionised state. Either way the incident particle loses energy to the host material and keeps doing so while going forward.

Bethe, Bloch and Bohr were among the first to study this energy loss process. Briefly the analysis proceeds as follows: Consider a charged particle of mass M, charge Ze and velocity V going past an electron as shown in Fig. 3.1(a). The electron is free and initially at rest. The distance b indicates the closest approach possible and is the *impact parameter* . As a result of the electrostatic interaction between the incident particle and the electron, an impulse I is transferred to the electron given by

$$I = \text{electrostatic force} \times \text{time of collision}$$

$$\sim \frac{(Ze.e)}{b^2} \cdot \frac{b}{V} = \frac{Ze^2}{bV}. \tag{3.1}$$

A more exact calculation gives

$$I = \frac{2Ze^2}{bV}. \tag{3.2}$$

As a result of the impulse given to it the electron acquires a momentum $p = I$, the corresponding kinetic energy being given by

$$\frac{p^2}{2m} = \frac{2Z^2e^4}{mV^2b^2}. \tag{3.3}$$

Let N be the number of electrons per cm^3. If we consider a cylindrical shell as in Fig. 3.1(b), the number of electrons in the shell would

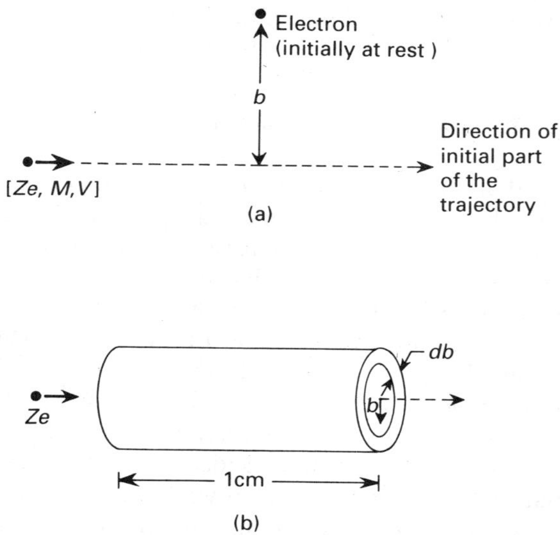

Fig.3.1 (a) shows a charged particle approaching an electron (initially at rest). The impact parameter b is the distance of closest approach. (b) One now considers several electrons to see how much energy would be transferred to them. The first step is to consider all the electrons in a cylindrical shell of thickness db and length 1 cm. This leads to the formula (3.4).

be $2\pi b.db.N$. The energy lost by the incident particle per cm of the shell (due to transfer of energy to electrons in the shell) is given by

$$dE(b) = \frac{4\pi Z^2e^4N}{mV^2} \cdot \frac{db}{b}. \tag{3.4}$$

The total energy loss due to transfer of energy to electrons in all shells in the range b_{min} to b_{max} is

$$-\frac{dE}{dx} = \frac{4\pi Z^2 e^4 N}{mV^2} \log\left(\frac{b_{max}}{b_{min}}\right). \tag{3.5}$$

The upper cutoff b_{max} merely says that beyond a certain value of b, the incident particle is unable to disturb the electrons in the atom. The lower limit b_{min} too can be understood from a physical point of view. The most that can happen is a "head-on" collision between the incident particle and the electron. In such a case, the maximum velocity that the electron can acquire is less than $2V$. The electron energy cannot therefore exceed $(1/2).m.(2V)^2$. Corresponding to this energy there is a certain value of momentum which in turn implies a certain minimum value for b.

In any event, formula (3.5) is approximate and I have provided its derivation merely to give you a flavour of how the argument goes.

The energy loss (dE/dx), also called the *stopping power*, is usually expressed in the units eV/gm-cm^2. Naturally the stopping power varies with the energy of the projectile, its type, and the nature of the material through which it passes. This variation is sketched in Fig. 3.2.

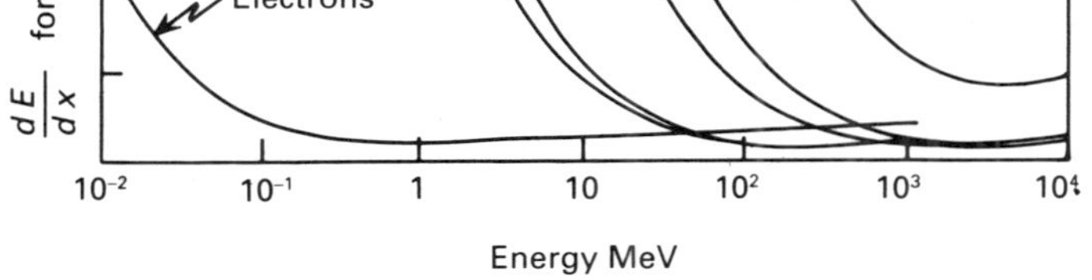

Fig.3.2 The stopping power of air for different particles at different energies.

Given the stopping power and the incident energy E_0, one can calculate the range R of the particle in the medium. This is the distance the particle would travel before coming to a stop, and is given by

$$R = \int_{-E_0}^{0} \frac{dE}{(dE/dx)}. \tag{3.6}$$

The general nature of the range–energy curve is indicated in Fig.3.3.

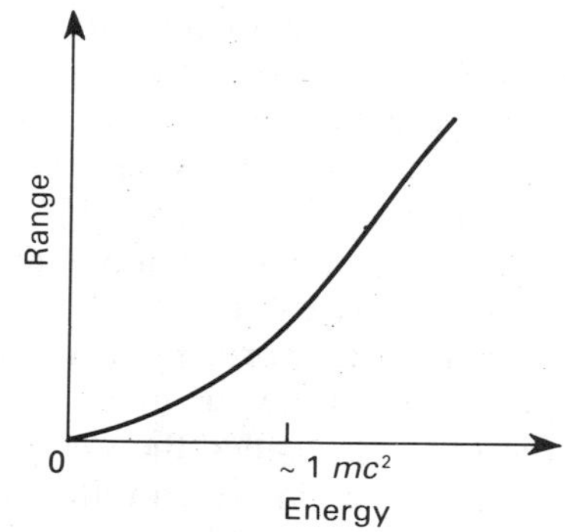

Fig.3.3 General nature of the range–energy curve.

The quantity (dE/dx) describes the *average* rate of loss of energy as the particle passes through the medium. This does not mean the particle goes undeflected, merely losing energy on the way. On the other hand, the particle generally follows a zig-zag path on account of random collisions on the way. This is particularly so when the incident particle is an electron.

Let the incident particle be scattered in a collision by an angle θ as sketched in Fig.3.4.

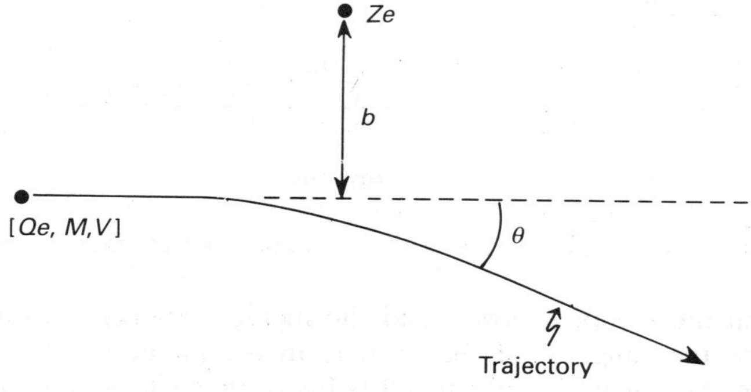

Fig.3.4 Scattering by a fixed particle.

Classical mechanics gives

$$\tan(\theta/2) = \frac{ZQe^2}{MbV^2} \tag{3.7}$$

where Qe is the charge of the incident particle. Here it is assumed that $V \ll c$ which implies that result (3.7) is valid in the nonrelativistic case. In the relativistic case,

$$\theta \sim \text{(impulse given/incident momentum)}$$

$$= (1/P) \cdot \frac{2ZQe^2}{Vb} \quad \text{(for small values of } q\text{).} \tag{3.8}$$

In the nonrelativistic limit, $P = MV$, which gives

$$\frac{\theta}{2} = \frac{ZQe^2}{MV^2b}. \tag{3.9}$$

In the limit of small θ, the classical formula (3.7) gives the same result as 3.9.

Let Θ denote the net angle of deflection of a charged particle as it passes through a foil making multiple collisions – see Fig.3.5.

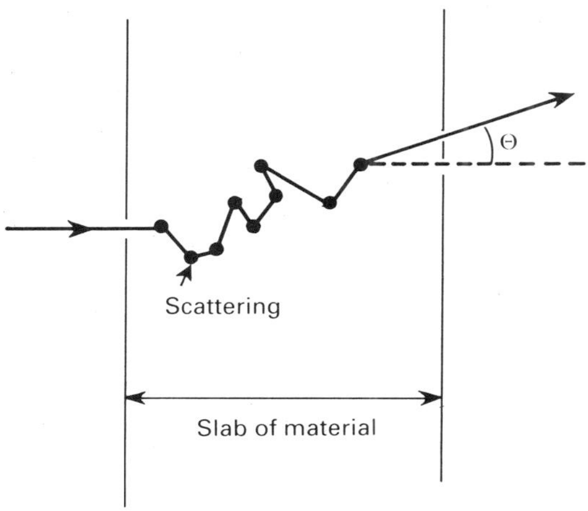

Fig.3.5 In a slab of a material there are many nuclei. Therefore as the incident particle passes through there are many scattering events each of which is like that shown in Fig.3.4. The angle Θ shown here is the cumulative effect.

This Θ is a statistical accumulation of the deflections in individual scatterings. The mean square value of Θ is given by

$$\langle\Theta^2\rangle = \sum_{i=1}^{N}\langle\theta_i^2\rangle \tag{3.10}$$

where θ_i is the scattering in the ith individual event, and N is the number of scatterings. Since statistically the individual events do not differ, we can write $\langle\theta_i^2\rangle = \langle\theta^2\rangle$ whence

$$\langle\Theta^2\rangle = N\langle\theta^2\rangle. \tag{3.11}$$

Detailed analysis shows that Θ^2 is proportional to Z^2; the scattering therefore increases rapidly as one goes across the periodic table.

Formulae for range and absorption must be interpreted with particle scattering in mind. Suppose a particle is just stopped by a foil of thickness L say. This does not mean that the particle has travelled a distance exactly equal to L before coming to a stop. On the other hand, the actual distance travelled could even be more.

Let E_0 be the energy of the incident particle and let x be the thickness of the foil. As x is increased, the number of particles emerging from the foil would naturally vary. With no scattering effects, the variation would be as in Fig.3.6(a) whereas with scattering effects included the variation would be rather like that in Fig.3.6(b). The difference is due to *straggling*, an effect particularly important for electrons.

When electromagnetic radiation passes through matter, there are three processes by which photons are either absorbed or lose energy, namely (i) photoelectric absorption, (ii) Compton scattering, and (iii) pair production. Briefly, they can be described as follows:

Photoelectric absorption When a photon of energy $h\nu$ interacts with the electron of an atom, there is the possibility of the photon being absorbed causing the electron in the atom to go to a higher excited state. This process is most favoured when the energy of the photon is exactly equal to the energy difference between atomic energy levels.

Compton scattering Soon after the discovery of the electron, J.J. Thomson noted that the electron could scatter the photon. This is known as Thomson scattering, and Thomson himself gave a theory for it. It applies when $h\nu \ll m_e c^2$, where m_e denotes the rest mass of the electron. When $h\nu \sim m_e c^2$, Compton scattering comes into play. Here the binding energy of the electron is small compared to the energy of the photon and therefore the electron can be regarded as free.

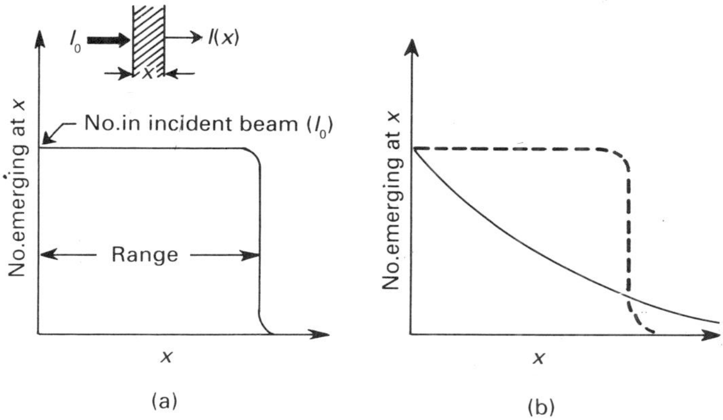

Fig.3.6 The effect of multiple scattering considered in the previous figure is to produce straggling. (a) shows how the emergent intensity $I(x)$ varies with foil thickness x when there is no multiple scattering. (b) shows the straggling introduced due to such scattering.

The incident photon collides with the free, stationary electron, transferring some energy as well as some momentum. Let θ be the angle of scattering of the photon. Compton showed

$$\lambda_S - \lambda_I = \frac{h}{mc}(1 - \cos\theta) \tag{3.12}$$

where λ_I and λ_S denote the wavelengths of the incident and scattered radiation. Remember, $\nu\lambda = c$. Soon after Dirac gave his theory of the electron, Klein and Nishina worked out the theory of Compton scattering in the light of the Dirac theory.

Pair production When the photon energy is greater than twice the rest mass of the electron (i.e., $h\nu > 2m_ec^2$), the photon can materialise into an electron – positron pair.

Consider a beam of photons of frequency ν, incident on a slab of thickness x. If I_0 is the incident intensity, the emergent intensity $I(x)$ is given by

$$I(x) = I_0 \cdot e^{-\mu x}. \tag{3.13}$$

Here μ is the mass absorption coefficient, expressed in units of cm^{-1} and has contributions from all the three processes mentioned above.

Using QM, μ can be calculated as a function of ν and its variation is sketched in Fig.3.7.

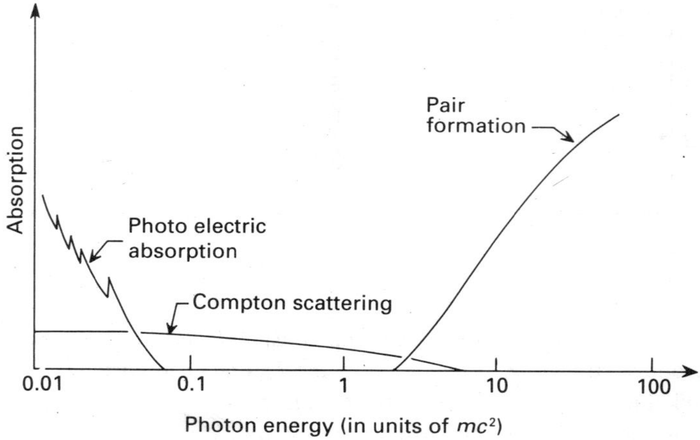

Fig.3.7 Variation of μ as a function of photon energy.

3.3 Some problems in positron physics

Bhabha's earliest papers dealt with positron physics and were published during the period 1934 – 1936. The positron had just then been discovered, the discovery being a great triumph for Dirac's theory. Positron physics was both new and exciting and no wonder Bhabha's attention turned towards it, especially as it meant working with his favourite tool, the Dirac equation. Bhabha's fascination for Dirac's work was lifelong.

This early work of Bhabha also formed his thesis work. The paper co-authored with H.R. Hulme, also of Gonville and Caius, appeared in the *Proceedings of the Royal Society*. Earlier Hulme had studied the photoelectric effect in heavy atoms; the two now combined forces to tackle the problem of photon production due to the annihilation of cosmic-ray produced positrons.

The background to this calculation is as follows: Soon after Anderson's discovery of the positron, Oppenheimer and Plesset interpreted pair-production as a kind of photoelectric effect. The usual photoelectric effect involves an atom absorbing a photon and an electron bound in the atom getting knocked out as shown in Fig. 3.8(a). Oppenheimer and Plesset viewed pair-production in a somewhat similar manner as sketched in Fig.3.8(b).

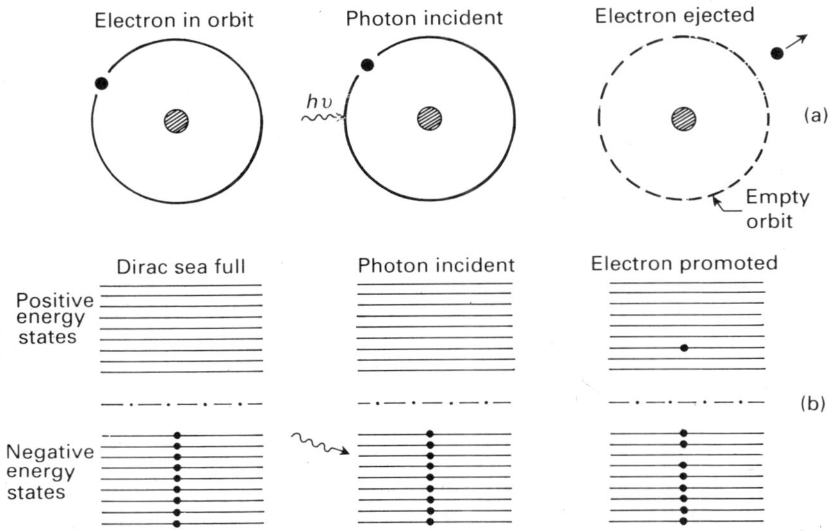

Fig.3.8 (a) illustrates the usual photoelectric effect – a photon is absorbed and a bound electron is knocked out. Oppenheimer and Plesset viewed pair-production in a similar manner, as shown in (b).

Now if a photon can materialise into matter, then the reverse also should be possible namely, the annihilation of an e^+–e^- pair into photons. Blackett and Occhialini used this idea to explain some interesting results obtained by Gray and Tarrant. The latter had investigated the scattering of high-energy gamma rays in matter and found that in addition to Compton scattering, the scattered radiation also contained a significant number of photons of energy 0.5 MeV (m_ec^2) and of energy $\sim$ 1MeV ($2m_ec^2$). These two groups of monochromatic photons were referred to as soft and hard components (of the scattered beam).

In 1933, Fermi and Uhlenbeck reasoned that these components are produced as follows: (i) The incident photon first materialises into an e^+–e^- pair. (ii) The e^+ then loses some of its kinetic energy by collisions. (iii) At the end of its path, it disappears by one of two processes: Either the e^+ annihilates with a free electron resulting in *two* photons each of energy 0.5 MeV (soft component) or it interacts with a K-shell electron and annihilates, resulting in a *single* photon. Would this latter process not create problems with the conservation of momentum? No, because the nucleus is there to take the recoil and help out. K-shell annihilation was thus considered to be the source of single-photon emission (hard component).

Fermi and Uhlenbeck calculated the rates R_1 and R_2 for the production of hard and soft photons, the former resulting from annihilation of e^+ with K-shell electrons and the latter by annihilation with free electrons. They used standard quantum mechanics of the pre-Dirac equation vintage, i.e., their calculation was nonrelativistic. For lead they got the result $R_1 = 2 \times 10^{-5}$ and $R_2 = 2.5 \times 10^8$. The ratio of the hard to the soft component is thus $\sim 10^{-13}$ but this result was too small to explain the experimentally observed results. Fermi and Uhlenbeck conclude: "Our results are that it is difficult to reconcile the explanation of the hard component of Gray and Tarrant as due to the destruction of positrons with the Dirac theory". (Fermi and Uhlenbeck seem to be having some problem with English!)

Bhabha and Hulme took off from where Fermi and Uhlenbeck left. The latter had confined themselves to the case of low-energy positrons (energy $\sim m_e c^2$). On the other hand it was already known that in cosmic-ray showers, a large number of positrons occur with energies $\sim 100 m_e c^2$ (50 MeV). At that time, there was even the feeling that the primaries themselves could partly be made up of positrons. So Bhabha and Hulme decided to calculate R_1 for high-energy positrons.

This called for a different approach, one based on the Dirac equation. The problem reduces to calculating the probability for the spontaneous transition of an electron from the K-shell to a state of negative energy. Of course this can happen only when a state of negative energy is empty as shown in Fig. 3.9. Bhabha and Hulme use two clever ideas. They first suppose that all the negative-energy states are empty, and that these states interact with the atom (via some agency). This is equivalent to the atom being exposed to a beam of positrons. In actual practice, all the incident positrons would not annihilate K-shell electrons; only some would. Bhabha and Hulme take care of this by multiplying "by the factor giving the ratio of the actual number of collisions (of positrons) to the number occurring if all the states of negative energy were free". Secondly, they suppose that the electron is induced or stimulated to make the required transition by photons. "But there are no photons," you

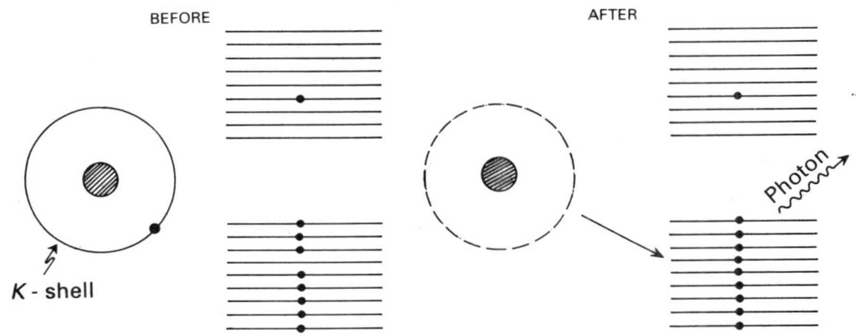

Fig.3.9 Bhabha–Hulme view of the origin of the hard component. The positron is a vacancy in the Dirac sea. Radiation is emitted when a K-shell electron jumps to fill this vacancy.

might argue. Bhabha and Hulme know this and they therefore eventually calculate the rate for *spontaneous* transition (which is what we want) from the stimulated rate. They find this route computationally more convenient.

Perhaps you haven't followed the details but it does not matter. Just note that Bhabha and Hulme performed a proper relativistic calculation for R_1. As for R_2, there was an estimate available from an earlier work of Dirac, based on the Dirac equation of course. Like Fermi and Uhlenbeck, Bhabha and Hulme also found that the ratio (R_2/R_1) was much larger than what the experiments indicated, despite the fact that they used the Dirac equation and considered positrons of much higher energies. Bhabha received the Ph.D. degree for this work.

3.4 Pair creation in particle collision

The next electrodynamic process studied by Bhabha was the creation of electron–positron pairs in the collision of fast-charged particles Let Z_2e be the charge of a particle fixed at the origin. Let a particle of charge Z_1e approach the other particle with a velocity V and an impact parameter b as shown in Fig. 3.10(a). Assume particle 2 is heavier. Let $F(r)$ and $G(r)$ denote the electrostatic fields produced

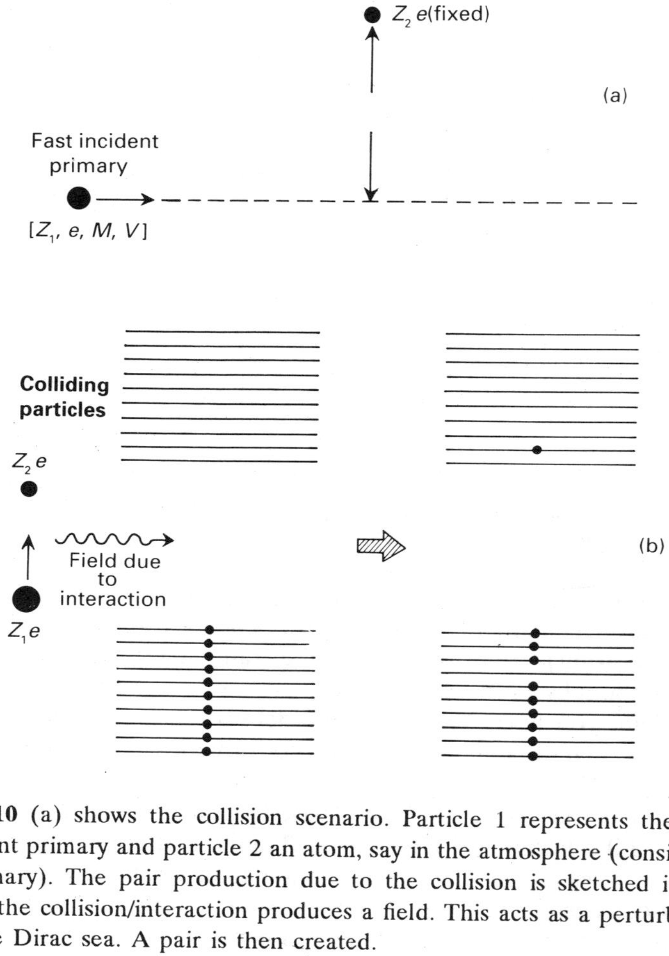

Fig.3.10 (a) shows the collision scenario. Particle 1 represents the fast-incident primary and particle 2 an atom, say in the atmosphere (considered stationary). The pair production due to the collision is sketched in (b). First, the collision/interaction produces a field. This acts as a perturbation on the Dirac sea. A pair is then created.

by the two particles respectively. Thanks to the relative motion, the particles do not interact via an electrostatic but an electromagnetic field. This field acts as a perturbation on the occupied negative-energy states (the Dirac sea – see Fig. 3.10(b)) and causes one of the electrons to make a transition to a state of positive energy; this is how the pair is created. Though Bhabha does not discuss in detail the motivation for this investigation, there are hints to suggest that he wants to model the creation of e^-–e^+ pairs in the upper atmosphere when cosmic-ray primaries collide with air molecules or when lead plates are introduced in cloud chambers. According to Bhabha, there is a transition from a *composite* initial state to a *composite* final state. The former is where the two particles 1 and 2 are headed for a collision, occurring against the background of the Dirac sea. The latter is where the particles 1 and 2 move away, having created an electron–positron pair. Bhabha identifies two ways in which this could occur.

Scenario I

1. Negative-energy sea is full.
2. Particle 1 interacts with the Dirac sea.
3. An electron–positron pair is produced.
4. Particle 1 now goes into an intermediate state.
5. Particle 1 then collides with 2.
6. Both 1 and 2 go to their respective final states.

Scenario II

1. Particle 1 collides with an electron in the Dirac sea.
2. An electron–positron pair is produced.
3. Particle 1 goes to its final state but the electron goes to an intermediate state.
4. The electron in the intermediate state interacts with particle 2.
5. Both the electron and particle 2 now go to their respective final states.

Schematic diagrams illustrating the two processes are given in Fig. 3.11. These are rather like the Feynman diagrams liberally used in the volume on QED but please note that these are NOT Feynman diagrams; they are just schematic illustrations to illustrate the sequences.

There are essentially four players in this drama – the colliding particles (1 and 2), the electromagnetic field produced by the action between 1 and 2 and the Dirac sea which starts off as an observer. The field perturbs the sea and tosses out an electron into a state of positive energy, in the process creating a pair. This is the overall physical picture which Bhabha converted into a mathematical theory, based of course on the Dirac equation.

The actual calculations were quite complicated and many nasty integrals had to be evaluated; and there were also many cases to be considered. Let E_-, E_+ denote the energies of the electron and the positron respectively, and p_- and p_+ their momenta. Define $\gamma = \sqrt{1-(V^2/c^2)}$. The cases considered are: (i) p_-, $p_+ \ll m_e c$, (ii) E_-, $E_+ \gg m_e c^2$, E_-, $E_+ \gg m_e c^2/\gamma$ (this case was earlier considered by Landau and Lifshitz) and (iii) E_-, $E_+ \gg m_e c^2/\gamma$ but $M_1 c^2/\gamma \gg E_-, E_+$.

There was also another delicate matter to be attended to. I have earlier taken $Z_2 e$ to be a bare charge fixed at the origin. Actually, this is supposed to represent an atom and we know that an atom not only has a nucleus but also a surrounding electron cloud. In Fig. 3.10 this cloud is missing. The presence of this electron cloud will *screen* the interaction between particles 1 and 2. Bhabha took this screening also into account.

This work spilled over into two papers. No comparison with experimental data was made but that possibly was due to lack of data at that time. Bhabha however notes that for fast protons colliding with heavy nuclei, the pair-production rate was several times higher than that earlier calculated for slow protons by Heitler and Nordheim.

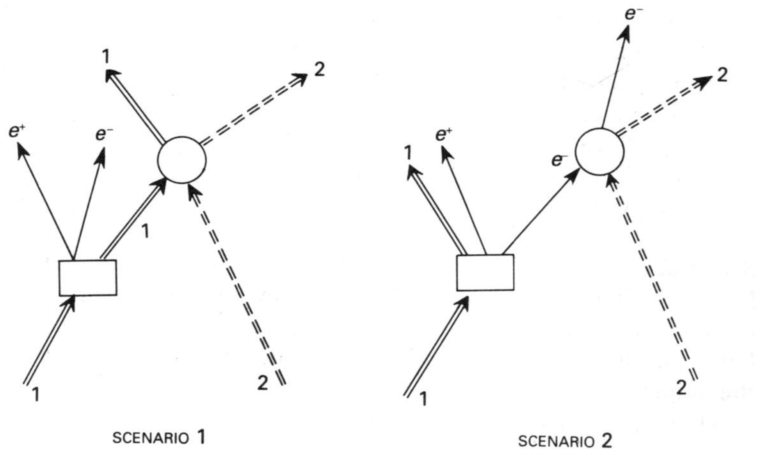

Fig.3.11 Schematic illustration of the two ways in which pair-production can occur due to collision between particles.

3.5 Bhabha scattering

We now come to the most important of the papers that Bhabha wrote in positron physics, i.e., the one dealing with what has come to be known as *Bhabha scattering*. Professor Virendra Singh refers to this paper as Bhabha's "crowning achievement" in the area of positron physics.

Bhabha scattering revolves around exchange effects in electron–positron scattering. Before discussing Bhabha's work, a few words about quantum mechanical exchange. In classical physics, individual particles belonging to the same species can be distinguished from each other. Watching two white billiard balls collide, we are able to say which ball went where even though the balls look identical. Basically this is because we are able to follow the trajectories of the individual particles. Classical physics allows the precise definition of particle trajectories, and that is why Boltzmann regarded atoms as distinguishable while setting up his kinetic theory of gases (see the companion volume *A Hot Story*).

QM ruined this pretty picture. How the apple cart was upset is explained in Fig. 3.12. The upshot of it all was that among particles of the same species (e.g., photons, electrons, protons, neutrons ...) one no longer distinguishes between the different members. This *indistinguishability* leads to important effects which are best discussed by examining what happens to the wave function of an assembly of identical particles.

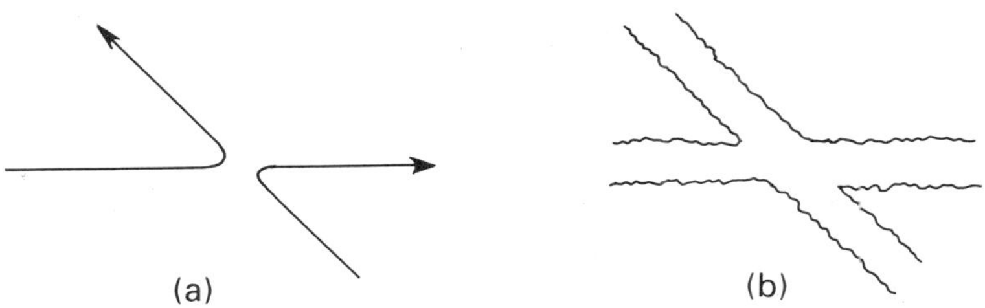

Fig.3.12 In classical physics, particles are distinguishable even if they belong to the same species. This is essentially because one can follow individual trajectories, as for example in the collision shown in (a). Thanks to the uncertainty principle, in quantum mechanics this distinguishability is lost as illustrated in (b).

Consider a set of N identical particles. Denote their coordinates by $q_1, q_2, \ldots, q_N$ and spin coordinates by $\sigma_1, \sigma_2, \ldots$ We shall use a shorthand notation and write the pair q_i, σ_i simply as i. Let Ψ $(1, 2, \ldots, i, \ldots, j, \ldots, N)$ denote the N-particle wave function. Swap *all* the coordinates of particles i and j. The array $(1, 2, \ldots, i, \ldots, j, \ldots, N)$ becomes $(1, 2, \ldots, j, \ldots, i, \ldots, N)$. Denote the wave function after the swap as Ψ'. The question is: How is Ψ' related to Ψ, i.e., how is the wave function modified by the two-particle exchange?

The answer depends on the type of particles we are dealing with. If the particles are Bosons (i.e., have integer spin), then $\Psi' = \Psi$. In the case of Fermions (half-integer spin), $\Psi' = -\Psi$. In the former case the wave function is said to be *symmetric* with respect to exchange (of a pair of particles) and in the latter it is *anti-symmetric*.

We now come to the problem of scattering, and consider first the scattering of electrons by electrons. In classical physics this problem is straightforward. In fact it was first discussed by J.J. Thomson himself. The important point is that Thomson regarded the electrons as *distinguishable* particles. In QM this distinguishability is lost and the effects of particle exchange have to be considered. The first to do so was Sir Neville Mott who studied this problem in 1929. He restricted himself to the nonrelativistic case and the type of scattering he discussed is referred to as *Mott scattering*. Shortly afterwards, Mϕller in Denmark extended Mott's work to the case of relativistic electrons. Relativistic electron scattering (with exchange effects included) is referred to as *Mϕller scattering*.

At this stage, people began to wonder whether there were any exchange effects in the scattering of electrons by positrons. According to one school of thought, there should be none since the positron could be clearly distinguished from the electron – after all, it had a different charge. But there were others who felt that the so-called positron was nothing but a hole in the set of negative-energy states of the electron, and therefore exchange effects must be included. The obvious way to resolve this doubt is via experiments but before doing experiments, one must compute the results for electron–positron scattering with exchange effects included. This is precisely what Bhabha supplied.

Let us look a bit more closely into the scattering problem. We start with Fig. 3.13(a) which shows a particle (1) at rest at the origin and another particle (2) rushing towards it. We shall assume that both 1 and 2 have the same mass. Assume that after collision, the particles bounce off as in Fig. 3.13(b). This is typically the way billiard balls scatter. Electrons don't scatter this way but there is a reason for discussing the billiard ball picture first.

Let us suppose a snapshot of the particles is taken before they collide. The photograph would reveal two frozen images. The midpoint of the line joining the two particles would be the centre of mass of the two-particle system. This centre of mass moves, even as particle 2 rushes towards 1. All this refers to scattering as it appears in the laboratory. This point of view is therefore referred to as the *laboratory frame*. Calculations are however easier from the point of view of an observer who rides with the centre of mass. As shown in Fig.3.13(c), this observer would first see two particles rushing towards him. There would then be an impact, after which they move away as, say, in Fig. 3.13(d). But then experiments are performed in the lab and not in the centre-of-mass frame. Therefore whatever

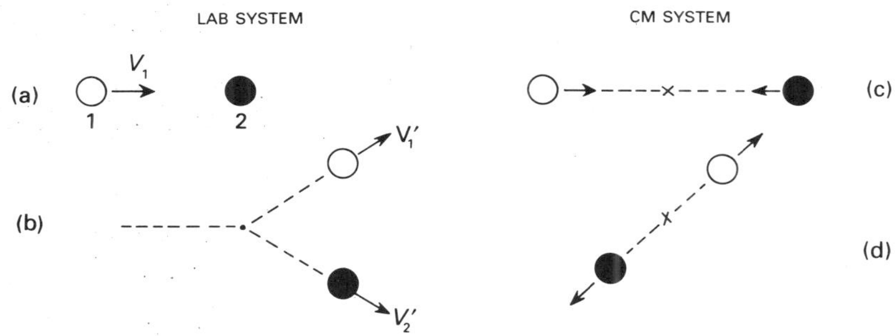

Fig.3.13 Illustration of the lab and the centre-of-mass frame points of view of the collision between two particles 1 and 2. (a), (b) show the lab-frame scenario and (c), (d) the CM-frame view.

theoretical results are obtained in the centre-of-mass frame must finally be transformed into the lab frame for the purpose of comparing with experiments. This is easily done and Box 3.1 explains how.

I must next introduce you to the word *cross-section*. Consider a beam of particles directed towards a sphere as sketched in Fig. 3.14. Clearly, only some particles would hit the sphere. If A is the cross-sectional area of the incident beam and a that of the sphere, then only a fraction (a/A) of the incident particles would hit the sphere. If I_0 particles cross the area A per second, then the *reaction rate* or the number of hits per second would be $I_0(a/A)$. In this simple example, $a = \pi r^2$ represents the *geometrical* cross-section of the target sphere, r being the radius of the latter.

The targets one deals with in microscopic physics seldom behave like hard spheres, and only in such cases is the idea of a geometric cross-section useful. Elementary particles always interact with each

Box 3.1 Here is some more on the lab and the centre-of-mass (CM) systems. Figure (a) shows a particle of mass m_1 and velocity v_1 moving towards a head-on collision with a particle of mass m_2 which is at rest. The CM moves with a velocity $V_{\rm CM}$ as shown. After the collision, the particles move as shown in (a) and our interest is in particle 1 which moves off at an angle θ_L. The view of the scattering in the CM frame is shown in (b). Figure (c) shows how the various velocity vectors are related.

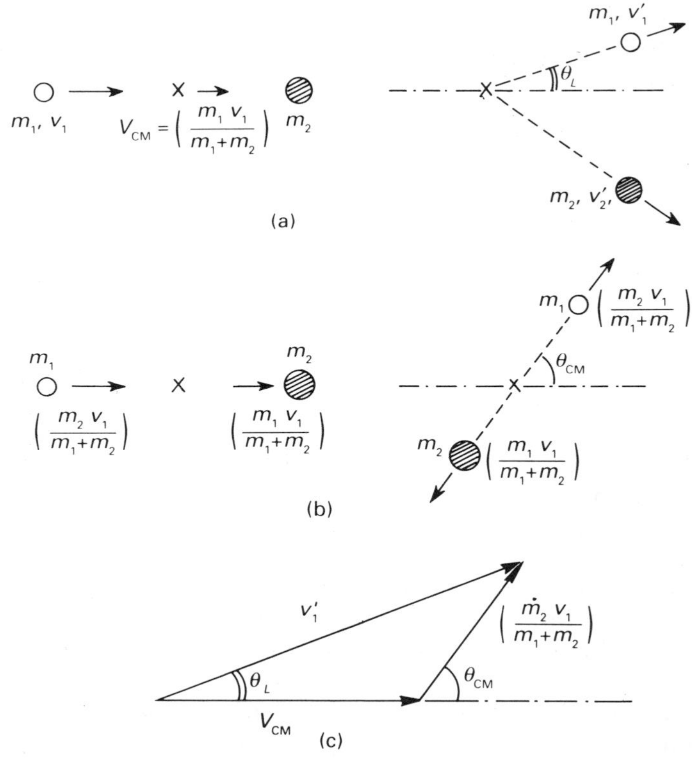

A little trigonometry shows

$$\tan\theta_L = \frac{\sin\theta_{\rm CM}}{m_1/m_2} + \cos\theta_{\rm CM}\ .$$

This is the way the two geometries are related. In theoretical calculations, one often deduces the scattering cross-section in the CM system and then converts the result to the lab system using transformations as above.

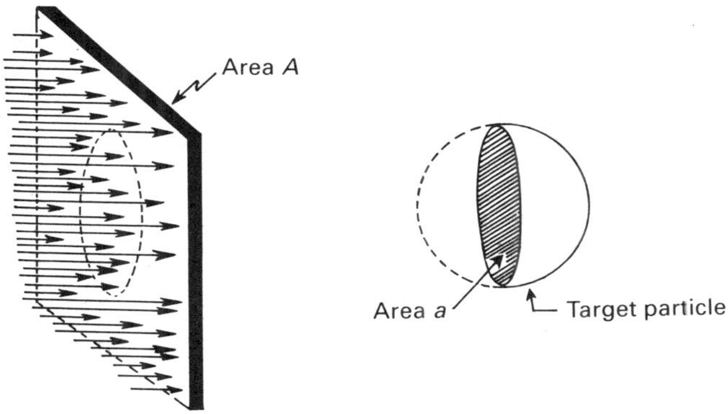

Fig.3.14 Concept of geometric cross-section. Explanations in text.

other even if they are not in direct contact. They do this via an appropriate force field. For example, electrons interact with each other and other charged particles via the electromagnetic field. Thanks to this somewhat longer reach, the interaction or *reaction* cross-sections are often much larger than the geometric cross-sections.

Cross-sections are expressed in units of 10^{-24} cm^2, this unit being called a *barn*. Way back in the mid-thirties, nuclear physicists were surprised to find some of the reaction cross-sections to be several thousand times the geometric cross-section. Someone then exclaimed, "The nucleus appears to be as big as a barn door!" And from this was born the name barn.

When a target is bombarded with a beam of particles, many things can happen. The particles in the incident beam can be absorbed, they can cause reactions, or they can be just scattered. There is a cross-section associated with each such process; here we shall be concerned only with scattering.

Consider Fig. 3.15(a). This shows various possible scenarios for scattering. Of interest in such a situation is the *differential* cross-section for scattering into a small angular interval as shown. In three dimensions, the angular interval considered appears as in Fig.3.15(b) and the required cross-section is denoted by $(d\sigma/d\Omega)$.

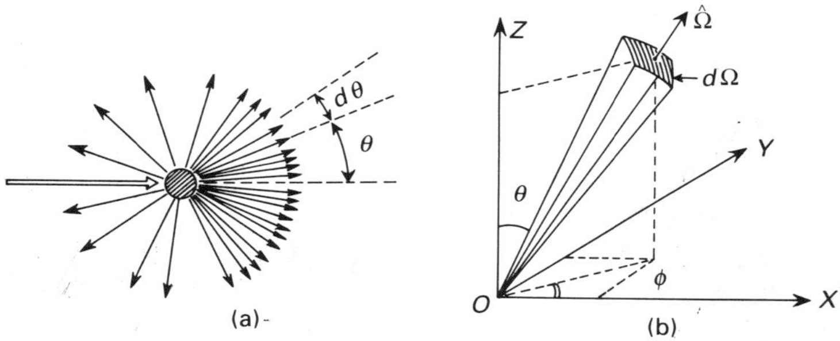

Fig.3.15 Scattering, as the very name implies, throws off the incident particles in various directions. The scattering angle could vary and differential scattering cross-section is a measure of the probability of scattering in different directions. If the scattering is in two-dimensions (as on a billiard table), one would ask for $(d\sigma/d\theta)$—see (a). In three-dimensions, the elementary angular interval $d\theta$ (of (a)) is replaced by the elementary solid angle $d\Omega$ shown in (b). Correspondingly, the differential cross-section is written $(d\sigma/d\Omega)$.

This is related to the probability of scattering in the direction $\widehat{\Omega}$. The total scattering cross-section σ is obtained by integrating the differential scattering cross-section over all angles, i.e.,

$$\sigma = \int_{\theta=0}^{\pi} \int_{\phi=0}^{2\pi} \frac{d\sigma}{d\Omega} 2\pi \sin\theta d\theta d\phi. \tag{3.14}$$

We are now ready to consider the work of Bhabha. He argued as follows: Let us start by supposing that the positron is distinguishable from the electron. Then we can talk only of positive-energy states and in this case the scattering involves transitions as in Fig. 3.16(a). On the other hand if we regard the positron as a hole in the negative-electron state, then the situation is as in Fig. 3.16(b). This is just (a) redone in the negative-energy picture. Bhabha describes this as "the normal scattering process". But there is also another process possible which is shown in Fig. 3.16(c). In both (b) and in (c), the initial and the final states are the same; however, the process (c) involves exchange. Today, one would rather describe these processes (b) and (c) via the Feynman diagrams shown in Fig. 3.17 (these diagrams are explained in *The Quantum Revolution: Part* II).

In (a), the electron and the positron interact via the exchange of a photon; (b) considers the virtual annihilation of the initial electron–positron pair and their subsequent recreation in their final states.

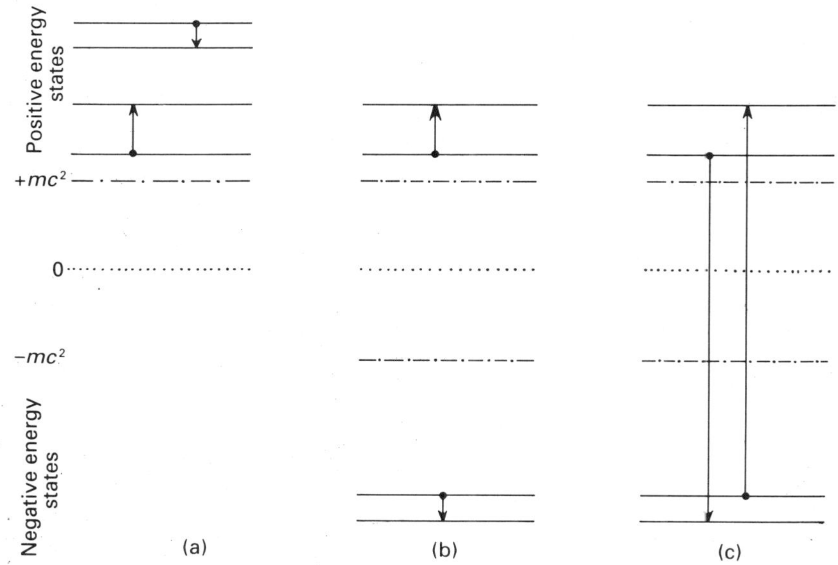

Fig.3.16 In (a), the positron is distinguishable and there is only one process to consider. If the positron is indistinguishable, we must consider the two processes in (b) and (c). These are called normal exchange processes respectively.

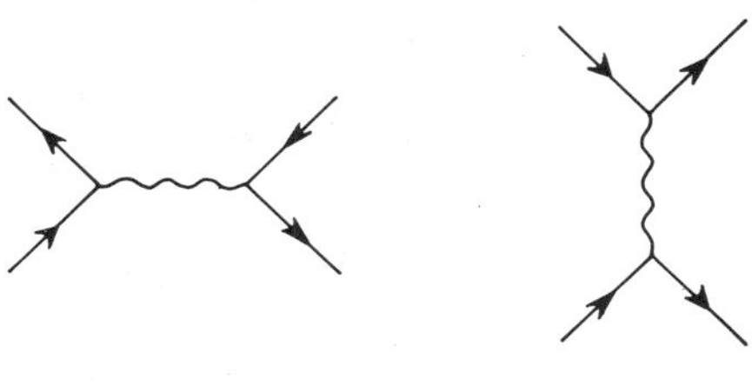

Fig.3.17 Feynman diagrams appropriate to the process discussed in the previous figure.

I shall not go into the details of Bhabha's work but instead jump to the experimental verification of the Bhabha formula. The first respectable set of measurements were made in 1954, eighteen years after Bhabha published his paper. Electrons and positrons from radioactive sources were directed at thin foils (e.g., of mylar) and the scattered particles were detected with suitable detectors. The differential scattering at a fixed scattering angle (90° in the centre-of-mass frame) was measured as a function of the incident electron energy. The results are shown in Fig. 3.18 and 3.19. As can be seen, there is good agreement between theory and experiment.

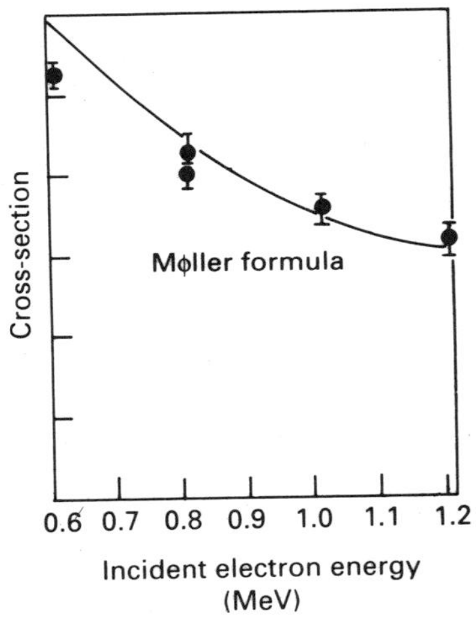

Fig.3.18 Variation of the electron–electron scattering cross-section as a function of incident electron energy, for a fixed angle of scattering. The solid line is based on Mϕller's formula.

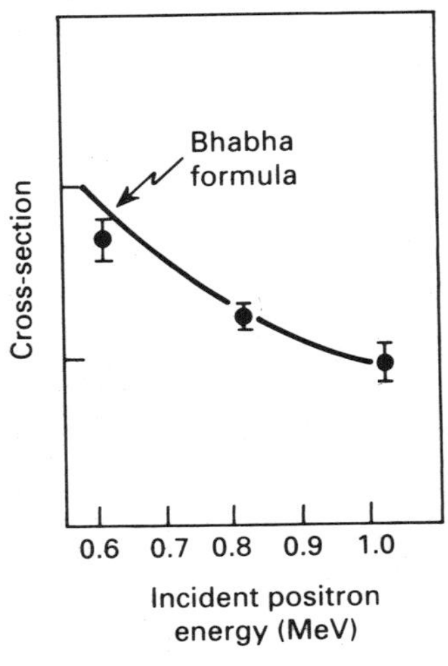

Fig.3.19 Verification of Bhabha scattering formula. The points are from experiments on electron–positron scattering and the solid line is from Bhabha's formula.

In his paper, Bhabha confined himself to the lowest order in perturbation theory. To use the jargon of quantum electrodynamics, he deliberately ignored radiative corrections. His object was to see if exchange made a big difference or not; and it did. Subsequently, experiments showed that exchange effects *must* be included. In recent times, the work of Bhabha has been extended to include the radiative corrections also. Figure 3.20 shows some results on Bhabha scattering obtained at high energies using colliding beams from accelerators – see Box 3.2. The agreement between theory and experiments is quite impressive.

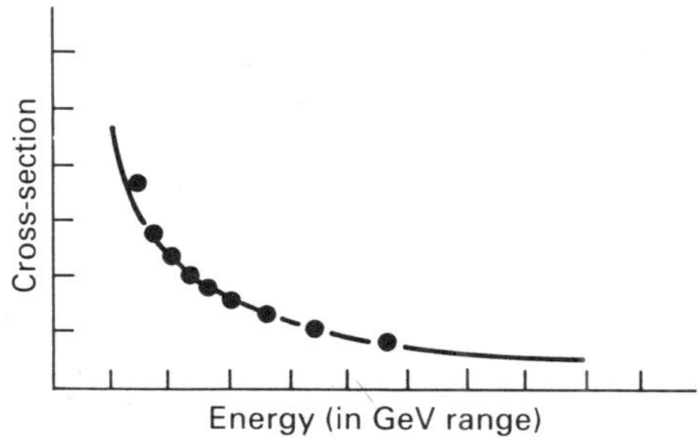

Fig.3.20 Cross-section for Bhabha scattering at high-energy as a function of energy. Points show the data obtained from collider experiments while the curve is from Bhabha's theory.

Box 3.2 In Bhabha's days, the only way of studying high-energy reactions was via cosmic-ray induced reactions, using for this purpose various types of detectors like Geiger counters, proportional counters, scintillation counters, Cerenkov counters, cloud chambers and photographic emulsions. Often, one used counters and cloud chambers in combination – one such combination operated by TIFR at Ooty will be described in a later chapter. Starting from the late fifties–early sixties period, high-energy accelerators came to be developed and they completely changed the course of experimental high-energy physics. In turn this produced a deep impact on theoretical physics. (A brief story on accelerators may be found in *Why Are Things the Way They Are?*).

In an accelerator, one typically accelerates the desired particles (electrons, protons, ...) to the desired energy. Reactions are then produced by bombarding a suitably chosen target with the beam of accelerated particles. In these reactions, one particle (i.e., that in the target) is stationary while the other (i.e., that in the beam) is moving. If the target particles also moved, the energy available for reaction would increase. For this purpose, one devised the colliding-beam arrangement. Essentially, one arranged for a beam of particles and antiparticles to be put into circulation in a storage ring. Here the two beams move in the opposite directions and do so for hours. At certain points their paths intersect, offering opportunities for reactions. At CERN, the large electron–positron (LEP) collider has a circumference of 28 km!

Professor Virendra Singh observes:

> Our faith in the correctness of Bhabha scattering formulas is such that they are now routinely used to calibrate the beams at large accelerators using positrons or other antiparticle beams.

3.6 Cascade theory

Another important contribution made by Bhabha while in Cambridge is the cascade theory of cosmic-ray showers, a theory which he developed in collaboration with Heitler. In the early thirties, Carl Anderson (who discovered the positron) measured the energy loss suffered by high-energy electrons as they pass through matter. He reported that an electron with an initial energy of 300 MeV would on the average lose about 35 MeV of energy while travelling through 1 cm of lead. Such energy loss can come about due to (i) ionisation of atoms in the slab, (ii) scattering of the incident particles by the nuclei, and (iii) production of radiation by Bremsstrahlung. (I have discussed this last process in the volume on QED. In brief, as the electron flies past the nucleus it suffers an acceleration. Bremsstrahlung is the radiation emitted by the accelerated electron.) In 1934, Heitler made a rough estimate of the cross-section for process (iii) and obtained the result

$$\sigma \sim \frac{Z^2}{137}\left(\frac{e^2}{mc^2}\right)^2,$$

where Ze is the nuclear charge. Shortly thereafter, Bethe and Heitler derived a detailed formula for the energy loss, taking due account of the screening of the nuclear charge. The basic step in their work was the calculation of the probability for the following transition:

Initial state:

$$\text{particle momentum} = p_0,$$

$$\text{particle energy} = E_0$$

Final state:

$$\text{particle momentum} = p$$

$$\text{particle energy} = E$$

$$\text{photon energy} = h\nu = E_0 - E.$$

The perturbation causing the transition is the interaction of the particle with the nuclear field $V = (Ze^2/r)$ on the one hand and with the radiation field on the other. Skipping the details, Bethe and Heitler found that the energy loss was around 550 MeV per cm of lead. Are you wondering how the electron can lose an energy of 550 MeV when it has only 300 MeV to start with? The answer is easy. It simply means that an electron of that energy (i.e., 300 MeV) would travel less than 1 cm in lead. The important point is that Bethe and Heitler had predicted a much higher energy loss than revealed by experiments. The authors wondered whether this implied the failure of quantum electrodynamics at high energies.

There were not many takers for the idea that quantum electrodynamics was failing. This is not to say that such a failure cannot occur; just that if it did, it would be at much higher energies. So what was the alternative explanation? Some cloud chamber experiments performed around that time offered a clue. It was found in these experiments that the incident particle often initiated a *shower* of particles as sketched in Fig. 3.21. Actually there are several types of

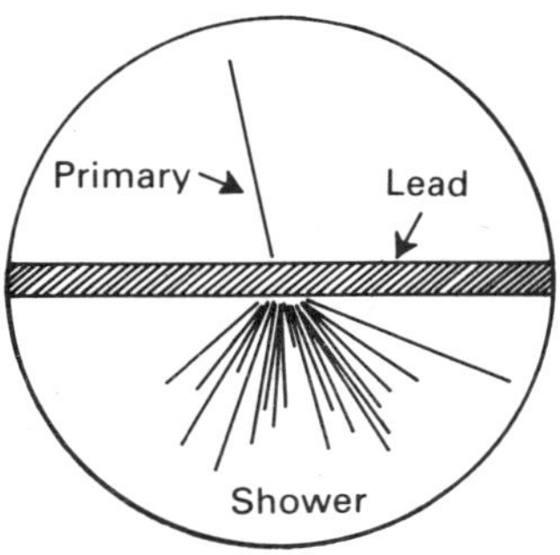

Fig.3.21 Schematic of a typical cloud chamber picture of a cosmic-ray induced shower.

showers possible but these details do not concern us here. Meanwhile, looking at such pictures Heisenberg wondered whether the incident particle while interacting with a nucleus caused a violent explosion and whether the observed shower was just the debris flying away. While this explanation might be OK in some cases, it was not capable of explaining extended showers in which there were a large number of electrons and positrons. Qualitative aspects of an alternative explanation are illustrated in Fig. 3.22. This is the famous cascade. The incident particle initiates a *whole chain of events*, and as a result there are many descendants down the chain, geometrically spread out. Thus the calculation of the energy loss requires a drastic revision of what Bethe and Heitler had earlier offered; and this is precisely what Bhabha and Heitler supplied.

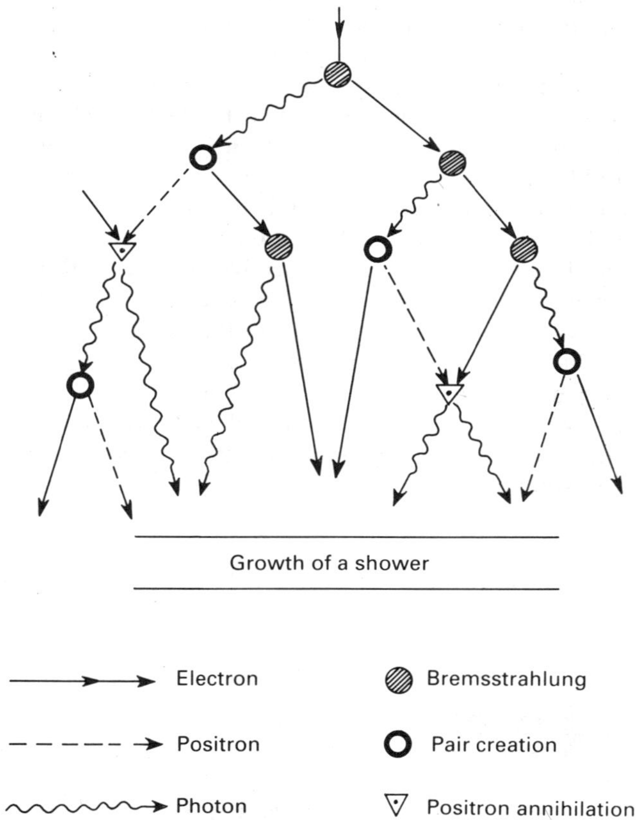

Fig.3.22 The Bhabha–Heitler picture of a shower produced by a cascade of processes.

The cascade idea seems to have been floating around for some time, and in their paper Heitler acknowledges earlier discussion on the subject with L. Nordheim while Bhabha thanks Carmichael for a similar exchange of views. Recalling their collaboration, Heitler later said:

> It [the idea for the cascade process] must have been 'in the air' and I am sure several physicists thought about it. We soon found ourselves, Bhabha and I, calculating what should, according to the theory, happen step-by-step when a fast electron passes through matter; the emission of several gamma-quanta, each of which would subsequently create a pair, which in turn would emit gamma-quanta, which again create pairs and so on till the energy was exhausted. This was the theory of showers.

Introducing the theory, Bhabha and Heitler comment in their paper that according to experiments, a fairly large number of fast electrons are observed at sea level. If these electrons are survivors of those that enter the atmosphere, then they must have travelled through 8km of air. On the other hand, the theory of Bethe and Heitler shows that they should all be stopped by the time they travel through 2km. Bhabha and Heitler offer their theory as a resolution to this paradox. They add:

> We may describe the theory which is put forth in this paper as the normal quantum theory of showers, inasmuch as it depends only on describing the interaction of matter and radiation by Dirac's relativistic wave equation, and the quantum theory of radiation. The limits of our theory are therefore the limits of relativistic quantum mechanics.

In their paper, Bhabha and Heitler address the following question: *Given an electron of energy E_0 which enters a thick layer of matter, what is the number of electrons with energy greater than E [obviously, $E < E_0$] found at any given point below the top of the layer?* To answer this question, they consider the loop of interlinked processes shown in Fig. 3.23.

Each process has its own rate-equation and the problem is thus essentially described by a set of coupled rate-equations. Naturally, there are constraints. We shall skip the details and straight away proceed to the results. Figure 3.24 shows the average number of electrons with energies larger than E produced by one primary electron with energy E_0. Curves are sketched as a function of the depth into

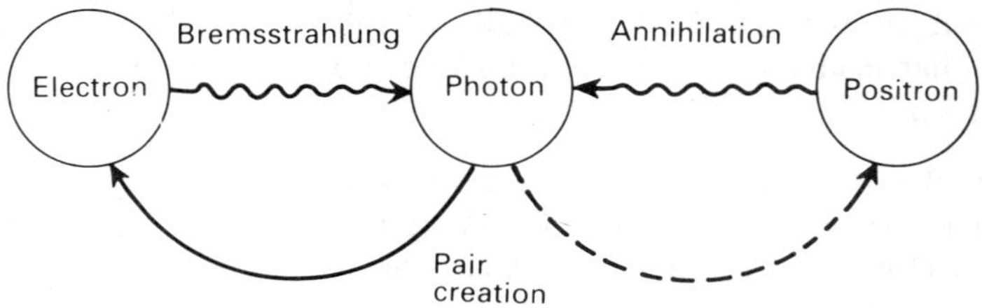

Fig.3.23 The loops involved in the generation of the cascade. The photon can be produced by Bremsstrahlung or positron annihilation. The photon in turn contributes to the population of electrons and positrons by pair creation.

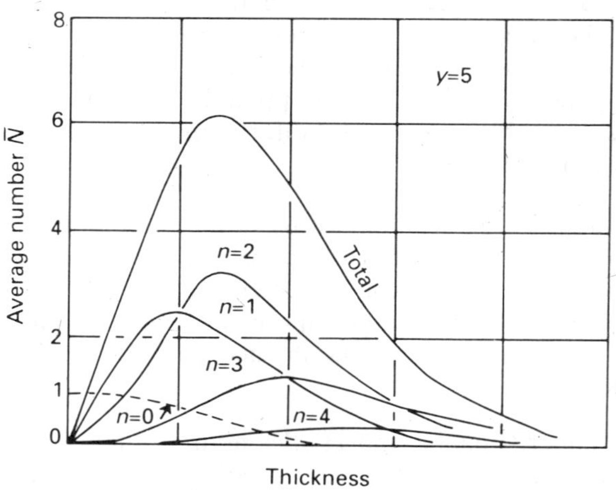

Fig.3.24 Variation (schematic) of the average number $\bar{N}$ of electrons (or positrons) with energies greater than a specified energy E produced by one primary electron (or positron) of energy E_0, as a function of thickness l of matter. The parameter $y = \log(E_0/E)$. The different curves (which are numbered) correspond to the distributions for finding 1, 2, 3, ... particles respectively. The total is the curve for $\bar{N}$. The dotted line $(n = 0)$ is the ordinary straggling curve for the primary particle. The results shown here pertain to the case $y = 5$. See Fig. 3.25 for similar results, for other values of y.

the slab of matter. The parameter y is defined by $y = \log(E_0/E)$. Figure 3.25 shows the curves for several values of the parameter y. From the theory it emerges that for a given E, the number of secondaries increases very rapidly with E_0. For instance, if a primary of energy 2×10^5 MeV were to pass through a lead plate 5 cm thick, as many as 600 electrons and 600 positrons with energies larger than 10 MeV would emerge from the lower surface of the plate. This is what Bhabha and Heitler refer to as a shower. They also note that such a shower would be accompanied by a large number of hard quanta. Further, the number of hard quanta is of the same order of magnitude as the number of electrons. In short, Bhabha and Heitler succeeded in demonstrating that "the penetrating power of fast electrons appears to be greater than a straightforward consideration of energy loss [i.e., the Bethe–Heitler theory] would indicate".

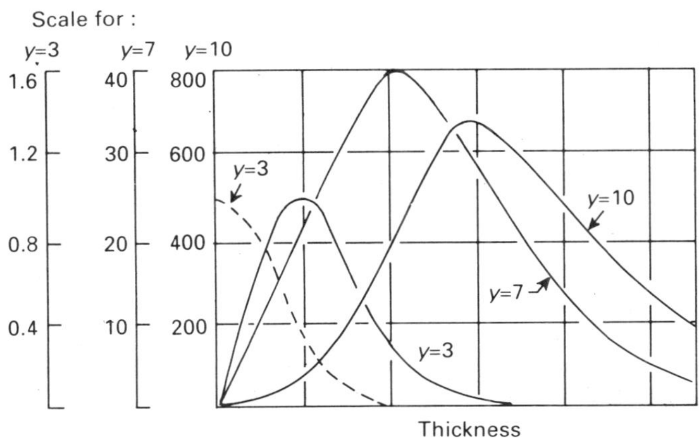

Fig.3.25 Curves for the average number $\bar{N}$ similar to that in the previous figure but for different y values. As in Fig. 3.24, the dotted curve is the ordinary straggling curve for the primary particle.

Earlier I remarked that several people got the idea of showers around the same time. Among these, Carlson and Oppenheimer alone developed a full-fledged theory almost identical to that of Bhabha and Heitler. Their paper which was published in *The Physical Review* was received for publication on 8 December 1936, whereas the Bhabha–Heitler paper was received by the Royal Society on 11 December 1936. Carlson and Oppenheimer also argued that "showers are built up by a long succession of elementary processes, and not by the simultaneous ejection of a huge number of particles in one elementary act". In other words, they too rejected the explosion idea of Heisenberg. There is no need to discuss this work except to mention that Bhabha and Heitler had sent a copy of the manuscript of their paper to Oppenheimer (today we would say that they sent a preprint). Based on this private communication, Carlson and Oppenheimer remark:

> Their results (i.e., of Bhabha and Heitler) differ from ours primarily because of their neglect of ionisation losses; apart from this the agreement between their values and ours is excellent. We do not agree with their conclusion that these calculations make it possible to ascribe the greater part of sea-level cosmic radiation to be degraded electrons and photons of high initial energy.

3.7 Enter the meson

The Bhabha–Heitler paper essentially dealt with the soft component of cosmic rays. Since this component was made up of electrons and positrons, the standard Dirac theory was adequate. The first step in going beyond the Dirac theory (this was needed to deal with certain problems in cosmic rays) was taken in 1937 when Bhabha examined the so-called "penetrating component of cosmic radiation". As Bhabha himself put it,

> [Since several experimenters had shown] that there are ionising particles in cosmic radiation which penetrate more than a metre of lead, and further, according to the theory, no electron of any reasonable energy can make its effects felt through more than about 15 cm of lead, it has become clear that the behaviour of the penetrating component faces us with at least one of the two following conclusions:
>
> (a) The theoretical formulae for the energy loss of fast electrons break down for energies above some critical energy ...
> (b) The penetrating component does not consist of electrons.

Professor Virendra Singh describes this paper of Bhabha as "a brilliant piece of cosmic-ray phenomenology". At the end of his analysis, Bhabha reached the conclusion that *the majority of the penetrating particles must have masses nearer to a hundred times the electron mass rather than ten times the same*. The year was 1937, and what we know as mesons today were not known then. Bhabha's conjecture is therefore quite bold; in fact, he was predicting the existence of a meson, *purely from an analysis of cosmic rays*.

At the time Bhabha wrote this paper (October 1937), he was not aware that Hideki Yukawa of Japan had already given in 1935 a theory of nuclear forces which called for a mediating particle, i.e., a meson. Soon after Bhabha communicated his paper, Heitler appears to have drawn Bhabha's attention to Yukawa's work.

I have already mentioned Yukawa's work in the previous chapter. Some further comments are necessary here. As remarked earlier, the Yukawa force acts between nucleons rather in the manner the electromagnetic force acts between charged particles, e.g., electrons. The quantum of the electromagnetic field is the photon. Thus, electron–electron interaction is interpreted in terms of exchange of photons. And the potential generated by the charge is given by

$$U = \frac{e}{r}. \tag{3.15}$$

Unlike the photon, the (Yukawa) meson has a mass, say m. From the relativity result

$$E^2 = m^2c^4 + p^2c^2$$

we have

$$\frac{E^2}{c^2} - p^2 - m^2c^2 = 0. \tag{3.16}$$

Recall the recipe for going over to quantum mechanics (*The Quantum Revolution: Part* I)

$$E \to i\hbar\frac{\partial}{\partial t}$$

$$p_x \to -i\hbar\frac{\partial}{\partial x} \text{ etc.}$$

Using this, (3.16) becomes

$$\left(\frac{1}{c^2}\frac{\partial^2}{\partial t^2} - \frac{\partial^2}{\partial x^2} - \frac{\partial^2}{\partial y^2} - \frac{\partial^2}{\partial z^2} + \chi^2\right) = 0 \tag{3.17}$$

where $\chi = (mc/\hbar)$. This is the wave equation for the meson. Suppose the meson field is generated by a neutron or proton. This field is analogous to the electromagnetic field generated by electric charge. There is in this case a quantity similar but not identical to electric charge; it is this quantity, which we shall call "charge" (for want of a better word). Let us denote the strength of this "charge" by g_1. Introducing this "charge" on the right side of (3.17), the solution is found to be of the form

$$g_1 \frac{e^{-\chi r}}{\gamma}. \tag{3.18}$$

This gives the potential at a point distance r from the "charge" g_1 and is to be compared with the familiar electrostatic potential given in (3.15). Unlike (3.15), the potential (3.18) falls away rapidly and its range is $(1/\chi)$. Just as the potential energy of interaction between two charges is (e/r), those between two nucleons is $\sim (g_1^2 e^{-\chi r}/r)$.

Like the electron, the nucleon also has a spin; in fact it is (1/2). The potential energy of interaction of two electrons does not depend on their spins but in the case of nucleons, it does. This is referred to as the "spin-dependence of the nuclear force". Thanks to this, there is in the nucleon case, a quantity g_2. The equivalent g_2 is zero for an electron (in classical theory). More will be said about some of these points in the next chapter.

As I mentioned earlier, by analysing the nature of the hard component of cosmic rays Bhabha conjectured (in 1937) that there existed an elementary particle with a mass that is intermediate between that of an electron and that of a proton. Once his attention was drawn to Yukawa's work, he wrote another long paper in February 1938 developing a theory of nuclear forces based on this new particle. Interestingly, Bhabha referred to this particle as a "heavy electron". He summarises this work as follows:

> A theory is developed based on the idea that the proton and the neutron are two states of the same particle [today we would describe this using the jargon *isotopic spin*], which can go over from one state to another by the emission of a charged particle of mass intermediate between those of the proton and the electron, as originally suggested by Yukawa. These "U-particles" are described by four wave functions. Quantisation of the theory leads as usual to positive and negative U-particles with a spin of one unit. The U-particles are identified with the heavy electrons of cosmic radiation. The theory leads uniquely to short range forces [involving g_2] ... The theory also leads to showers

> but consisting mainly of heavy electrons, a few electrons, and some heavy particle.

Several things are of interest. (i) Bhabha is yet to introduce the word meson – that actually came later. (ii) Bhabha, following up on his earlier work, now identifies the particle he had then conjectured about with the *U*-particle of Yukawa, i.e., the hard component is linked to the *U*-particle. (iii) Bhabha also refers to this particle as the "heavy electron". (iv) Bhabha notes that the *U*-particle "must have an integral spin and obey Einstein–Bose statistics". (v) Bhabha further comments that since the *U*-particles as proposed by Yukawa were charged, they could not lead to neutron–proton forces (except in higher order). On the other hand, there was already enough evidence to show that the neutron–proton force was similar to the proton–proton force, a symmetry often referred to as the charge-independence of the strong force. Bhabha therefore declares, "In order to have a proton–proton interaction of the same order as the proton–neutron force, it appears necessary to introduce a neutral particle *N* obeying Bose statistics ...".

Meanwhile, Anderson discovered a new particle with a mass between that of the electron and the proton and named it mesoton. However, on the advice of Millikan he changed the name to mesotron although he (Anderson) did not agree with it. Bhabha then sent a short paper to *Nature* (in February 1939) in which he proposed the name meson. His argument went as follows:

> The name 'mesotron' has been suggested by Anderson and Neddermeyer for the new particle found in cosmic radiation with a mass intermediate between that of the electron and the proton. It is felt that the 'tr' in this word is redundant, since it does not belong to the Greek root 'meso' for middle; the 'tr' in neutron and electron belong, of course, to the roots "neutr" and "electra" ... It would therefore be more logical and also shorter to call the new particle a meson instead of a mesotron.

The name given by Bhabha has remained to this day and is used for a class of elementary particles. This name arose during conversation with friends one of whom (Kemmer) recalls:

> The decision to use the word meson (for the Yukawa particles) was made in a certain private house in Cambridge (that of Egon Bretscher) by Maurice Price, Homi Bhabha and myself.

I have already told you that there are actually two particles namely the π and the μ, with masses intermediate between that of the proton and that of the electron. In the thirties, people did not realise that there were two such particles. All they knew was (i) Yukawa had predicted one such particle and (ii) Anderson had discovered one such particle in cosmic-ray experiments. It was assumed by everyone (Bhabha included) that these two particles were one and the same. However, Yukawa who thought deeply about this matter, later felt there were some discrepancies and apparent contradictions between various pieces of experimental data. In June 1942, a young physicist in Yukawa's group named Shoichi Sakata proposed there were actually two different particles but then the war was in full swing and nobody even knew that such a suggestion had been made.

After the war, there was a conference of physicists organised at Shelter Island in America (see *The Quantum Revolution: Part* II). While this meeting was preoccupied with Lamb's discovery, infinities in QED and all that, there was some discussion on cosmic rays also. During this discussion, Robert Marshak of Rochester proposed that there were two particles with two different masses. One was produced in the upper atmosphere by cosmic-ray collisions while the other resulted from the decay of the first. In short, Marshak not only introduced the idea of π and of μ but also of $\pi - \mu$ decay. The idea was well received at Shelter Island. By the time he returned to Rochester, Marshak was startled to find that British physicists had already recorded such a decay event in emulsions.

With hindsight, we can make the following remarks: (i) Bhabha, like others of that period, did not realise there were two particles, one which was absorbed easily and the other which wasn't. Oppenheimer once referred to the $\pi - \mu$ confusion as a cruel, ten-year joke. (ii) Today we know that besides the π^+ and the π^-, there is also a π^0. It would seem that Bhabha's N-particle was the forerunner of π^0. (iii) At the present time, the μ-meson is identified with the electron (or the so-called *lepton*) family. Technically, the μ is no longer regarded as a meson. (iv) For a while, the muon used to be called the heavy electron, a term which Bhabha also used. This term is no longer in vogue.

So, it took about two decades to get the following facts straight: (i) There were two components in the cosmic rays. (ii) The soft component is related to showers, which are best described by the Bhabha–Heitler theory. (iii) The hard component is related to muons. (iv) Muons are born from pions and it is pions which come close to Yukawa's U-particle.

3.8 Meson and time dilatation

The meson story would not be complete without reference to the subject of relativistic time dilatation. In the volume *At the Speed of Light*, I have not only explained how time appears to flow slowly for a moving object but have also described an experiment involving μ-mesons which clearly demonstrates this effect. Bhabha was the first to point this out, in a paper which he published in January 1938. Of course, at that time one did not know that there were actually two mesons—the pion and the muon, and that the pion first decayed into a muon which later decayed into an electron. According to the view then prevalent, there was only one particle, namely the U-particle which had a dual role. Firstly, it participated in the processes,

$$N \rightleftharpoons P + U^-$$

$$P \rightleftharpoons N + U^+ .$$

It was this kind of exchange that kept the neutrons (N) and protons (P) bound together in the nucleus. Today we would say that it is the π-meson, if any, which plays this gluing role.

Nuclei also emit electrons. This is the familiar β-decay. Now one knows there are no electrons in the nucleus. (Can you say why?) How come then the nucleus is able to emit electrons? It was argued that the U-particle decays according to the scheme

$$U^- \rightarrow e^- + \nu$$

where ν denotes the neutrino. This would, among other things explain the radioactivity of the neutron which decays according to

$$N \rightarrow P + e^- + \nu.$$

In this scheme, β-decay actually happens in two steps:

(i) $N \rightarrow \overrightarrow{P + U^-}$

(ii) $U^- \rightarrow e^- + \nu.$

As mentioned earlier, in the thirties it was believed that cosmic rays contained *U*-particles. Coming now to the time dilatation business, Bhabha noted:

> A positive *U*-particle at rest may disintegrate spontaneously into a positive electron and a neutrino. This integration being spontaneous, the *U*-particle may be described as a "clock", and hence it follows merely from considerations of relativity that the time of disintegration is longer when the particle is in motion.

At the time when Bhabha wrote this, there were no detailed results available to back up the hypothesis. Bhabha merely observed:

> We believe that this may have to do with the fact observed by Blackett and others that below 2×10^8eV, most cosmic-ray particles are electrons; above this energy, heavy electrons.

Unfortunately, people forget Bhabha when describing time dilatation effects associated with the muon. Actually, I too am guilty of this, but it was due to ignorance rather than forgetfulness. It is only when I gathered material for this book that I became aware of Bhabha being the original proposer of the idea. As they say, it is better late than never!

The last paper Bhabha wrote in Cambridge prior to departure to India was entitled *Classical Theory of Mesons*. This was published in the *Proceedings of the Royal Society*. Appropriately, the paper was communicated by Dirac. This was a new track for Bhabha on which he traversed quite some distance in Bangalore. It seems better to describe this work separately along with others similar in scope and objective. Summarising Bhabha's work in Cambridge, his important contributions were:

- The explanation of relativistic exchange scattering (Bhabha scattering).
- The theory of production of electron and positron showers in cosmic rays (Bhabha-Heitler theory).
- Speculations about the Yukawa particle, related to which was his suggestion of the name meson.
- Prediction of relativistic time dilatation effects in the decay of the meson.

All this earned for Bhabha a high reputation in Cambridge and indeed in scientific circles everywhere. It was at this juncture that

Bhabha decided to come to India for a vacation. As you know, he stayed back to continue his research in India. We pick up that story in the following chapter.

4 *Research in the Backwaters*

We come now to the most interesting and also the most important part of Bhabha's research career, namely the work he did in India. Undoubtedly there was a continuation of earlier interests but there was also a change in philosophy for which two factors were responsible. Firstly, thanks to the war (1939–1945) experimental results became scarce. Secondly, experienced colleagues like Heitler were not available. Net result – Bhabha's work became more "inward looking". What this implies would be made more clear later.

Bhabha's work in India dealt with (i) cosmic rays and (ii) elementary particles. As far as cosmic rays are concerned, Bhabha continued his study of showers. He also dabbled a bit in experimental work (as described in Chapter 1). Once TIFR was founded, he left experimentation to other people but kept in touch with the experiments. His research in theory continued for a while but soon organisational work forced him to retire from research in physics altogether; that story is reserved for the following chapters.

4.1 Showers continued

In Bangalore, Bhabha resumed his work on showers but it was essentially a tightening up of the earlier analysis performed in collaboration with Heitler. Now for some details.

The first stage of the improvement of the Bhabha–Heitler theory was done in collaboration with S.K. Chakrabarthy. In their paper, Bhabha and Chakrabarthy say:

> It is generally accepted that the cascade theory put forward by Carlson and Oppenheimer (1937) and Bhabha and Heitler (1937) correctly describes all the general features of the behaviour of the soft component of cosmic radiation. Moreover, it appears to be in rough quantitative agreement with the observed absorption curve of cosmic radiation in the atmosphere and the production of electron showers in heavy materials by fast electrons. Nevertheless, a very exact comparison between theory and experiment has not yet been made,

> due on the one hand, to inaccuracies in the theory introduced by the inexactness of the physical assumptions and approximations in the mathematical treatment, and on the other hand to uncertainties in the experimental data itself. A stage is, however, being reached when the gradually increasing data on the atmospheric absorption curves at different latitudes makes a more accurate knowledge of the theoretical behaviour of cascade processes necessary in order that a more exact comparison between theory and experiment may be made with a view to finding out whether experiment reveals other processes besides those explained by the cascade theory, and to what extent.

Bhabha and Chakrabarthy then go on "to give a more accurate theoretical treatment of cascade processes than has been done hitherto". There was no conceptual advancement but only improved mathematical elegance. This effort was spread over three papers with a follow-up in a fourth which was authored by Bhabha alone.

The cascade theory of Bhabha and Heitler or Carlson and Oppenheimer or even Bhabha and Chakrabarthy allows one to calculate only the *mean* or *average* number of particles in a shower started by a primary electron or photon of a given energy, that is the mean number after the shower has traversed a given thickness of material. However, shower production is essentially a statistical process and while analysing experimental data it sometimes becomes necessary to pay attention to fluctuations from the mean. In 1950, Bhabha and Alladi Ramakrishnan turned to this problem. It was not as if others had not worried about fluctuations in cosmic-ray showers. Many in fact had, and all except Scott and Uhlenbeck had analysed the problem by making approximate models for the shower. The only treatment of fluctuations based on actual quantum mechanical cross-sections for radiation loss and pair creation was done by the two just mentioned. Bhabha and Ramakrishnan went further than Scott and Uhlenbeck "in strictly carrying through the calculations to the end". Specifically, they calculated the following quantities: Let $N(E_1, E_2)$ be the number of particles whose energies lie between E_1 and E_2. This could be the energy spread after the shower, started by a primary of energy E_0, has traversed material of thickness t say. Let $\langle N(E_1, E_2)\rangle$ be the mean value of N and $\langle N^2(E_1, E_2)\rangle$ the mean of the square. Bhabha and Ramakrishnan obtained an expression for the quantity

$$\langle N^2(E_1, E_2)\rangle - \langle N(E_1, E_2)\rangle^2.$$

Later Bhabha gave a formula for $\langle N^k(E_1, E_2)\rangle$ for an arbitrary integer k. Once this quantity is known for all k from $k = 1$ to $k = \infty$, the theory of statistics enables one to obtain $P\{N(E_1, E_2)\}$, the probability of there being N particles with energies in the interval E_1 to E_2. The quantities $\langle N^k \rangle$ are referred to as the *moments of the probability distribution P*.

I have here touched only upon the major work of Bhabha on cosmic rays; there are several other papers he wrote on cosmic rays or was a co-author of, e.g., on experimental studies. Interesting though they are, I am afraid I have to skip them as I now have to turn to his work on the classical theory of the meson and what has come to be called the *Bhabha equation*. Over now to these topics.

4.2 Dirac's return to classical theory

There are two clear phases in Bhabha's work on elementary particles. Between 1939–1945 (or so), he was preoccupied with classical theories but after that he turned towards a possible quantum theory. For both, the inspiration came from Dirac.

The take-off for the classical theories was a paper due to Dirac which appeared in 1938, exactly a decade after the discovery of the Dirac equation. (For a deep background, see the companion volumes on *The Quantum Revolution*; *Parts* I and II.) After the initial excitement associated with the Dirac equation, especially after the discovery of the positron, there followed a period of disappointment owing to the "plague of infinities". In brief, electrodynamics based on the Dirac equation predicted infinity as the answer for many quantities which one knew were finite. This was disturbing, and at that time no one quite knew what to do. Meanwhile, many became disenchanted with quantum electrodynamics (what I have elsewhere referred to as QED II), and this included Dirac! Thus it was that in 1938, Dirac went back to a classical theory of the electron.

By way of explanation, he said:

> One may think that this difficulty [divergence difficulty of quantum electrodynamics] will be solved only by a better understanding of the structure of the electron according to quantum laws. However, it seems more reasonable to suppose that the electron is too simple a thing for the question of laws governing its structure to arise, and thus quantum mechanics should not be needed for the solution of this difficulty. Some new physical idea is now required, an idea which should be intelligible both in the classical theory and in the quantum theory, and our easiest path of approach to it is to keep within the confines of the classical theory.

Before describing Dirac's work, a brief reference is necessary to the earlier work of Lorentz done at the turn of the century. (Some of this is also discussed in *The Quantum Revolution*: *Part* II.) Lorentz was interested in the force produced on an electron due to the electromagnetic field generated by its own motion, i.e., back reaction. He pictured the electron as a sphere of radius a with a distribution of charge inside. Lorentz then calculated the resultant force arising out of the action of the field due to the charge at one point, acting on the charge at another point. The electron as a whole was supposed to move with a velocity v. Lorentz obtained the result:

$$\text{Force} = \frac{e^2}{c^2 a}\dot{v} - \frac{2}{3}\frac{e^2}{c^3}\ddot{v} + \ldots \tag{4.1}$$

Here $\dot{v} = (dv/dt)$ denotes acceleration, while $\ddot{v} = (d^2v/dt^2)$ denotes the rate of change of acceleration. The first term on the right-hand side of (4.1) is the inertial force while the second is the radiation reaction. We are used to writing the inertial force as (mass $\times$ acceleration). Remembering this, the quantity (e^2/c^2a) can be interpreted as the mass of the electron. Dirac refers to this as "one of the most attractive ideas in the Lorentz model of the electron, the idea that all mass is of electromagnetic origin". Unfortunately, this idea is not acceptable because we would then have a problem explaining the mass of the neutron. By the way, there are several other terms on the right-hand side of (4.1) but these are not shown.

Once we give up the idea that the mass of the electron is electromagnetic in origin, we have no compelling reason to cling to the belief that the electron has a finite size. In fact, finite size is embarassing because if the electron moves at a speed close to c (which it is possible to achieve), it would lose its rigidity. Thanks to this difficulty, people switched to the idea of a point electron. While this made sense from the relativity point of view, the point electron brought in its own difficulty, namely, *self-energy divergence*. This means the following: Suppose that initially the electron is in the form of tiny bits and fragments which are far from each other. We now try to "assemble" the spherical electron by bringing the various pieces together. The total work done in this process is the self-energy. If the final object is a point electron (i.e., $a = 0$) then the self-energy is infinity – this is the divergence difficulty of classical electrodynamics. As explained in the volume on QED this divergence difficulty becomes worse when one makes calculations using the Dirac equation. It was at this point that Dirac went back to the classical electron and tried to view it in a new light.

Prior to Dirac, Born had suggested that perhaps Maxwell's equations needed modification to tackle the problem of divergence. Dirac rejected this idea – Maxwell's equations were too beautiful to be tampered with. His own view was:

> We shall retain Maxwell's theory to describe the field right up to the point-singularity which represents our electron and shall try to get over the difficulties associated with the infinite energy by a process of direct omission or subtraction of unwanted terms ... The scheme must be mathematically well-defined and self-consistent, and in agreement with well-established principles, such as the principle of relativity and the conservation of energy and momentum.

The last remark is very important because it highlights the modern approach to constructing theories of physics. Whatever be the underlying assumptions, certain basic principles must be adhered to, namely, that all the fundamental conservation laws must be obeyed and all the important symmetries respected. Actually, conservation laws and symmetries go together; we shall come to that fine point shortly.

Consider an electron moving in space-time (this concept is explained in the volume on QED). For illustration, we consider the case of 1 space + 1 time dimension as in Fig. 4.1. The electron moves due to a force generated by the electromagnetic field which is partly external and partly due to the motion of the electron itself, i.e., self-generated. To a certain extent, the electron drives itself. Lorentz's analysis led him to equation (4.1) which is a series in (e^2/c^n). Dirac on the other hand arrived at:

$$\text{Force} = m\dot{v} - \frac{2}{3}\frac{e^2}{c^3}\ddot{v} - \frac{2}{3}\frac{e^2}{c^5}\dot{v}v. \qquad (4.2)$$

In stating all this, I admit I have taken some liberties and oversimplified matters. However, that is not too serious. The point simply is, as Dirac puts it, "these are the same equations of motion obtained from the Lorentz theory of the extended electron by equating the total force on the electron to zero, if one neglects [in the result of Lorentz] terms involving higher derivatives of v than the second." Dirac regards (4.2) as "giving exact description of the motion of an electron in a specified incident field [which produces the force]..."

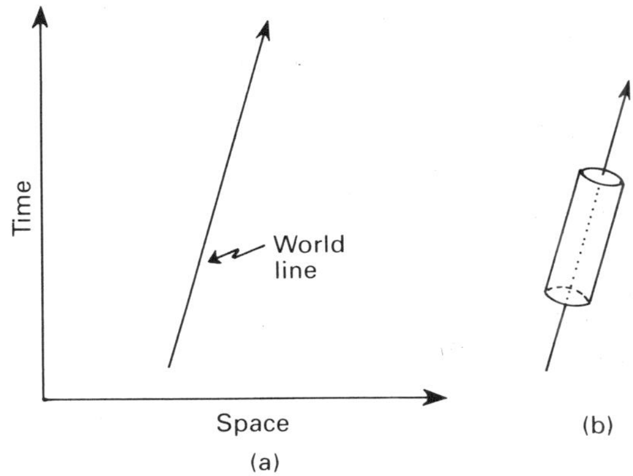

Fig.4.1 (a) shows the usual world line familiar in special relativity (for the 1 space + 1 time dimension case). (b) Tube around the world line which is later shrunk. The use of this tube is discussed in the text.

and then goes on to study various consequences. Bhabha used a similar approach in dealing with the motion of the neutron and the proton. Before discussing Bhabha's work, there is one aspect of Dirac's work worth drawing attention to.

Let us go back to Fig. 4.1. Since the motion of the electron generates a current, one can talk of a current density. This current density vanishes everywhere except on the world line where it is infinitely great. There is thus a singularity on the world line. Equation (4.2) determines this world line. Dirac considered a small, thin "tube" around the world line (as shown in Fig. 4.1(b)) and then analysed the flow of energy and momentum in and out of the tube. The conservation of energy and momentum are invoked at this stage. Dirac then shrunk the tube so as to make it drape the world line. This was Dirac's way of subtracting infinities (a topic which kept us busy in the volume on QED). As Dirac puts it:

> If we want a model of the electron, we must suppose that there is an infinite negative mass at the centre [associated with the kinetic energy within the tube] such that, when subtracted from the infinite positive mass of the surrounding Coulomb field [i.e., associated with the energy outside the tube], the difference is well defined and is just equal to m [observed rest mass of the electron].

All this may sound confusing but in a nutshell, Dirac assumed that point electrons were given and that one had no business trying to imagine the electron as the limit of a large sphere of charge e compressed to a point. Bhabha adopted a similar point of view which is what we shall now turn to.

4.3 Classical theory of the meson

Inspired by the paper of Dirac just summarised, Bhabha wrote close to a dozen papers dealing with protons, neutrons, their motions and their interactions with mesic forces. His motivation was roughly the following: (i) Quantum electrodynamics (as it then existed) was doing a poor job, predicting infinity instead of finite answers for many quantities like the self-energy. (ii) These divergence difficulties were expected to be worse in the case of strong interactions (see Fig. 7.2 in *The Quantum Revolution*: *Part* II), and (iii) in any case one did not have as yet the analogue of the Dirac equation for neutrons and protons (Bhabha himself was to have a crack at this problem but that comes later). The best bet, under the circumstances, seemed to be to follow in the footsteps of Dirac, i.e., move in the direction of his 1938 paper (on the classical theory of the electron). As Bhabha himself put it:

> The difficulties in the classical theory arise by first letting the charge occupy a certain finite volume and then considering a point charge as the limit of this distribution when the volume is made to tend to zero, the amount of charge inside the volume remaining constant. The work done against electrostatic forces in compressing a charge which was originally distributed over a finite volume into a point is naturally infinite...
>
> There is, however, no reason why a point charge should be regarded as the limit of a finite distribution. One may simply regard the point charges in Nature as given. The only idea of energy which now has a meaning is the mutual energy of the point charges.

This was the new point of view proposed by Dirac, and it was used by Bhabha as a stepping stone. The similarities and the differences between the electromagnetic and the meson case, can be appreciated better via the following schematic:

Electron	**E.M. field**	**Electron**

	Neutral field	
Mass: m	Photon	Mass: m
Charge: e	Mass: 0	Charge: e
Spin: 1/2	Charge: 0	Spin: 1/2
	Spin 1	
No dipole moment	Only trans. polarisation	No dipole moment

Nucleon	**Meson field**	**Nucleon**

	Charged / Neutral	
Mass: M	Mass: 0	Mass: M
"Charge": g_1	Charge = 1, 0, −1	"Charge": g_1
Spin: 1/2	Spin: 1	Spin: 1/2
"Dipole moment" g_2	Longitudinal and transverse polarisation	"Dipole moment" g_2

Compared to the electromagnetic field, the meson field has many complications.

1. The meson has a finite rest mass while the light quanta have zero mass. As a result, longitudinally polarised meson waves may exist, besides the two transversely polarised waves known in the theory of light.
2. Both g_1 and g_2 enter in the interaction of the meson with the nucleon. Of these, g_1 is like the charge of electrodynamics while

g_2 is the analogue of the magnetic dipole moment. The magnetic dipole moment of the electron is purely quantum mechanical in origin. Therefore, the equivalent of g_2 is zero in the classical theory of the electron. (Remember, Bhabha is interested in a classical theory.)

3. The electromagnetic field is neutral whereas the meson field could be either neutral or charged.

It must be stressed that g_1 is not the nuclear charge Ze. Rather, it is the analogue of the electrostatic charge in the force that produces nuclear binding, i.e., strong interactions. These complications show that as compared to the electromagnetic problem, there are many more cases to be studied in the meson problem.

Bhabha's first paper on the classical theory of the meson was written shortly before his departure for India. Once back home, he went into details and considered the consequences of the various interactions possible, e.g., interaction of the transverse polarisation of the charged field with the nucleon "charge" g_1, interaction of the longitudinal polarisation of the uncharged meson field with the "dipole moment" g_2, etc. (See Fig.4.2 for a pictorial representation of some of the cases possible.)

Fig.4.2 The meson field can be either charged or uncharged. Further, there are two polarisations possible. The nucleon carries a "charge" g_1 and a "dipole moment" g_2. Thus many interactions are possible. A sample is shown above.

I shall not go through Bhabha's findings in detail because most of them have been overshadowed by subsequent developments. But three things are worth commenting upon. The first is that as a part of this exercise, Bhabha collaborated with Harish Chandra to set up "an exact classical theory for point-particles interacting with any field". Later Harish Chandra turned to mathematics and achieved undying fame (see Box 4.1). The second is the scattering of neutral, transversely polarised mesons by nucleons with $g_1 = 0$. Figure 4.3 shows the result obtained by Bhabha for this case and the standard quantum mechanical result due to Heitler. Clearly, ordinary QM fails.

Bhabha also noticed a difference between the case of the charged and the neutral meson. Concerning this difference, Bhabha corresponded with Pauli while he (Bhabha) was still in Europe. In India, Bhabha pursued the matter and came up with the novel idea of nucleon isobars. We take up that topic now.

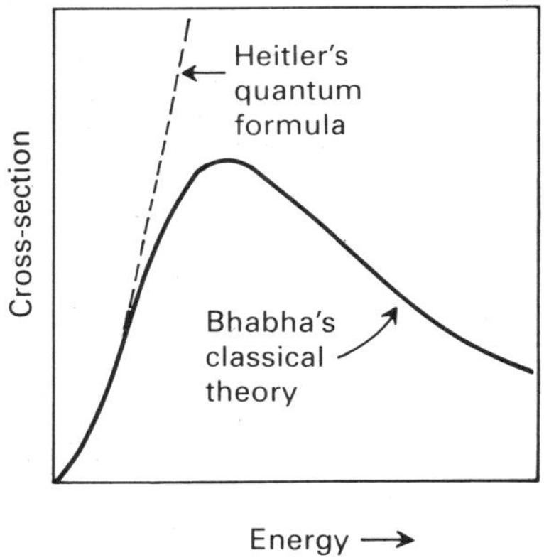

Fig.4.3 Cross-section for the scattering of transversely polarised neutral mesons by nucleons via the g_2 interaction. The dashed line is the result due to the quantum theory of Heitler. It diverges at high energies, which is unacceptable. The solid line is due to Bhabha's classical theory, and predicts a better behaviour.

Box 4.1 Harish Chandra (that was his full name!) was born in Kanpur in October 1923. His father was a civil engineer who worked in the U.P. Irrigation Department. After school and Intermediate studies, Harish Chandra joined the Allahabad University from where he obtained the M.Sc. degree in Physics. The paper in acoustics in the final exam was set by C.V. Raman and one question was on the vibrations of the membrane in the *mridangam*. This is a complicated problem which Raman had solved (see the companion volume *Raman and His Effect*), and he wanted to see if there was any student bright enough to tackle it. Harish Chandra did. It was the only question he could answer for the answer was long and complicated. Nevertheless, Raman was so impressed and pleased that he gave him 100 out of 100. He said: "Here is a boy who has attempted a question no other student has. And he has presented an original solution. If he had time, he would have cleared all the other questions. He does not have to convince me of his ability by giving answers to all the other routine and standard questions."

Meanwhile, Harish Chandra discovered Dirac's book on QM in the library and promptly mastered it. In 1942, Sir K.S. Krishnan (again see *Raman and His Effect*) was appointed Professor of Physics in the Allahabad University and from him Harish Chandra borrowed advanced books on physics and mathematics to improve his learning.

In 1943, Harish Chandra got his M.Sc. degree and, armed with a letter of recommendation from Krishnan, went to Bhabha in Bangalore. Harish Chandra worked with Bhabha for two years. With a recommendation from Bhabha he then went in 1945 to Cambridge to study under the great master, Dirac.

In Cambridge his personal contacts with Dirac were infrequent. He attended Dirac's lectures but soon dropped out when he discovered that they were almost the same as his book. However, Harish Chandra did not miss the weekly seminar run by Dirac. Of Dirac he later said, "He was very gentle and kind yet rather aloof and distant ... [I felt] I should not bother him too much and went to see him about once each term".

Harish Chandra's Ph.D. topic was the *Classification of Irreducible Representations of the Lorentz Group*. The topic was proposed by Dirac.

Harish Chandra's work was now bordering mathematics but as a work of mathematics, his paper was not rigorous enough. Harish Chandra himself said later:

> Soon after coming to Princeton, I became aware that my work on the Lorentz group was based on shaky arguments. I once complained to Dirac about the fact that my proofs were not rigorous and he replied, "I am not interested in proofs but only in what Nature does." This remark confirmed my growing conviction that I did not have the mysterious sixth sense which one needs in order to succeed in physics and I soon decided to move over to mathematics.

The switchover occurred in the following way. In 1947–48 Dirac was a Visiting Professor at the Institute for Advanced Study in Princeton, and Harish Chandra was appointed his assistant. Already in Cambridge, Harish Chandra's appetite for mathematics had been heightened by his attending the lectures of J.E. Littlewood and Philip Hall. And in Princeton he took in more lectures besides reading more of mathematics. The change was now made, irrevocably.

As a mathematician, Harish Chandra drifted through many places – Harvard, Columbia, Paris ... He even spent a year (1952–53) in TIFR.

During this visit to India, he made a brief trip to Bangalore where he was received at the airport by Raman. Bhabha tried to make Harish Chandra stay on but did not succeed. In 1961, Harish Chandra came back to the Institute for Advanced Study, Princeton, and this time he stayed, till he passed away in 1983.

In 1969 he had his first heart attack. Doctors advised physical exercise and mental rest. The first part of the advice he took, the second part he did not. In October 1983 there was a conference in Princeton in which Harish Chandra took an active part.

On the last day of the conference, Harish Chandra invited many participants to his home. Later in the afternoon, after the guests had departed, he went for his customary walk. He did not return alive. His ashes were spread in Princeton and immersed in the Ganges at Allahabad.

A big conference in his honour had been planned in 1984 to celebrate his 60th birthday. The conference was duly held but the man in whose honour it was being held had passed into eternity.

4.4 Nucleon isobars

Bhabha resorted to a classical theory of mesons more or less for the same reasons that made Dirac go back to a classical theory of electrons, i.e., divergence difficulties; in the case of protons and neutrons of course, these difficulties were much worse. Dirac had shown that his classical theory did not suffer from this difficulty. And, following in his footsteps, Bhabha had shown that one could construct a similar theory for the neutral meson. But where charged mesons were concerned, he was a bit hesitant. As he put it, "I think it is only to be regarded as satisfactory that a classical theory of a charged meson does not seem possible ..." Why? Bhabha himself provides the answer.

Now the interaction between two protons or two neutrons can be understood in terms of the exchange of a charged meson. Bhabha comments:

> In a classical theory the jump of heavy particle [meson] from the proton to the neutron state would have to be replaced by a continuous process in which the electric charge gradually left the heavy particle and spread into space in the form of a charged meson field.

And this is where the problem crops up. In the classical theories of Dirac and Bhabha, the point charges are regarded as *given*. One can't now have this point charge spreading out into a cloud and then getting compressed back again into a point charge (which is what happens when the charge hops from the proton to the neutron). Such a charge compression would, as explained earlier, produce infinities. In short, a classical theory of charged meson field would bring back the curse of the infinities. So what was the alternative? Bhabha had one. As he explained:

> The above difficulty, however, does not exist for a quantised meson field. For now, although when a proton turns into a neutron the electric charge becomes distributed over a finite volume as a charged meson field, the distribution is only statistical, and we may regard the charge as always concentrated in a point ... The above considerations make it plausible that a solution of those specific difficulties which occur in the theory of charged but not neutral mesons and their interactions with heavy particles, is only to be found on a quantum mechanical basis.

Bhabha developed such a (quantum) model in a paper entitled *On Elementary Heavy Particles With Any Integral Charge*. This paper was written shortly after his return to India and was communicated to the *Proceedings of the Indian Academy* by Raman. The paper is interesting not because its predictions have come true but because an idea in that paper later came to be widely accepted (with appropriate modifications of course). Bhabha describes this idea as follows:

> We may formulate it [the central idea of the paper] thus. A heavy particle can exist in any state with an electric charge ne where n is a possible integer, or zero, the rest mass in the corresponding state being M_n.

Why all this? Because Bhabha wanted to achieve some symmetry between the neutral and the charged meson field cases. Let me explain.

Recall first that in second-order perturbation theory in quantum mechanics, scattering proceeds via an intermediate state. It turns out that when neutral mesons are emitted and absorbed, there are twice the number of intermediate states involved as when charged mesons are exchanged. Bhabha had noted this even while in England. The new idea proposed by him was intended to remove this difference.

According to him, besides the proton (with a charge $+e$), there were other particles with charges $+2e, +3e, ...$ on the one hand and particles with charges $-e, -2e, ...$ on the other. Let M_0 be the mass of the neutron. In Bhabha's theory, the mass M_n of a particle of charge ne is given by

$$M_n = M_0 + \Delta M_n.$$

The variation of ΔM_n with n (as given by Bhabha) is indicated in Fig. 4.4. We observe that apart from the proton (P) and the neutron (N), there are several new particles, all charged. Just as the P and N have nearly the same mass (but different charges), $P(2+)$ and $P(-)$ have nearly the same mass but different charges. Likewise, $P(2-)$ and $P(3+)$. In nuclear physics there are many nuclei with different charges but (nearly) the same mass, e.g., Ca^{40} and A^{40}. Such nuclei are called nuclear isobars. Analogously, Fig. 4.4 introduces what might be called *nucleon isobars*.

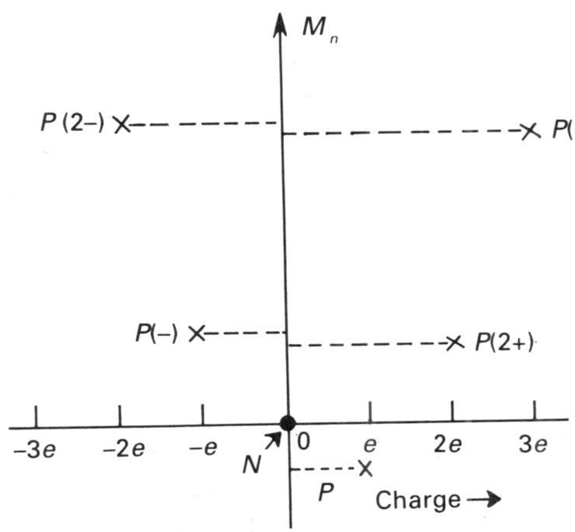

Fig.4.4 Schematic variation (according to Bhabha) of the charge of elementary particles with their mass.

What are these new particles? For example, is the particle with charge $-e$ i.e., $P(-)$, the anti-proton? Bhabha answers that one.

> It is clear that the particle of charge $-e$ is not the "anti-proton" since its mass is appreciably different from the mass of the proton. Since the existence of an anti-proton of exactly the same mass as a proton is a consequence of the Dirac equation, the acceptance of the above idea would probably necessitate rejecting the Dirac equation for a relativistic theory of heavy particles ...

Over the years, Bhabha's idea has metamorphosed, if one might say so. Later I shall make a brief reference to more recent developments. For the present, let us get on with the Bhabha story.

Consider now the interaction of two protons. Bhabha's picture leads to two possibilities for the intermediate state as indicated below:

$$P+P\rightarrow\left\{\begin{array}{c}P+U^{-}+P(2+)\\ \\ P+U^{+}+N\end{array}\right\}\rightarrow P(2+)+N$$

Intermediate state

Here $P(2+)$ is the particle of charge $+2e$ and $U^{\pm}$ are charged mesons. Similarly, for N–N collision one has:

$$N+N\rightarrow\left\{\begin{array}{c}P+U^{-}+N\\ \\ P(-)+U^{+}+N\end{array}\right\}\rightarrow P(-)+P$$

Intermediate state

where $P(-)$ is the particle of charge $-e$. Observe that the number of intermediate states is now the same, both for P–P and N–N scattering, unlike in the classical picture.

Bhabha argued that particles like $P(2+)$ and $P(-)$ would be produced in high-energy nucleon–nucleon collisions. In those days, cosmic rays were the only source of high-energy data. Analysis of available data did not reveal any conclusive evidence and Bhabha therefore made various suggestions for fresh experiments. Reacting to these, Prof. H.J. Taylor of Wilson College, Bombay then exposed photographic plates in the Himalayas to try and obtain evidence for such isobars in cosmic-ray interactions. However, no evidence was found. Fifteen years after Bhabha's prediction, Fermi observed the first resonance in pion–nucleon scattering (see Appendix to this chapter). This opened the floodgates and soon numerous resonances were discovered among which could be identified isobars. True, isobars are understood and explained today in a somewhat different manner but that should not deter us from admiring Bhabha's foresight and vision. (We must also not forget a few others who were on a similar track.) After all, don't we give credit to our ancients for having conceived of the atom thousands of years ago?

4.5 Looking inward

We come now to Bhabha's work on what has come to be called the *Bhabha equation*. Basically, it is a quantum mechanical equation, inspired by and rather like the Dirac equation and intended as a gateway to the world of elementary particles. It did not quite work out that way but that does not make Bhabha's work any less beautiful. Later I shall add a few more remarks about the abstract and aesthetic beauty of this equation. Let me just mention here that after dabbling for a while with the classical theory of the meson, Bhabha decided that one could not put off the confrontation with a *proper* quantum theory of the meson. If the work on the nucleon isobar was a sort of warm-up exercise, the work on the Bhabha equation was a more intense and serious effort. It is this work which I earlier described as inward looking. Why? Because in it Bhabha goes to his roots as an admirer of mathematics on the one hand and of Nature on the other and tries to use the elegance of the former to reconstruct the beauty of the latter. Here he is in a world all by himself, his signposts being the mathematical theory of groups. And so, we must get a brief glimpse of what symmetry and groups are all about if we are to understand and appreciate Bhabha's motivations as well as style.

4.6 On invariance

We start with the concept of invariance. Invariance means absence of change. With respect to what? In physics it implies absence of change with respect to some particular operation (rather, transformation) or a set of operations.

Let us consider the example of geometric invariance. Consider the equilateral triangle in Fig. 4.5. If the triangle is rotated clockwise or anticlockwise by 120°, the triangle goes into coincidence with itself. Suppose you look at the triangle and then close your eyes; meanwhile I rotate it by 120°. When you open your eyes again you cannot say whether I have rotated the triangle or not. I could have

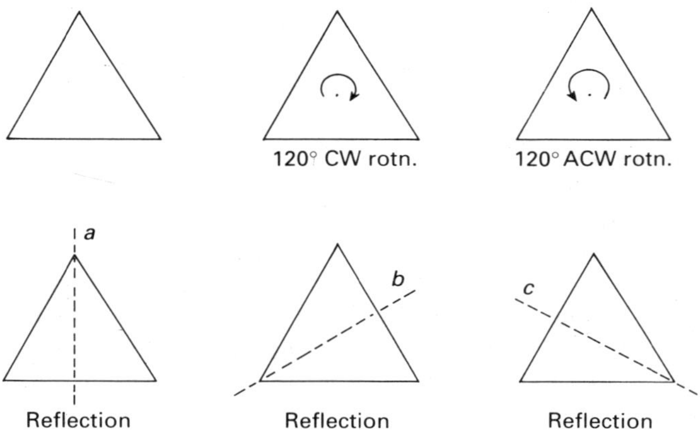

Fig.4.5 Equilateral triangle and some of the (geometric) operations which leave the triangle invariant, i.e., bring it into coincidence with itself. Such operations are called symmetry operations.

rotated 120° clockwise or anticlockwise or even reflected. Everyone of these operations brings the triangle into coincidence with itself, making "before" and "after" equivalent. This is the meaning of invariance.

Geometric invariance flows from the geometric symmetry. In physics we extend the concept of symmetry and invariance to Hamiltonians and Lagrangians, and in fact this is where most of the action is.

Suppose we wish to calculate the energy levels of an atom. We would do this by first setting up a Hamiltonian and then diagonalising it – this is the standard quantum mechanical route (see *The Quantum Revolution*: *Part* I). To specify the Hamiltonian we must have a coordinate frame of reference. Question: Will the energy levels depend on how we choose the coordinate axes? Obviously it should not, which means that the starting Hamiltonian must be suitably tailored to guarantee this. In other words, the Hamiltonian must be invariant with respect to either the translation of the frame of reference or rotation of the axes about the origin. In such a case, one says the Hamiltonian has translational and rotational symmetry. Note, we are now speaking of the symmetry of a mathematical entity, i.e., the Hamiltonian, as opposed to that of a geometric object, e.g., a cardboard piece in the shape of an equilateral triangle.

4.7 On symmetry

Symmetry is big business in physics. In fact, much of the progress in high-energy physics has come through the discovery of beautiful and totally unsuspected *hidden* symmetries, i.e., symmetries beyond those we normally associate with space and time. This is a subject in itself, too big to be discussed here. Let me just say that symmetry leads to richness in the physical system that possesses the symmetry. For example, in the case of the atom, it is the rotational symmetry that leads to the classification of atomic states in terms of angular momentum etc. In fact, this classification can be done even without knowing the detailed structure of the Hamiltonian — all one has to know is the symmetry of the system. In the case of elementary particles, this is particularly helpful because one knows more about their symmetries than the way they interact. Thus, using symmetry arguments, one has been able to classify the large number of particles into families with hierarchy etc.

4.8 On groups

Closely related to symmetry is the concept of groups, with which we must now become familiar.

You must have heard of sets — a set of animals, a set of numbers, and so forth. Let us say we have a set (E, A, B, C, D, F). This is a finite set consisting of six elements. For the moment, we don't bother about what these elements are. We just regard them as abstract entities. It is possible to have operations (or compositions) between elements of a set. What this means is that if the set consists of the numbers (0, 1, 2, 3, ...), then an operation betwen two elements could mean adding two numbers, multiplying two numbers, etc.

When element A operates on B, we express it as AB. The result of the operation could be another element belonging to the set, e.g., $1 + 2 = 3$. Obviously, the operation here is addition. We would be interested in such cases, and write the result as $AB = C$.

A group G is a very special kind of set which has the following properties:

1. For every element (e.g., A and B) in G, the operation AB results in an element contained in G.

2. There is associativity, i.e., $(AB)C = A(BC)$. It means that B can first act on C, and then A can act on the result, or A first acts on B and the result of that is made to act on C. Both sequences are equivalent.
3. There is a special element E in G such that if you operate on any element with E, you get back the same element, i.e., $EA = AE = A$, $EB = B$ and so on. This element E is called the *identity* element.
4. For every element A in G, there exists some other element Y say, such that $AY = YA = E$. Often, Y is written as A^{-1}, and read A *inverse*.

Consider now the table below. It is a multiplication table which tells you what happens when one of the elements of our set acts on another, e.g., $BA = E$. Using this table, you can convince yourself that all the group properties are obeyed by our set (E, A, B, C, D, F).

Element acting first	Element acting second					
	E	A	B	C	D	F
E	E	A	B	C	D	F
A	A	B	E	F	C	D
B	B	E	A	D	F	C
C	C	D	F	E	A	B
D	D	F	C	B	E	A
F	F	C	D	A	B	E

The set (E, A, B, C, D, F) thus forms an *abstract* group. You may ask, 'So what? Is there any use?' Yes, and to see that let us go back to the equilateral triangle. We now identify the symmetry operations of the triangle with group elements A, B... etc., as below:

> A = 120° clockwise rotation, B = 120° anticlockwise rotation, C, D, F = 180° flips about the dotted lines a, b, c in Fig. 4.5, and E = identity.

We then find that the geometrical operations defined above obey the multiplication table we had before. In other words, the set of operations we can perform on an equilateral triangle is a *practical* realisation of an abstract group.

Once we know that a physical system has group structure, using that knowledge we can then describe many of the properties of the system. For instance, using group theory one can sketch the different modes in which the membrane of a drum can vibrate. We don't need to know anything else about the drum such as its diameter, the density of the membrane, etc. Group theory is very powerful, and has many uses. See also Box 4.2.

Box 4.2 It was mentioned in the text that symmetry is related to invariance. In the case of geometric symmetry, this relationship is fairly easy to grasp but in other cases, this relationship is more subtle. As Feynman puts it:

> The symmetry of physical laws are very interesting ... In quantum mechanics, *for each of the rules of symmetry there is a corresponding conservation law* ...

What does Feynman mean? Let me illustrate with one example. Consider the Bohr model of the atom. In this we have an electron of charge $-e$ interacting with a nucleus of charge $+Ze$. The potential energy of interaction is

$$-\frac{Ze^2}{r}, \tag{1}$$

where r is the distance between the electron and the nucleus. Suppose the nucleus is held fixed at the origin of coordinates. The potential energy is given by (1) no matter where the electron is, provided it is on the surface of a sphere of radius r. The potential energy is insensitive to the *direction* of the vector $\mathbf{r}$, and depends only the scalar magnitude r. We may also look up this invariance in a slightly different way, as illustrated in figure (a).

Here the nucleus and the electron maintain their respective positions but the axes of coordinates are rotated. However, this does not alter the energy of attraction between the electron and the nucleus. In short, direction plays no role and the potential energy is insensitive to it. More formally, the potential energy remains invariant under rotation or is *spherically symmetric*. This is the symmetry (rotational symmetry in this case) that Feynman is talking about. The corresponding conserved quantity is angular momentum.

There are three conservation laws we learn about when we begin studying physics namely, conservation of linear momentum, conservation of angular momentum and conservation of energy. These are respectively related to symmetry under translations in space, symmetry under

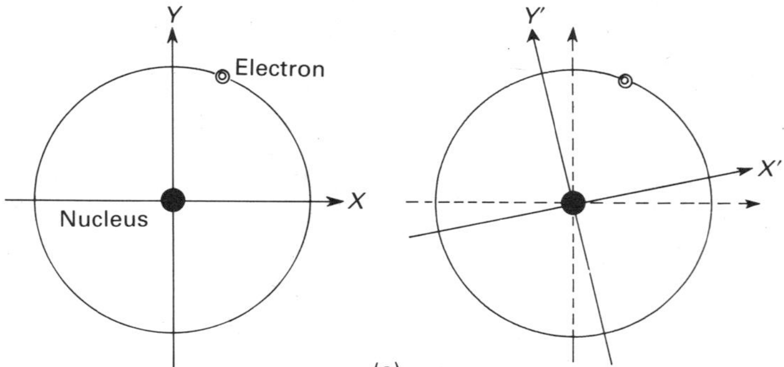

(a)

rotations and symmetry under translations in time (if I drop a stone and do measurements on it, I would get the same results today, tomorrow, etc., provided the conditions of the experiment remain the same). Feynman refers to these connections between symmetry and conserved quantities as "among the most beautiful and profound things in physics". He adds:

> There are a number of symmetries which appear in quantum mechanics which have no classical analog ... One of these is as follows: If ψ is the amplitude for some process or the other, we know that the absolute square of ψ is the probability that the process will occur. Now if someone else were to make his calculations, not with this ψ, but with a ψ' which differs merely by a change in phase (let Δ be some constant, and multiply $e^{-i\Delta}$ times the old ψ), the absolute square of ψ', which is the probability of the event, is then equal to the absolute square of ψ.
>
> $$\psi' = \psi e^{-i\Delta}; \qquad |\psi'|^2 = |\psi|^2.$$
>
> Therefore the physical laws are unchanged if the phase of the wave function is shifted by an arbitrary constant ... The conservation law which is connected with the quantum mechanical phase seems to be the *conservation of electrical charge*. This is altogether a very interesting business!

Changing the phase by Δ is called *gauge transformation*. The fact that physics is unchanged by such a transformation is called *gauge symmetry*. Group theory thus reveals that charge conservation is a natural sequence of gauge symmetry. In recent decades, many new conservation laws have been discovered like the conservation of strangeness, charm, etc. Corresponding to each of these, there is an internal symmetry. The discovery of these hidden symmetries is one of the great triumphs of modern physics.

4.9 Groups and their representations

In mathematics, groups are considered at a purely abstract level. In physics on the other hand, group operations are assigned physical meaning. Further, one considers in detail what is called the *representation* of groups. I shall now explain this by considering the group of the square. To start with, forget groups, representations and all that and just focus on the square in Fig. 4.6(a). Among other things, this square goes into coincidence with itself under the following operations: (i) 90° clockwise rotation, (ii) diagonal reflection, and (iii) "midway" reflection. The effect of these operations is illustrated in Fig. 4.6(b). If you think of the square as made up of a piece of cardboard, say, you would not be able to distinguish between "before" and "after"; nor would you be able to say which operation was performed, if any. Next, note that

> "midway" reflection = diagonal reflection ×90° clockwise rotation, i.e., the operation on the left is able to produce the same effect as the combination on the right.
>
> This is one example of the combination rule $C = AB$ mentioned earlier.

Now consider the four patterns in Fig. 4.6(c). Say c(i) is the starting pattern. Observe it is different from a blank square. If we rotate this pattern by 90° clockwise, we get c(ii). If now on c(ii) we perform a diagonal reflection, we get c(iii). On the other hand if we perform a "midway" reflection on c(i) we obtain c(iv). However, c(iv) is indistinguishable from c(iii). The message is: The patterns c(i)–c(iv) follow the multiplication rule given earlier. Notice something very important. Operations that leave the square invariant do not, in general, leave the patterns themselves invariant. However, the abstract rules of combinations of the operations are mimicked by the patterns. This is the key point about the representation business. The following page shows a list of operations associated with the group of the square.

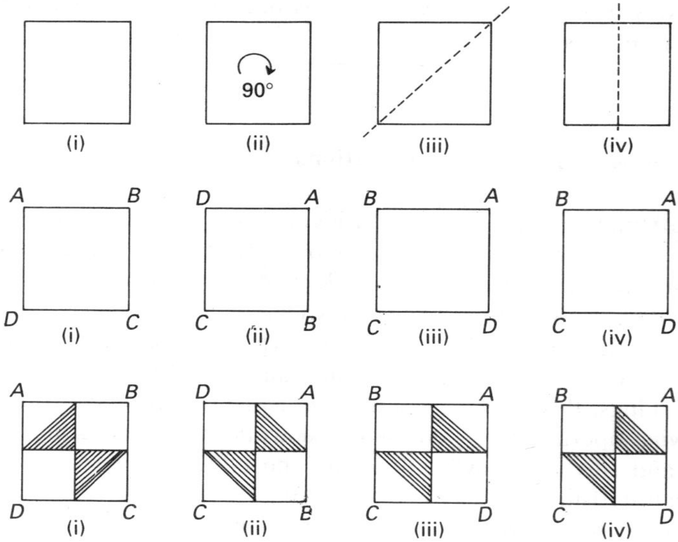

Fig.4.6 (a) The square and some of the operations which leave it invariant. (b) The manner in which the corners are shuffled by the operations of (a). (c) Pattern changes and how they respect the group multiplication table. (i) is the starting pattern. A 90° rotation produces (ii). When this is followed by diagonal reflection, we get (iii). A midway reflection on (i) leads to (iv) which is the same as (iii). They are consistent with the combination rule stated earlier.

Group of the square

Identity, 90° rotn., 180° rotn., 270° rotn., diagonal refln. 1, diagonal refln. 2, midway refln. 1, midway refln. 2.

I suggest you spend some time using these to construct the multiplication table. Next, consider the set of decorated patterns in Fig. 4.7. Try now to convince yourself that when the group operations are applied to members of this set of patterns, they faithfully follow the multiplication table. The set of patterns in Fig. 4.7 constitutes a *representation* of the group of the square.

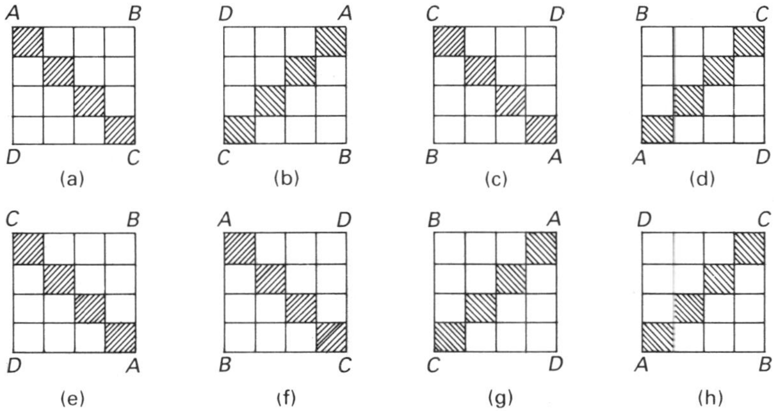

Fig.4.7 A set of patterns which form a representation of the group of the square. Each pattern is identified with a group element, (a) being associated with the identity element. The patterns follow the group multiplication table.

Now comes an important question: How many representations can a group have? And the answer is: The sky is the limit! This might appear to make the whole business of representations messy and hopeless; fortunately not. Why? Because, in the world of representations, there are what are called *irreducible representations* which are like building blocks. Depending on the situation, the number of irreducible representations can be finite or infinite. Even if they are infinite, they do not pose any serious problem. Once one has access to these irreducible representations, then one can do lots of things in physics. In a nutshell, the abstract group is like Lord Vishnu and the irreducible representations are like His Avatars!

4.10 The Lorentz group

In physics, one deals with a variety of groups. For example, in the world of molecules and crystals one is interested in groups related to the geometric structure of the molecule or the crystal as the case may be. Such groups are rather like the groups of the triangle and of the square I introduced you to earlier. In the world of the atom, one is interested in the group of all possible rotations about all possible axes passing through the centre of a sphere. The rotation group also is a geometric group. Of course, while actually working out the theory of the atom one adds a few frills but for our purposes, that is a matter of detail.

Geometric groups (i.e., those related to geometric symmetry) are one example of groups. There are many others, an important one being the Lorentz group. In the volume *At the Speed of Light*, I have discussed how two observers, say O and O' riding respectively two inertial frames S and S' in uniform relative motion would describe events to each other. Say there is an event P and that O uses (x, y, z, t) to describe it. O' (who is riding S') similarly uses (x', y', z', t'). There exists a transformation called the *Lorentz transformation* which relates these two sets of space-time coordinates. What has all this to do with groups? We are coming to that! For a minute, consider a circle whose equation is

$$x^2 + y^2 = a^2$$

The physical import of this is that as long as we are on the circle, the sum of x^2 and y^2 is a constant. In other words, the quantity $(x^2 + y^2)$ is invariant with respect to a rotation about an axis perpendicular to the circle and passing through the centre – see Fig. 4.8. Similarly,

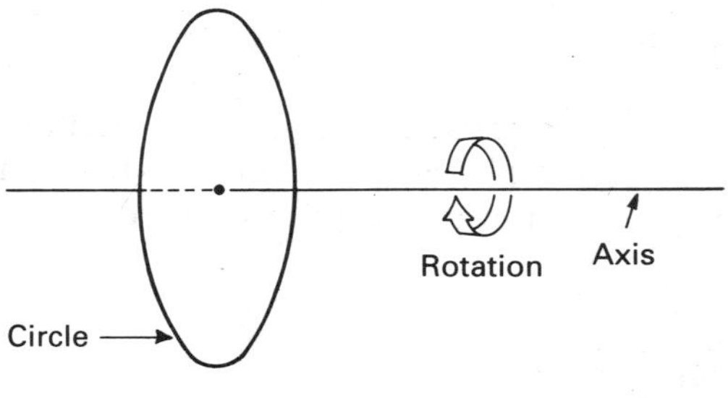

Fig.4.8 The circle is invariant when rotated about the axis, no matter what the rotation angle.

in the case of a sphere, the quantity $(x^2 + y^2 + z^2)$ is invariant with respect to rotations about all possible axes passing through the centre, and through all possible angles.

Now to special relativity. Suppose a flash of light is emitted at the origin of coordinates at time $t = 0$. The light wave will propagate as an expanding sphere described by the equation

$$x^2 + y^2 + z^2 - c^2t^2 = 0. \tag{4.3}$$

Let us now consider an observer moving with a uniform velocity v relative to the coordinate system Ox, Oy, Oz. Let $O'x', O'y', O'z'$ be the coordinate system of this observer and further let the origins O and O' coincide at time $t = t' = 0$. Now according to special relativity, the velocity of light is independent of the motion of the observer. Thus the observer in the second frame also sees a spherical wave front, this one being described by

$$x'^2 + y'^2 + z'^2 - c^2t'^2 = 0. \tag{4.4}$$

Of course, (x, y, z, t) and (x', y', z', t') are related by Lorentz transformations. What (4.3) and (4.4) tell us is that the quantity $(x^2 + y^2 + z^2 - c^2t^2)$ is invariant under a Lorentz transformation. Thus, by analogy, *we can regard Lorentz transformations as rotations in four-dimensional space.* And associated with these rotations there exists a group which is the *Lorentz group.*

The Lorentz group plays an important role in many branches of physics. Bhabha relied heavily on it and explains why.

> One of the primary requirements of every theory of elementary particles is that it shall be in keeping with the principles of the special theory of relativity. Any mathematical quantities which appear in the equations must therefore have well-defined transformation properties for changes in the frame of reference, and these must be combined in the fundamental equations in such a way that the latter remain unaltered by any transformation of the Lorentz group involved in going from one Cartesian frame to another moving relative to it with uniform velocity.

Nobelist Steven Weinberg has this to say about the Lorentz group:

> I don't know why Nature has all these symmetries but Lorentz invariance, for example, the most important symmetry of all, is not only a symmetry which governs the form of the equations [describing the elementary particles], it tells us what the equations are all about.

The Lorentz group deals with the symmetries of space–time. In addition, there are other symmetries called inner symmetries. The corresponding groups are called *gauge groups*. They are very important in elementary particle physics. Weinberg adds:

> In a sense, if you have an elementary particle, and you describe how it behaves under various symmetry transformations, including translations, rotations, gauge transformations, then you have said everything there is to say about the particle. The identity of the particle is fixed by its symmetry properties. The particle is nothing else but a representation of its symmetry group.

4.11 Some more background

I am sorry I am loading you with a lot of preamble but I am afraid it is necessary if we are to get some feel for what Bhabha was after and what he did vis-a-vis the theory of elementary particles. So far, I have been telling you something about groups and their representations because Bhabha made heavy use of these concepts. I must digress a bit more before making contact with the Bhabha equation.

In the late-thirties early-forties period the situation with regard to elementary particles was roughly the following:

1. The known species of elementary particles (as then defined) consisted of (i) the electron, (ii) the positron, (iii) the proton, (iv) the neutron, (v) the neutrino (whose existence was inferred from β-decay studies) and (vi) the Yukawa particle, whatever it was.
2. Elementary particles appeared to have spin 0, 1/2, or 1.
3. Spin 1/2 particles obeyed Fermi statistics while spin 0 and spin 1 particles obeyed Bose statistics. (For more about particle statistics, see the companion volume *Bose and His Statistics*.)
4. The electron (and the positron) could be described within the framework of the Dirac equation.
5. Quantum electrodynamics based on the Dirac equation was not faring well.

One could perhaps add many footnotes but I shall skip them. What I should stress is that people suspected that there could be other elementary particles as well, indeed possibly with spin greater than 1, e.g., 3/2. The problems people were grappling with were two-fold. On one hand, there was the battle against the infinities in QED (see, *The Quantum Revolution*: *Part* II). And on the other, there was the problem of understanding nuclear forces as well as new particles steadily being discovered, especially in cosmic-ray experiments.

At this stage the game becomes rather technical and I am sure you wouldn't want me to tax you with details (important though they are!). Let me therefore confine myself to the highlights of what Bhabha attempted and achieved (in the above context).

4.12 An approach via postulates

Bhabha was interested in giving a theoretical description of elementary particles. This is an exercise in theoretical physics. Now what is the aim of theoretical physics? Bhabha defines it as follows:

> The aim of theoretical physics must be to find a complete set of mutually consistent mathematical postulates or axioms from which the properties of Nature, meaning thereby the result of every conceivable experiment, can be deduced in the form of theorems.

Of course, Bhabha is interested only in elementary particles. Specifically, he would like to discover equations which do the same job for the entire family of elementary particles, which the Dirac equation does for the electron. How exactly does one define an elementary particle? Bhabha helps us out. He says:

> The only quantities of this description [i.e., which remain invariant under Lorentz transformations] are tensors and spinors, and one should expect that only those would occur in the theory of an elementary particle which are *irreducible*, that is, which cannot be split into two or more parts in a relativistically invariant way. Correspondingly, we should expect the equations describing an elementary particle-field to be irreducible, that is, incapable of being split into separate sets of equations in a relativistically invariant way.

In short,

> An elementary particle-field is one described by an irreducible set of equations.

Lots of highbrow jargon I agree, but if you stay with me some of it will soon begin to make sense. In essence, Bhabha is looking for wave equations like the Dirac equation, which describe the elementary particles in a "Lorentz invariant" manner.

Let us go back to the question of axioms or mathematical postulates. What kind of postulates does Bhabha prefer? He discussed this in a series of lectures he gave at the Canadian Mathematical Congress held in 1949. Bhabha starts with the following:

Postulate 1

The predictions of any theory which one formulates, must not violate the principle of special relativity.

Postulate 2

A function ψ called the wave function, whose value is defined at all points of space-like surfaces, exists such that it provides the maximum possible amount of information which can be obtained by observation about the state of the physical system.

Postulate 3

The fundamental laws of Nature are such that given the values of the wave function Ψ at all points of a space-like surface, it is possible to calculate its values at all points of a later space-like surface.

Postulate 4

Besides Ψ, Ψ^*, and the derivatives of these, the equation of motion shall contain only universal constants.

Postulate 5

The equation of motion must be derivable from a suitable Lagrangian by a variational principle. (This principle is a central concept in theoretical physics, and has been briefly touched upon in the volumes *The Quantum Revolution*: *Part* I *and Part* II.)

An important requirement is that the Lagrangian of the theory must be invariant with respect to the operations of the Lorentz group. A Pundit would simply say: The Lagrangian must be *Lorentz invariant.*

Reduced to brass tacks Bhabha was exploring equations of the form

$$\left(i\hbar\frac{\partial}{\partial x^k}\alpha^k + \chi\right)\psi = 0 \tag{4.5}$$

a special case of which is the Dirac equation. Equation (4.5) is referred to as the Bhabha equation. Before I tell you more about it, a few words of history.

4.13 Similar quest by others

As you know, the Dirac equation was a terrific success (that is if one ignored its performance on the electrodynamics front!). So, understandably, there was a general curiosity about and search for similar equations for the proton, neutron, etc. People also wondered if there were particles of spin higher than 1.

Many had a go at this problem. The route to follow was indicated by the experience of classical electromagnetic theory where one had the celebrated first-order (i.e., Maxwell's) equations which describe the electric and magnetic fields, and the second-order equation for wave propagation. In the case of elementary particles also, the search was on for something similar. There were good reasons why people did so; and Bhabha himself has explained them. He says:

> The requirement that the formulation of the natural laws shall be invariant for all transformations of the Lorentz group, that is, all transformations which leave the form $(x^2+y^2+z^2-c^2t^2)$ invariant, has as a consequence that the simplest invariant differential operator is
>
> $$\frac{\partial^2}{\partial x^2}+\frac{\partial^2}{\partial y^2}+\frac{\partial^2}{\partial z^2}-\frac{1}{c^2}\frac{\partial^2}{\partial t^2}.$$
>
> The simplest invariant partial differential equations for one function are therefore the wave equation
>
> $$\frac{\partial^2 u}{\partial x^2}+\frac{\partial^2 u}{\partial y^2}+\frac{\partial^2 u}{\partial z^2}-\frac{1}{c^2}\frac{\partial^2 u}{\partial t^2}=0,$$
>
> and the generalised wave equation
>
> $$\left(\frac{\partial^2}{\partial x^2}+\frac{\partial^2}{\partial y^2}+\frac{\partial^2}{\partial z^2}-\frac{1}{c^2}\frac{\partial^2}{\partial t^2}+\chi^2\right)u=0,$$
>
> where χ is an invariant.

So there should be two things in the tool kit – a first-order equation which defines the field and a second-order equation which describes evolution in space-time (see above). And, for the first-order equation, people were looking for something like a Dirac equation.

Action moved on roughly two paths. One stream was pursued by Dirac, Fierz and Pauli. A positive outcome was that along the line, Pauli was able to show the connection between spin and statistics. (I have briefly touched upon this in the volume *Bose and His Statistics*.) It all had to do with quantising the wave field in a manner that made physical sense. Pauli found that for particles with integer spin, quantisation implied Bose statistics and for particles with half-integer spin, quantisation implied Fermi statistics. In practical terms this meant defining commutation rules in one case and rules for anti-commutators in the other case. Echoes of this might perhaps come to you from *The Quantum Revolution*: *Part* I *and Part* II, (that is, if you have read those volumes). One unsatisfactory feature with the Dirac–Fierz–Pauli (DFP) scheme was that to describe the particle field, many subsidiary conditions had to be imposed. And for particles of higher spin (i.e., greater than 1), this business of subsidiary conditions became really messy.

4.14 The Bhabha equation

I now come to the so-called second route. This was taken by Bhabha who was essentially looking for a way of not resorting to the subsidiary conditions. To see what Bhabha did, we have to go back to equation (4.5)

$$\left(i\hbar\frac{\partial}{\partial x^k}\alpha^k + \chi\right)\psi = 0.$$

This is written in the four-vector notation of relativity (which I have explained in *At the Speed of Light* and in *The Quantum Revolution*: *Part* II). If we remember that and take $\chi = \beta mc^2$, we have the Dirac equation, provided the α's and β are suitably interpreted, i.e., as described in Chapter 3 of *The Quantum Revolution*: *Part* I. Don't feel lost if these details overwhelm you. They are not important right now. Just note that Bhabha wrote down (4.5) as a possible generalisation of the Dirac equation.

Now when Dirac wrote his equation, he told us what his set of α's were. What about the present case? Bhabha showed that his α's satisfied a certain equation and that this equation could be solved knowing the irreducible representations of the Lorentz group in five dimensions. Note that this Lorentz group relates to five, not four, dimensions. It is like a rotational group in five dimensions and its identification tag is SO(5). Next time you hear somebody talk about SO(5), don't be too scared – you can shrug and dismiss it simply as rotations in five dimensions!

Perhaps you now have a glimpse of how group theory enters into the picture. In essence, as follows:

(i) Bhabha writes first-order equation for the wave field ψ rather like Dirac did. This ψ is supposed to describe elementary particles.
(ii) Bhabha's equation features α-matrices like Dirac's did.
(iii) The α-matrices now have to be defined. Bhabha says: They can be found by solving such-and-such an equation.
(iv) How to solve it? Bhabha says: Take help from the irreducible representations of SO(5).

After all this trouble, what did Bhabha discover? He found that "each irreducible representation [of SO(5)] gives one irreducible equation for an elementary particle-field". So? Well, this equation

> has solutions in which energy and momentum are connected by the equation ($E^2 = p^2c^2 + M^2c^4$), with M given respectively for integral or half-odd integral n [this n is a quantity associated with the irreducible representation] by
>
> $$\pm\frac{\chi}{n},\ \pm\frac{\chi}{n^{-1}},\ \pm\frac{\chi}{n^{-2}}, \ldots \pm\chi \quad \text{or} \quad \pm 2\chi.$$
>
> The particle-field therefore describes particles with several different values of the rest mass, but these must all be considered as different states of the same physical entity, just like the positron and electron, since the equations are irreducible.

There it is! Bhabha found that except in the case of particles of spin 0, 1/2 and 1, "all elementary particles must appear with several values of the rest mass which bear well-defined and simple numerical ratios to the lowest value".

Have such particles been found? That is a long story. After the advent of high-energy accelerators any number of particles have been found, yes including with spin greater than 1, but they do not follow Bhabha's classification scheme. This is only to be expected. In the forties when Bhabha did his work, one hardly knew of the existence of various "hidden" symmetries, i.e., various non-classical degrees of freedom. Sure one knew about spin discovered by Goudsmit and Uhlenbeck but one little suspected that there were a whole lot of other symmetries (like strangeness, charm, etc.). Once these symmetries were discovered, people tried the same game as Bhabha, adding the invariances demanded by these new symmetries to the good old Lorentz invariance which of course continued to remain at the top of the requirement list. In short, apart from the Lorentz group, one had to respect appropriate gauge groups. As far as starting from a minimum set of postulates, using symmetry and linking it all to a variational principle was concerned, the style set by Bhabha (and independently by a few others of his period), is still very much in vogue.

Bhabha knew for sure that his equation could not be the last word. Being firmly of the view that Nature cannot be unravelled by "pure thought" he was fully alive to the fact that experimental findings would influence and refine the postulates and assumptions one makes. Indeed this has happened.

Apart from this, are there any other problems with the Bhabha equation? Yes, two. First of course there is the problem of infinities. If it is any comfort, this problem which is associated with strong interactions (see Chapter 7, *The Quantum Revolution*: *Part* II), is not peculiar to the Bhabha equation. In this connection I would also like you to recall the conversation between Dirac and Feynman which I have quoted in the above chapter. Incidentally for spin > 1, "no totally consistent, relativistic, massive, interactive wave equations have yet been discovered." (I am quoting an expert.) The other problem? For higher spins, the solutions imply negative probabilities. (Technically, the system has what is called an indefinite metric. Doesn't matter if you don't follow. I don't!)

4.15 Some more history

A bit of history again. It starts in 1936 when Proca wrote down a second-order equation for spin 1 particles. Two years later Kemmer realised that Proca's equations could be described as a set of coupled first-order equations, and he also wrote them down for the analogous spin 0 case. Shortly after that, Kemmer's work was discussed at a seminar in Purdue University which inspired a mathematician named Duffin to publish a paper on the subject. When Kemmer saw Duffin's work he wrote to Duffin saying that he knew how to extend Duffin's work but would give place to him (Duffin) in case he wanted to publish more. Duffin replied that he was involved with other research and that Kemmer could go ahead if he wanted to. All this happened before 1939. Bhabha was a friend of Kemmer and presumably he was aware of these developments, called the Duffin–Kemmer–Proca or DKP formalism. Bhabha took off where DKP left. It would also appear that in Bangalore, Bhabha aroused the interest of Madhava Rao on the subject. Later (around 1945), Bhabha put his stamp by establishing the connection with SO(5).

This is not all. During the same period Taketani and Sakata in Japan independently did somewhat similar work but before they could complete it, Taketani was put in prison by the Japanese Government. Earlier, Taketani had written an article in which he said science was international and that scientists should be regarded as members of an international community. The then military government of Japan did not like the article. Though Taketani used a pseudonym, it was not difficult for the secret police to track him and throw him into prison. By the time Taketani was released, Duffin and Kemmer had skimmed the cream so to speak; so the Japanese went on to doing something different but related. Another person whose name deserves mention is Lubanski who published his work in Netherlands in 1941. Unfortunately, since Netherlands was then under German occupation, few took notice of his work.

Let me wind up the story of the Bhabha equation by quoting Professor Virendra Singh. He says:

> The fascination with relativistic equations, in general, and with Bhabha equations, in particular, has continued undiminished in view of their aesthetic appeal, despite the fact that they have still not found significant physical applications.

4.16 Bhabha as a physicist

From the next chapter onwards, we shall be seeing Bhabha in an entirely different light. It is therefore worthwhile to pause and reflect on Bhabha the physicist. Given his tastes in mathematics, it was inevitable that Bhabha's first love would be theoretical physics because that provided the ideal meeting ground between abstract beauty and natural beauty.

Theoretical physicists come in several varieties, two broad types being phenomenologists and formal theorists. A phenomenologist usually speculates, builds models, etc., all for computing numbers which can be compared with experimental data. A formal theorist, on the other hand, is interested in creating a framework, an edifice, which others could use. Bhabha tried both, although his natural instincts lay in the direction of formal theory. At the same time, he did not take the extreme view that Einstein did when he (Einstein) said, "... pure thought can grasp [physical] reality ..." According to Bhabha,

> It is most important to distinguish this approach [theory tempered with experiment] from the one which assumes that one can arrive at the laws of Nature by pure thought and epistemological reasoning. The latter approach has neither met with much success, nor proved particularly fruitful in promoting an understanding of the physical world. In our approach, on the contrary, we recognised that it may be possible to build many logically consistent theories which have nevertheless nothing to do with the actual structure of the physical world.

One must therefore employ the minimum number of assumptions and develop a formal theory not only of maximum mathematical elegance but also capable of giving the best possible description of Nature. Today, even a graduate student knows that this is the way one must work but way back in the forties this outlook was confined to a handful. Bhabha not only shared this belief but also articulated it effectively in his papers. Dirac's influence on Bhabha's thinking is clearly visible. Later we shall catch glimpses of other aspects of Bhabha's fascination with beauty.

Perhaps you are wondering what happened in the field of elementary particles subsequent to Bhabha's investigations. A brief description of that can be found at the end of the Appendix to this chapter.

Appendix to Chapter 4

As you know, the study of elementary particles commenced with the discovery of the electron and the proton. Both these are stable. After the advent of high-energy accelerators, a large number of particles were discovered. Almost invariably, they are unstable. Many of these are resonances. This Appendix is mainly an introduction to particle resonance.

The word resonance implies something is "in tune" or "in harmony" with something else. Suppose we have a swing that is stationary. The swing is like a pendulum and therefore has a natural frequency of oscillation. Suppose we set the swing into gentle or low-amplitude oscillations. We now stand on one side and everytime the swing comes towards us we give it a gentle push. If given properly, the push would help the swing to oscillate with larger and larger amplitude. In this case, the force that we apply is in resonance with the swing. On the other hand, if we give the pushes erratically, the applied force and the natural oscillating tendency of the swing would not be in harmony with each other and the oscillations would fail to build up. Children playing with swings know this instinctively.

In particle physics, we deal with particle interactions. These are typically produced by bombarding one species with another. The former constitutes the target and the latter the incident beam. In high-energy physics, almost invariably the beam is derived from an accelerator. If we are dealing with neutrons (energy 1 MeV or less), it is more natural as well as convenient to derive the beam from a reactor.

Let us now consider slow neutron resonances. Say we have an experimental arrangement as in figure (a). The neutrons come from the reactor and their energy spectrum would be a Maxwellian with a temperature equal to that of the moderator in the reactor. [Question: Neutrons are Fermions. How come they have a Maxwellian distribution and not a Fermi–Dirac distribution? For a clue, see *Bose and His Statistics*.] The energy selector enables us to select neutrons of a given energy E, say. The great Enrico Fermi devised a mechanical rotating shutter called a chopper which can do this. We shall not bother about these details, but you might like to amuse yourself by reinventing the chopper concept. It is not very difficult really, and you would have the satisfaction of doing independently something that Fermi did!

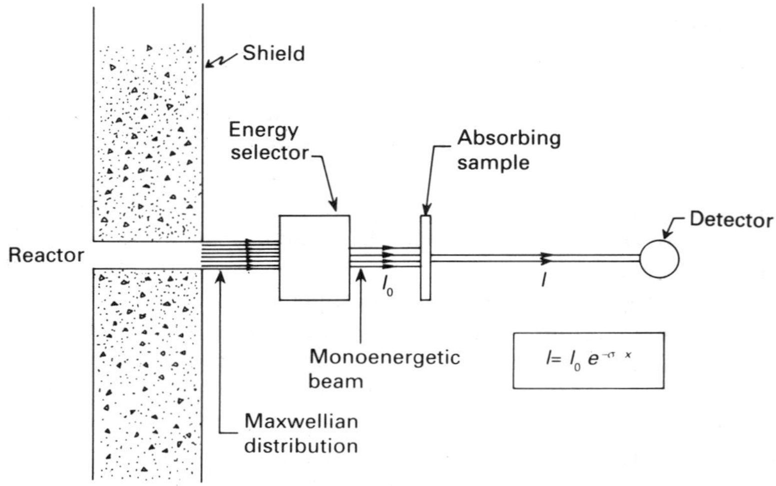

(a)

OK, so this energy selector produces for us a monoenergetic neutron beam. We allow this to fall on a target and behind the latter is placed a neutron detector. By measuring the neutron counts without and with the target present, we can get an idea of the extent to which neutrons of energy E are absorbed by the target material.

Suppose we repeat this experiment at various neutron energies and represent the results as a plot of the absorption cross-section σ_a (of the nuclei in the target), and neutron energy. Say we get a curve as in figure (b). The peak at E_0 in σ_a is referred to as a

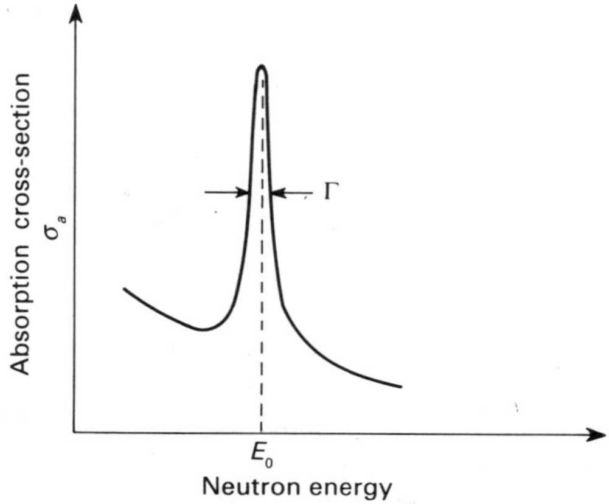

(b)

neutron capture resonance. Neutrons of this particular energy E_0 are preferentially absorbed by the target nuclei, as compared to neutrons of other energies.

What is the explanation for the capture resonance? Say our target is indium and that the nuclei are all In^{115}. In^{115} captures a neutron to become In^{116}. This nucleus (In^{116}) has many (internal) states and when it is formed by neutron capture, it is left in an excited state. Let us denote it by In^{116^*}. This new nucleus does not remain in the excited state for ever; it sheds its excess energy by emitting a gamma ray and goes to the ground state. So In^{116} stays in the excited state only for a certain time. Say the average lifetime of the excited state is τ.

For a minute, go back to the swing. Suppose we set it in full oscillatory motion and then simply watch. After a while the oscillations would damp and the swing would come to a stop. The de-excitation of In^{116^*} and its transition to the ground state is analogous to the swing coming to a stop. The resonance width Γ in figure (b) is related to the lifetime by $\tau \cdot \Gamma \sim \hbar$. This is nothing but a practical application of the uncertainty principle in the form $\Delta t \cdot \Delta E \sim \hbar$.

We now come to the elastic scattering of π^+- and π^--mesons by protons. From a naive point of view, one could describe this as one does billiard-ball scattering but that won't do as Fermi first discovered. In the early fifties Fermi was doing experiments on pion–proton scattering and he found the scattering cross-section rising as in figure (c). A clear peak which is an unmistakable signature

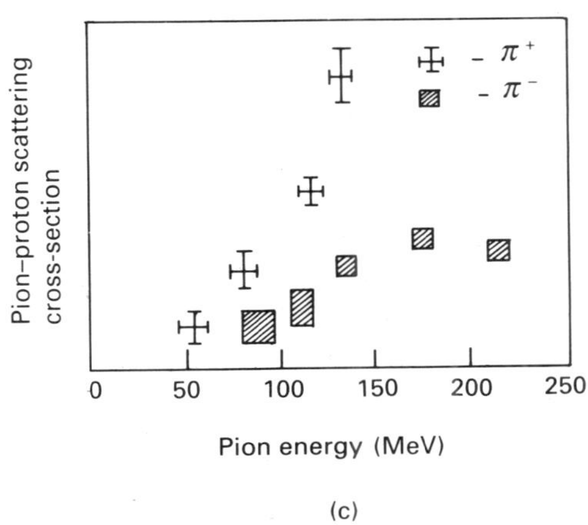

(c)

of resonance was found only later – see figure (d). But even at that time, there were strong indications that the rise in cross-section was signalling a resonance. How did people come to this conclusion? By what is called phase-shift analysis. A few words about that now.

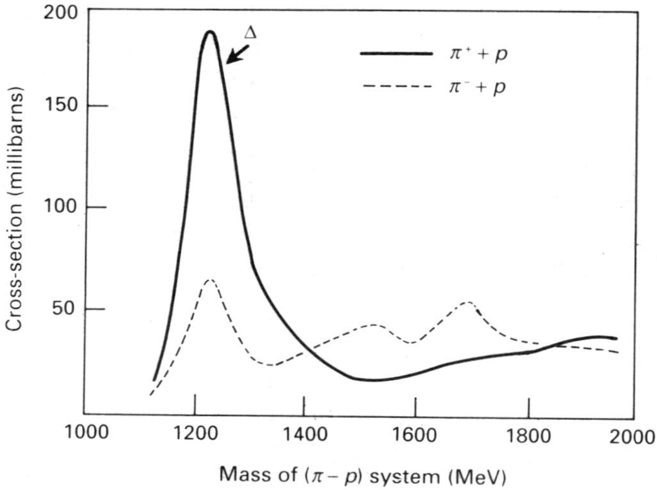

(b)

In quantum mechanics, it is convenient to analyse scattering in terms of waves. The incident particle is visualised as a plane wave and the scattered particles as a spherical wave as sketched in figure (e).

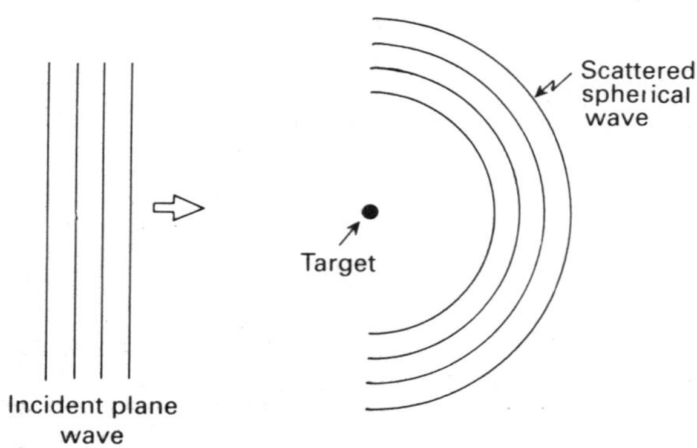

(e)

Phase shifts provide a convenient way of characterising the effect of scattering. The basic idea is illustrated in figure (f). Shown here is the phase shift between the unperturbed and the perturbed wave – in a manner of speaking, between the incident and scattered wave. Actually, I must be a bit more careful. Both the incident and scattered waves can be regarded as made up of waves of various angular momenta. These are called *partial waves* and the quantum number l is used for identifying the partial wave associated with angular momentum $l\hbar$. The phase shift associated with the partial wave is denoted by the symbol δ_l.

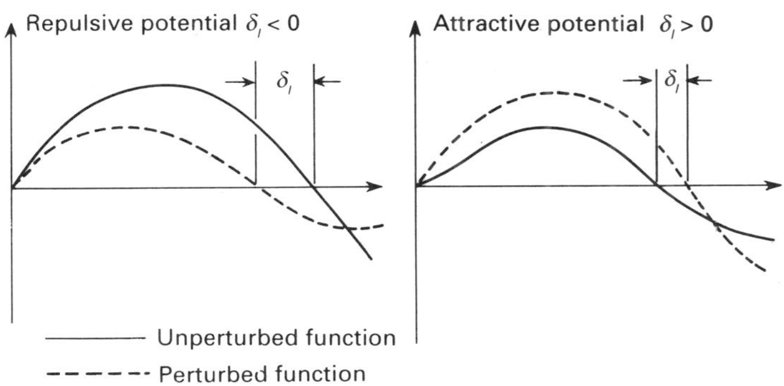

(f)

The phase shifts δ_l are very useful. For example, the total cross-section σ is given by

$$\sigma = \frac{4\pi}{k^2}\sum_{l=0}^{\infty}(2l+1)\sin^2\delta_l$$

where $k \sim (2\pi/\lambda)$, λ being the wavelength of the incident wave. The phase shifts δ_l depend on the potential $V(r)$ presented by the target to the incident particle on the one hand and the energy of the incident particle on the other. When $\delta_l = (\pi/2)$, there is a resonance corresponding to the lth partial wave. A pictorial way of visualising such resonances is indicated in figure (g). In figure g(1) we have a situation far from resonance; the incident particle just bounces off. In figure g(2), the two particles temporarily form

a bound state rather like a Bohr atom; but this bound state is short-lived.

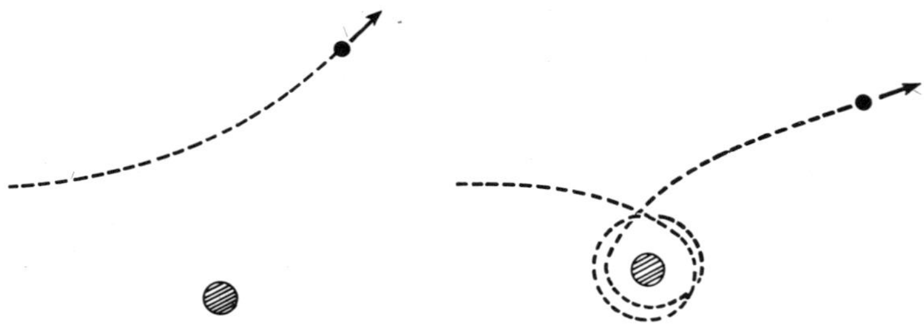

(1) (2)

(g)

In figure (h) is given another view of the resonance. On the right is sketched the potential $V(r)$ and on the left is the variation of (total) cross-section as a function of the energy. The dashed line on the right is the resonance state.

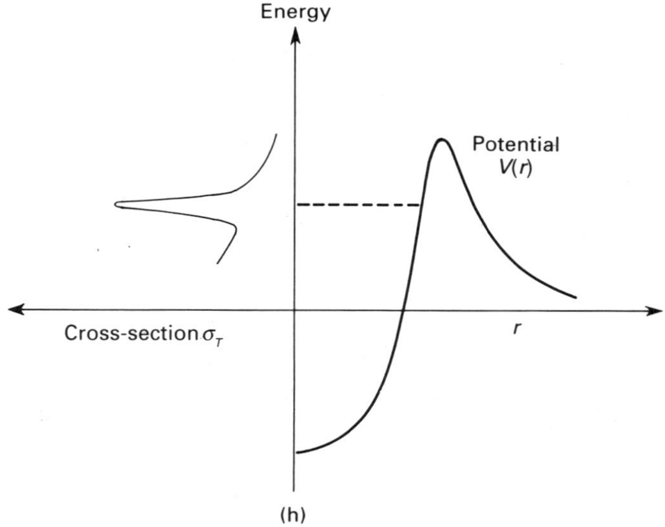

(h)

Now for some history, which starts with extracts from a lecture given by Prof. H.L. Anderson of Chicago in 1955 during a meeting to honour Enrico Fermi. Prof. Hans Bethe (Nobelist) of Cornell University was in the chair. Anderson said:

> Let me tell you about the time we [Fermi and Anderson] decided to work together with π-mesons. At Chicago, we had just completed a large synchrocyclotron which could accelerate protons to 450 MeV. Fairly intense meson beams, rather well-defined in energy, could be obtained from this machine ...
>
> Fermi's idea was that we should do scattering measurements. This was the classical way to study nuclear interactions, since Rutherford's time. Even if the method was not very novel, it had the merit of being simple and direct. From Earl Long, who had constructed a liquid-hydrogen plant, we could have ample quantities of liquid hydrogen. So we could do directly, the most fundamental of scattering experiments, pions and protons.

The arrangement used by Fermi is shown in figure (i). The pion beam (it could be π^+ or π^-) is made to pass through a liquid hydrogen target and the counter on the other side measures the number of transmitted pions. From this, the cross-section is evaluated. Go back now to figure (c) which shows the results obtained by Fermi. It shows that (i) π^- has less cross-section than π^+ and (ii) the cross-section for π^+ rises more steeply than that for π^-. Why? Let us hear Anderson again.

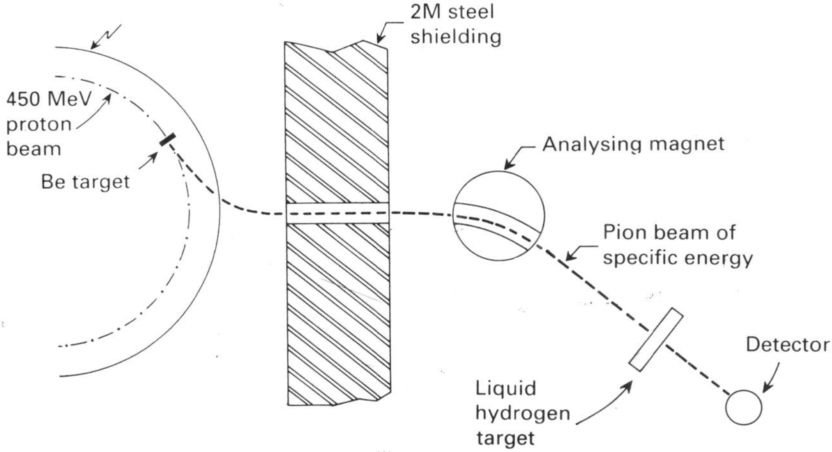

(i)

> This [π^+ having greater cross-section] seemed strange in view of the greater multiplicity of reactions with π^-.
> For π^- we have
>
> $$\pi^- + P \rightarrow \pi^- + P \qquad \text{elastic scattering}$$
>
> $$\pi^- + P \rightarrow \pi^0 + N \qquad \text{exchange scattering}$$
>
> $$\pi^- + P \rightarrow N + \gamma \qquad \text{radiative capture}$$
>
> while for π^+ only
>
> $$\pi^- + P \rightarrow \pi^+ + P \qquad \text{elastic scattering}$$
>
> seems possible.
>
> This obviously puzzled Fermi very much. I recall the day we were measuring this cross-section. Fermi was running the counters. He had a stop-watch in one hand, a slide-rule in the other, the desk calculator was chattering away, and his eyes were keeping a close watch on the flashing neon indicators to detect any possible misbehaviour. After he recorded each count, he would calculate the cross-section. He kept shaking his head because it kept coming out so high.
>
> There was little for me to do that I just sat back and began to go through my mail. On this day there was a preprint of a paper by Keith Brueckner on meson-nuclear scattering. "Enrico", I said looking at some of the curves, "here's a guy who seems to think the π^+ cross-section should be higher than the π^-". Fermi was disparaging in his retort. "How should he know anything about it?"
>
> "But Enrico", I persisted, now taking the trouble to scale off Brueckner's curve, "this fellow Brueckner says we ought to be getting about 120 millibarns for the cross-section". "We're getting even more than that," admitted Fermi. "Let me have a look at the paper". Then, "Will you take over for 20 minutes while I go up to my office?"

To cut the story short, Fermi, by his own analysis, came to the conclusion that the π^+ cross-section should indeed be higher than that for π^-. OK, so the π^+ cross-section was higher and continuing to increase with energy but did that imply there was a resonance? This is where phase-shift analysis came into the picture — see figure (j).

This shows the phase shift δ_l for $l = 1$ as a function of pion energy. Observe the phase shift is $\pi/2$ at pion energy $\sim$ 200 MeV. Clearcut peaks in the cross-section curves at this same energy were also established later, as shown in figure (d).

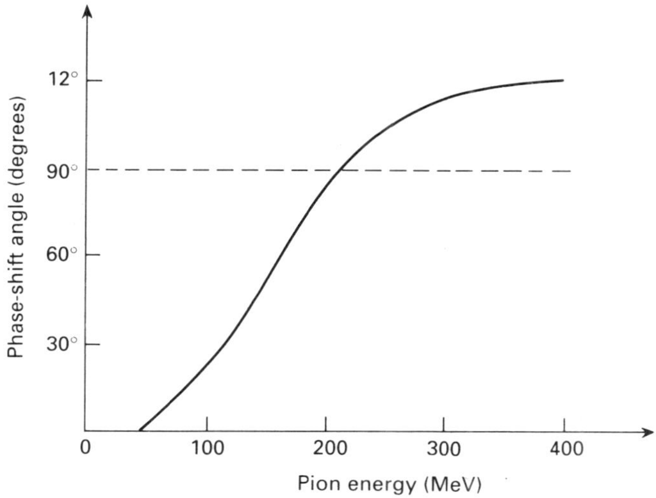

(j)

What has all this got to do with Bhabha? Just that he was one of the earliest to speculate that there could be particles of higher charge and higher mass than the proton. The $\pi - P$ resonance is a short-lived nuclear particle called Δ. Just as the various nuclei are combinations of protons and neutrons, this Δ is a composite made up of the proton and the pion.

In what way does this composite form? This would be determined by how the spin and the isotopic spins of the two particles can combine. The proton has spin (1/2), the pion has spin 0, and relative orbital angular momentum is 1; so the total angular momentum can be either 1/2 or 3/2 (in units of h, of course). This is not all. The neutron and the proton can be regarded as two states of the same particle, i.e., the nucleon, the two states being characterised by two different values of the isotopic spin. For the nucleon, the isotopic spin I is 1/2, the proton corresponding to projection $I_z = +1/2$ and the neutron to $I_z = -1/2$. The isotopic spin of the pion is 1 since it can exist in three charge states $+e$, 0, $-e$ corresponding to $I_z =$ 1, 0, -1 respectively. The two isotopic spins, i.e., of the nucleon and the pion can combine in two ways: Total isotopic spin = 3/2 or 1/2. The resonance Δ discovered by Fermi corresponds to charge $+2e$, total spin I = 3/2 and total isotopic spin I = 3/2. Therefore this particle is also called the (3/2, 3/2) resonance state. The Δ is a virtual bound state of the proton and the pion. Recall our earlier description of the neutron as a proton p, π^-. In that sense, the (p, π^-) resonance can be regarded as an excited state of the neutron. If that is conceded, then the resonance particle has the same mass as the neutron, barring the excitation energy. Therefore it could be regarded as an isobar of the nucleon. Today, particle resonances are described in terms of the quark model and our picture of isobars is more sophisticated.

Maybe, this is the place to add a few words about the state of particle physics today. Immediately after the Second World War when basic research was resumed with renewed vigour, people began observing in cosmic-ray experiments, particles not known earlier (recall Table 1.2). Almost invariably, these particles were short-lived. And when the big machines arrived on the scene in the fifties, the population of these so-called elementary particles increased very rapidly. Many of these particles were identified as resonances (like the Δ described above). Clearly it was meaningless to talk of two hundred or so elementary particles. Which was when Gell Mann came up with the idea of the quark model. According to it all particles other than the leptons, i.e., the electron and its cousins like the muon, are built up from quarks. The quarks have fractional charge and spin 1/2. Today, all known particles other than the leptons can be visualised as suitable combination of quarks.

5 *The Institution Builder*

We turn now to other aspects of Bhabha's multifarious personality and start with his founding of the Tata Institute of Fundamental Research (TIFR). Today TIFR is the National Centre for Nuclear Science and Mathematics. Those who visit the Institute and see its superb facilities, beautiful settings and all that would scarcely believe how small and humble its beginnings were.

5.1 Getting started

The story of TIFR goes back to August 1943 when Bhabha was a Reader in Bangalore. He was personally doing well in research but was nevertheless wondering about the development of science in India. Would science develop at the rate the country really needed? He shared his thoughts in a letter to J.R.D. Tata in which he said that he had an idea of going back to the west after the war, and perhaps take up a job in Cambridge or Princeton. However, if suitable facilities were made available, he was ready to continue in India as "it is one's duty to stay in one's own country and build up schools comparable with those in other lands." J.R.D. was touched and in a warm reply said (in part):

> If you and/or some of your colleagues in the scientific world will put up concrete proposals backed by a sound case, I think there is a very good chance that the Sir Dorab Tata Trust ... will respond ...

Bhabha accepted J.R.D.'s advice, and on March 12, 1944 he wrote a formal letter to Sir Sorab Saklatvala, Chairman of the Sir Dorab Tata Trust, proposing the creation of an institute. This letter was written in one sitting and Bhabha concluded it as follows:

> The scheme I am now submitting to you is but an embryo from which I hope to build up in the course of time a school of physics comparable with the best anywhere.

Bhabha's letter was first studied by Professor R.D. Choksi a member of the Trust who recommended support. The Trustees then formally considered the proposal at a meeting held on April 14, 1945. Bhabha was asked to be available and he waited in the anteroom while J.R.D. pleaded Bhabha's case that fundamental research was necessary. The Trust was persuaded by the argument. The official minutes of the meeting said:

> After a discussion of the financial implications of Dr. Bhabha's proposal as embodied in his letter, the Trustees decided to undertake the responsibility. They were of the opinion that this responsibility should be shared from the outset with the Bombay University and the Bombay Government ... Dr. Bhabha was present at this stage of the meeting and entered into the discussion. He readily accepted the Trustees' views regarding the sharing of responsibility.

Indeed, Bhabha later evolved a neat formula according to which there was a triangular arrangement between the Tata Trust, the Government of Maharashtra and the Government of India (operating through the Department of Atomic Energy). Much earlier, the I.I.Sc., was operated via a triangular arrangement between the Tata Trust, the Government of India and the Government of Mysore. Bhabha adopted this pattern. This "Bhabha formula" has since been repeatedly used not only by the DAE itself (for example in extending support to the Saha Institute of Nuclear Physics), but also by the Department of Science and Technology, which offers grant-in-aid to many research institutes (e.g., the Indian Association for the Cultivation of Science in Calcutta).

5.2 The seed

On June 1, 1945, TIFR began functioning in Bangalore. But Bangalore did not seem the right place to grow the new Institute, and six months later Bhabha had it shifted to Bombay. At that stage, the Institute received Rs.45,000 per year from the Tata Trust. Later Rs.25,000 came from the Government of Bombay (as it was then called) and Rs.10,000 from the Government of India.

What about buildings for the new Institute? No problem; Bhabha rented one-half of a building named *Kenilworth* on Peddar Road, and owned by his aunt Ms. Coover Panday. In fact, Bhabha was born in this building. (Today the old two-storey bungalow is gone. In its place stands a multi-storeyed apartment complex (with the same name), occupied mainly by the officers of BARC). TIFR paid Ms. Panday a rent of just Rs.200 per month!

Sir John Colville the Governor of Bombay inaugurated the Bombay premises on December 19, 1945. Speaking on the occasion, he said:

> We are embarking on an enterprise of importance to the country's development, in which great wealth, wisely husbanded and applied, individual initiative and government support are all blended. I do not think there could be a better combination for progress.

Prophetic words.

In those days, the Institute was small if not tiny. Since the nearest tea shop was over a kilometre away, Ms. Panday allowed tea for the Institute staff to be prepared in her kitchen, and she herself served tea to her favourite nephew in fine chinaware.

As a mathematical physicist, Bhabha naturally had big plans for promoting research in theoretical physics and mathematics but his Bangalore experience in high-altitude experiments convinced him that TIFR should also have a strong programme in experimental physics. Obviously, cosmic rays was the area to start with. Such experiments needed Geiger counters and the wizard who made these was one H.L.N. Murthy whom Bhabha brought with him from Bangalore.

Murthy started his career as a glass blower for Raman. He was so gifted that Bhabha not only took Murthy with him to Bombay but even sent him to the University of Bristol in England for training. And at Bristol they liked Murthy so much that they wanted him to stay! In 1959 I met a Canadian scientist who had done his Ph.D. in Bristol. He told me that his complex glass cryostat for studies on liquid helium was built by Murthy. In fact, a few years later Murthy built for me a neutron spectrometer which is still working in Trombay. This called for some intricate machining, and even today I have not figured out how Murthy did it. In 1960, he developed a heart problem. Bhabha then arranged for him to be operated in America and the doctor who operated was informed that Murthy was "not just a glass technician but an asset to India." After the operation, Bhabha arranged for Murthy to spend several months in America and Europe during which period he picked up experience in leading labs.

One of the earliest to join TIFR was B.V. Sreekantan who later rose to become the Director. Bhabha interviewed him twice in one day, and having selected him asked him whether he [Sreekantan] wanted to be a theoretician or an experimenter. Sreekantan replied, "Sir, I leave it to you. You have interviewed me and you are the best judge." Thereupon Bhabha said,

> Look here, if you start doing experimental work, there is a possibility that if you are really interested, you may be able to do theoretical work also, but the other way is almost impossible. [Recall Bhabha's own reverse transition.] Moreover, you have some background in electronics; if I were you, I would work in an experimental area. Of course the final choice is yours.

At that time, Sreekantan was a research student at I.I.Sc. whose facilities, i.e., workshop, library, etc., were substantial. Compared to that TIFR was just a few rooms, a few shelves of books and about a dozen people. Yet Sreekantan chose to leave I.I.Sc. and join TIFR because the leader was Bhabha. Soon Bhabha collected people with expertise in various subjects and the Institute now really got going. Some of those so recruited had met Bhabha during his travels abroad.

5.3 The shoots

By 1949, Kenilworth became too small to accommodate all of the Institute's activities. The Institute was then moved to a more spacious (and also beautiful) building next to the famous Gateway of India. Earlier, this building was occupied by the Royal Bombay Yacht Club. At present, the offices of the Atomic Energy Commission are located there, and even today the building is referred to as the Old Yacht Club (OYC). Despite this migration, Kenilworth was not completely given up and work continued there also (for a few years).

In 1950, Bhabha organised an International Conference on Elementary Particles. Leading physicists from many countries participated, and it was a source of great inspiration to the young scientists of the Institute, especially as their work received the personal appreciation of these leaders. Speaking at the concluding session Prof. Blackett said:

> I must say in my experience I have never attended a conference which was both so interesting scientifically and so well organised and in such a beautiful place. Actually I have found this conference exceptionally valuable to me. Then again it pleases me to see so many young Indian scientists from whom we expect great things in the future...

Indeed this has happened for in later years TIFR produced (and continues to produce) outstanding scientists in various disciplines.

In 1950, Bernard Peters came to India to do cosmic-ray experiments. Peters was born in Germany and in his younger days had participated in anti-Nazi protests. When Hitler came to power, Peters escaped to America and joined Rochester University. Peters met Bhabha in 1949 in New York and during their conversation, Bhabha told Peters about TIFR and its programme which included balloon flight experiments, i.e., experiments in which equipment was carried to great heights by unmanned balloons. Peters was planning similar experiments, and they now decided to collaborate. That is how Peters first came to India.

In October 1950, Peters arrived in Madras to conduct balloon flight experiments in the spacious campus of the Madras Christian College located in a suburb called Tambaram. I was then a student in that college. Peters wanted student volunteers and I was one of those who offered to help. The day before the flights commenced, we volunteers were given a sumptuous tea party. I was greatly excited to be associated with a major experiment, even though my own role was quite minor. We were asked to report at 4.00 a.m. in the cricket field to assist in the balloon launch. That night I could not sleep. However, when morning came I was not sure whether I did a wise thing in volunteering because to reach the cricket grounds one had to go a long distance through thick bush! But I did go because I had attended the tea party and felt a moral obligation. Later I had no regrets for I had a great time during the four or five flights that Peters conducted. When the flights were over there was a small farewell party during which I learnt that Peters was facing a rough time in America. Those days, there was a Senator there named McCarthy who was engaged in a witch-hunt against people with even the slightest of leftist leanings. In his youth in Germany, Peters had joined communists in protesting against the Nazis, and this was his crime.

At this stage, Bhabha invited Peters to join TIFR, which Peters readily agreed to. He joined the institute in 1951 and served there till 1958 when he left for Denmark for personal reasons. With the arrival of Peters, Bhabha left to him the overall responsibility for cosmic-ray experiments. The experiments also diversified, leading to the emergence of several distinct types of activities. Initially all these centred around cosmic rays – naturally. Right from his days in Bangalore, Bhabha was fully conscious of the advantages India offered for cosmic-ray research. These are:

1. India lies close to the magnetic equator (in fact, as I mentioned earlier, this passes close to Thiruvananthapuram). If you remember Fig.2.3, you will realise that the low-energy component is cut off at low latitudes. Thus the high-energy component can be conveniently studied.
2. India has the highest mountain range in the world. Therefore, cosmic rays in rarefied atmosphere can be studied for extended periods, unlike in balloon flights which last only a few hours each.
3. India has the deepest mines in the world (the Kolar Gold Mines). This facilitates special studies.

Naturally the different experiments possible on account of these advantages called for their own techniques. Thus one group concentrated on designing special balloons for high-altitude experiments, another on electronic payloads, a third on emulsions and so on. But it was not all balloons and high-altitude experiments. In 1950, Bhabha asked Sreekantan to take a cosmic-ray telescope down the Kolar Gold Mines, measure the vertical intensity and to check whether the penetrating particles were all just muons. More about all this soon.

Bhabha also recognised very early the need to give strong support to mathematics. Thanks to the Indian tradition in mathematics, there was no dearth of students or people aspiring to do mathematics, and the phenomenal, inspiring and legendary success of Srinivasa Ramanujan had greatly increased the thirst for studies in higher mathematics. But there were only a few experts to guide these aspirants and they lay scattered across the country, unable to be effective and coherent. Bhabha wanted to change all this and decided that TIFR must have a strong and independent department in mathematics. One of the first mathematicians Bhabha invited to join TIFR was Prof. D.D. Kosambi. Though mathematical statistics was his field, Kosambi was versatile and a scholar in many subjects. Until the end, he commuted daily from Pune!

In 1949, Bhabha invited Prof. K. Chandrasekharan who was then working at the Institute for Advanced Study, Princeton (which is where Einstein also worked). The maths programme then really got going and has never looked back. Today the mathematics faculty of the Institute is one of the best in the world, and foreign mathematicians eagerly look forward to a visit to TIFR; some eminent ones are regular visitors. One of them, Laurent Schwartz a winner of the Fields Medal (this is, if you like, the 'Nobel Prize' of mathematics) said after his first visit in the fifties: "I have met students in the Tata Institute who are the salt of the earth!" And in 1971 he wrote: "I consider the Tata Institute is a remarkable achievement and is without parallel in any country." It is also worthy of mention that the only Indian mathematician to be elected a F.R.S. after Ramanujan and Harish Chandra is from TIFR. See also Box 5.1.

Box 5.1 Srinivasa Ramanujan recorded all his earlier work on what has come to be known as Ramanujan's Notebooks. They have become famous. One of the first things that TIFR did was to bring out a reproduction of the notebooks which were available. Below is a sample page.

From Ramanujan's Notebooks

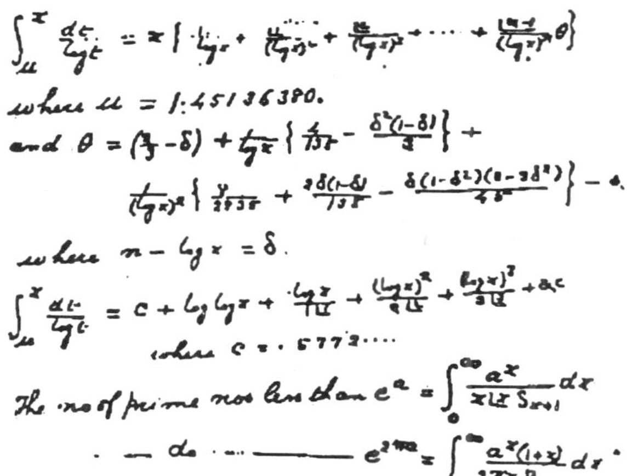

5.4 The sapling

We were now in the early fifties. The Institute activities were growing so fast that even the Old Yacht Club became inadequate. In part this was because a lot of the spade work for India's atomic energy programme (about which I shall say more in the next chapter) was being carried on under the umbrella of TIFR. And so Bhabha was on the lookout again for space, this time also for a spot which would be the setting for the permanent buildings of the Institute.

His eyes fell on a spacious area in the very tip of the Bombay island. This part known as Colaba was largely under the control of the Ministry of Defence. Bhabha made an application to the Ministry requesting the donation of some land but the Ministry turned it down. The Defence Minister at that time was V.K. Krishna Menon, an old friend of Nehru from his England days. Bhabha refused to take 'No' for an answer and went to Nehru who overruled Menon. This was no mean achievement because Menon was a close confidant of Nehru and rarely did Nehru contradict Menon.

The Colaba premises covered about 25,000 sq.metres and consisted, at that time, of a series of World War II barracks; and into these moved the various experimental groups. The Library, the Workshop, the theory and maths groups, however, continued to function at OYC. Bhabha's office also was at OYC. There was no canteen at Colaba and all working there came to OYC at lunch time as there were many eating places in that area.

One of the reasons for our limited intellectual growth (at least where science and technology are concerned) is that we are somewhat cut off from the mainstream. Today with lots of visitors coming and going, the situation is not so bad but forty years ago there were hardly any foreign scientists who visited India. In the late forties, Bhabha arranged for many young scientists to go abroad for training but with the Institute rapidly growing, it seemed simpler to invite leading scientists to visit TIFR and lecture there. Many eminent physicists and mathematicians visited in this manner, Dirac being one of them. All visitors gave courses of lectures. Students were assigned the task of carefully preparing the lecture notes, getting them typed, and later corrected by the visiting professor. Copies were then made for distribution. These lecture notes were also made available (on request) to other institutions. I still have with me many such notes, including those of Dirac's lectures.

In Cambridge, Bhabha had learnt the value of scientific seminars and colloquia. He himself belonged to an informal club called the Kapitza Club which used to meet once a week to discuss the latest scientific developments. In TIFR, Bhabha insisted on such activities, and right from the beginning, an important event every week was the 'Wednesday Colloquium'— it continues to this day. Bhabha rarely missed the colloquium (unless he was out of station), and rarely did he come on time! Usually one did not start till the big man showed up. (It once happened in my case also.) Later when atomic energy began to occupy most of his time, Bhabha reserved Wednesday for TIFR; thus Wednesday became his 'TIFR day'.

5.5 The tree

In between all these scientific and administrative preoccupations, Bhabha made plans for the permanent buildings of TIFR. Wanting his Institute to match the best in the world in every respect, Bhabha invited a well-known American architect to prepare the plans. In 1954, Nehru laid the corner-stone. The building took eight years to come up, not surprising since Bhabha was fussy about even the smallest detail. Finally it was inaugurated in 1962, by Nehru of course. A week of "celebration" followed, consisting of lectures by leading scientists from all over the world. One of those who spoke on that occasion was T.D. Lee, famous for his prediction (along with C.N. Yang) of the breakdown of parity. I had the good fortune of escorting some of these leading lights during their visit to the Atomic Energy Establishment, Trombay.

Having gone into a lot of trouble to have a magnificent building for the Institute, Bhabha was equally particular about its upkeep. Some months before the buildings were formally declared open, Bhabha issued an order to the Institute staff in which he said:

> These buildings are as fine as any corresponding buildings to be found anywhere in the world and no pains have been spared in providing the members of the Institute with good conditions of work and amenities for their comfort and well-being as are to be found anywhere in the world ... These buildings have been made available to the staff of the Institute by the people of India through the taxes they have paid. [By now most of the funds for TIFR came from the Government of India, through the Department of Atomic Energy.]
>
> Each member of the staff should have a sense of personal pride in these buildings ... and it is his duty to see that he himself uses them in such a way as to maintain their quality and cleanliness ...
>
> The strictest norms of cleanliness should be maintained throughout the buildings, more especially in the lavatories. Feet should be wiped on a mat before entering the buildings, and marks from dirty hands should not be left on the walls. Lavatories should be used properly and kept spotlessly clean.

It did not stop with just orders. I have personally seen very senior members of the administrative staff supervising the cleaning operations. Indeed, in the early days they even used to teach the janitors how to use a mop since they (the cleaners) were not used to it. Bhabha was very touchy about the proper usage of facilities and many are the stories of his pulling up people. Dissatisfied with the response to his circular, he even issued a warning in 1965 in which he said:

> Those who continue to behave in an unhygienic and unsocial manner will have to leave the Institute.

Today, the TIFR buildings are over thirty years old, but their upkeep remains what it was in Bhabha's days, in all respects. In fact, the building continues to look as good as new, something that can be said of few buildings in India. Several additions have also been made, but in full harmony with what was originally built by Bhabha. No trace remains of the leaky, army barracks in which so many of us started our careers – only nostalgic memories. In their place one now sees exquisite gardens, stretching out to the Arabian Sea.

5.6 People and programmes

From the story so far it should be clear that Bhabha did not wait for buildings to start work. For him a good programme began with finding first the right person; and once the person was found, all that remained was to give full backing. Throughout his life Bhabha followed this philosophy. He also differed from most other institution builders in another important respect. Typically, when an eminent scientist becomes ambitious enough to start an institute of his own he seeks to create an institute devoted to his pet subject which may be theoretical physics, astronomy, crystallography, molecular biology or whatever. Bhabha was not like that. He wanted TIFR to support diverse disciplines in pure science, subject of course to there being (a) excellent programme leaders and (b) sufficient funds and space. Actually, (a) was the main constraint rather than (b).

Two areas which were started only in the sixties and in which the Institute has excelled are: Radioastronomy and molecular biology. Bhabha himself has narrated that story in the last ever lecture he delivered (a couple of days before his tragic death). This was an address to the International Council of Scientific Unions (ICSU). Bhabha was then the ICSU Chairman, and the council meeting was being held in TIFR. He said:

> It may be of interest to give two more examples of building projects and development around people. As early as June 1944, Sir A.V. Hill had written to me that biophysics was a neglected subject in India and that it should be taken up under the wing of the Institute.

[Sir A.V. Hill had come to India in 1944 to advise the Government about what it should do in CSIR in the post-war years.] While I agreed with his suggestions, I did not think that it would be wise to embark on this line till someone was found, mature enough to be able to work on his own and build up a group. When however in 1962 my attention was drawn by the late Dr. Leo Szilard [a pioneer in atomic energy] to a very promising Indian molecular biologist, it was decided to start work in microbiology, which has since then been growing very satisfactorily.

Another example is provided by the Radioastronomy Group [see Box 5.2]. Four Indian radioastronomers had jointly written identical letters to the Chairman of the University Grants Commission, the Director General of the Council of Scientific and Industrial Research [CSIR], and to me as the Chairman, Atomic Energy Commission offering to return to India as a group and establish radioastronomy here if facilities and support could be given to them. Having ascertained that the members of the group had considerable original work to their credit and were of sufficient maturity to be able to work on their own in India, it was decided to take up radioastronomy here in the Institute ... A project has been developed for a large cylindrical radiotelescope for studying quasars and other radio sources and locating them accurately by lunar occultation. The telescope, which will have four to five times the collecting area of Jodrell Bank [the reference is to what was then one of the largest radiotelescopes in the world], will be designed and built entirely by Indian scientists and engineers ... Work on the site at Ooty has already started ...

Box 5.2 The traditional form of astronomy is optical astronomy, based on (visible) light received from celestial objects. Light is nothing but electromagnetic radiation and it is now known that celestial objects can emit radiation in different parts of the spectrum. This has therefore given rise to various new types of astronomy such as radioastronomy, microwave astronomy, infrared astronomy, X-ray astronomy and gamma-ray astronomy. TIFR is involved in most of these.

The "promising molecular biologist" referred to by Bhabha is O. Siddiqui who has now founded a flourishing school in TIFR in this new area. The story of radioastronomy is largely the story of Govind Swarup, one of the four mentioned by Bhabha. More of that story may be found in Boxes 5.3–5.6. It is of interest that Siddiqui and Swarup were later both elected F.R.S.

Box 5.3 Here is Swarup's recollection of Bhabha.

> I first met Bhabha during his visit to the National Physical Laboratory (NPL) in New Delhi 1951 ... In 1955 he visited the Potts Hill Station near Sydney where many remarkable discoveries had been made ... Bhabha's interest in our work and in the field of radioastronomy was most encouraging ... In September 1961 T. Krishnan, M.R. Kundu, T.K. Menon and myself wrote a proposal for the formation of a radioastronomy group in India and sent it to a number of institutions in India, including Bhabha ... M.G.K. Menon, then Dean, TIFR, forwarded our proposal to Bhabha who was then visiting Geneva. Bhabha promptly called us to meet him in Washington D.C. in November 1961. After meeting Bhabha, T.K. Menon wrote: "He talks quite happily of final outlays of 50 to 100 lakhs. Unbelievable for us at present."
>
> Bhabha's telegram dated 20 January 1962 reads, "We have decided to establish radioastronomy group Stop Letter follows with offer." A prompt action indeed by any standards in the world!

Box 5.4 Swarup has also recollected how the Ooty radiotelescope [see Box 5.5] was launched:

> I joined TIFR in April 1963 ... In June 1963, while reading two papers in *Nature* ... the idea flashed to me that the lunar occultation method could offer an excellent means of measuring the angular sizes of a large number of extra galactic radio sources for distinguishing between the big bang and the steady-state models of the Universe ...
>
> In August 1963, Bhabha called me for a brief meeting. It was an extraordinary and memorable experience. He soon became quite interested in the proposal, grilled me for a couple of hours ... Finally, Bhabha gave me the 'go ahead'. On my enquiry concerning the type of project report required, he remarked: "Young man, do not waste your time writing a project report. Your main problem would be to collect a team ..."
>
> In January 1965 a site was selected for the 530m × 30m large cylindrical telescope near Ooty. Bhabha's keen interest in this enterprise was very helpful. Although the Collector of

Nilgiris wondered why we were in such a hurry when the life of a star is billions of years, Bhabha got a prompt response from R. Venkataraman, then Minister of Industries in Tamil Nadu [later to become the President of India], and we were allotted the site and electrical power connections in a few months.

Box 5.5 As mentioned in Box 5.2, radioastronomy is based on observations of celestial objects using the radio waves emitted by them. Just as an optical telescope is used to gather light, a radio telescope is used to gather the radio waves. The collector element in a radio telescope is usually a large dish (rather like the dish used for picking up TV signals from satellites) as shown in figure (a). Typically, the dish is completely steerable meaning that it can be made to point in any direction in the sky. At the time Swarup was planning the Ooty telescope, the largest radio telescope in the world was at Jodrell Bank, England. The larger the collection dish the greater is the sensitivity of the telescope; the greater the sensitivity, the fainter the object which can be spotted.

Swarup wanted to build a telescope with a collection area exceeding that of the Jodrell Bank instrument. However, if the telescope were made completely steerable (as at Jodrell Bank), it would have meant enormous engineering problems. Instead, Swarup decided to have a parabolic dish capable of being steered around its axis – see figure (b). Clearly there was less flexibility compared to the spherical dish but as opposed to that, one could now make the collection area really large without too much difficulty.

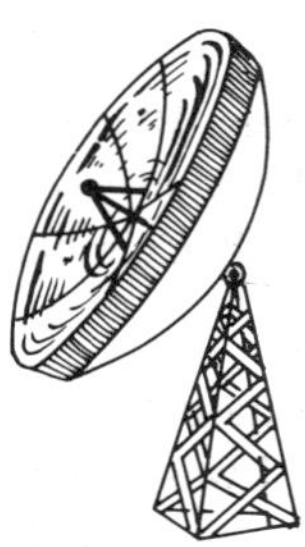

(a)

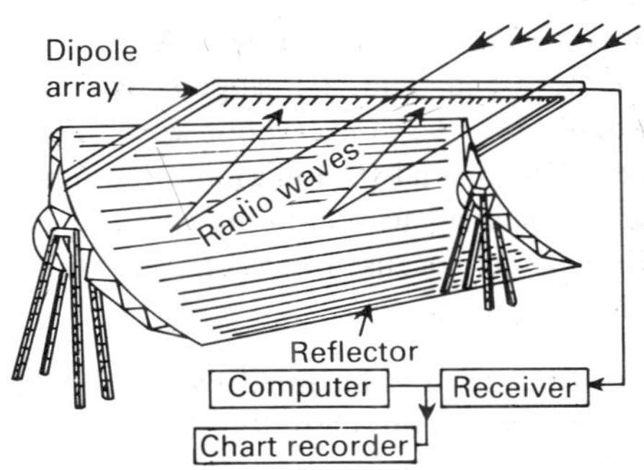

(b)

Swarup had another bright idea. If the telescope were to be tilted to the ground at an angle equal to the latitude, (see figure c(i)), then the axis of rotation of the telescope would be parallel to the axis of rotation of the Earth (see figure c(ii)). Suppose one is making observations on a particular object in the sky. Now even as the observations are in progress, the Earth would be rotating. So it would be necessary to readjust the telescope continuously. If the telescope is arranged as in c(ii), this readjustment is quite easy – one has merely to rotate the parabola about its axis.

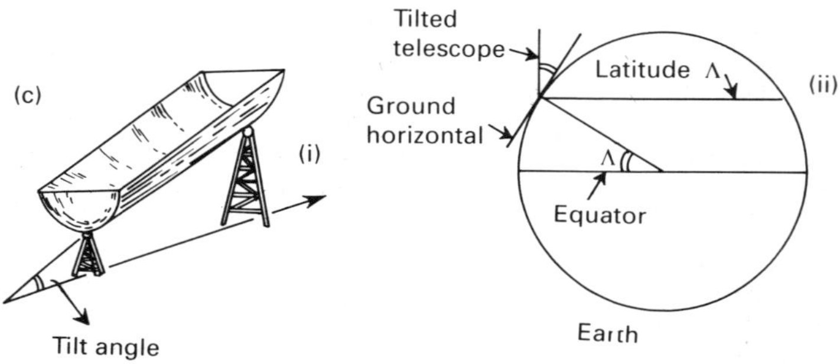

The latitude of Ooty is about 11°N. If the telescope has to be given a tilt of 11° by mechanical structures, it would cost a lot of money. So Swarup went hunting for a hill slope which was 11°! Who said we can't be clever or original in India? By the way, right now Swarup is engaged in building one of the largest radio telescopes in the world.

Box 5.6 Dr. Ramesh Sinha of TIFR tells this story about the selection of the Ooty site. The proposed site was to be a hill slope parallel to the spin axis of the Earth (recall Box 5.5). It had to be at least 500m long, the northern end being not less than 100m higher than the southern end. The N–S slope should not be too high also because that would mean large excavation costs. Four sites were short listed – one near Kodaikanal (S. India) and the other three near Ooty. Bhabha had spent many a vacation in the Nilgiri hills and preferred a site there over Kodaikanal because of easier access to big cities, especially Coimbatore. Sinha says:

> Bhabha, accompanied by M.G.K. Menon and Bernard Peters arrived at the Ooty Raj Bhavan from Bangalore ... I was asked to guide Bhabha to the sites that Govind Swarup and I had

short-listed. We began with the Pykara Lake site in Wenlock Downs, a picturesque north–south slope just about 500m long running right into the blue waters of the lake. The slope was bordered by a rich clump of trees. On one side there is a small but very prominent Toda village. In our earlier visit, a Toda woman had told us that their ancestors had lived on the grounds from the time of the Mahabharatha, tending their *mahishas* (buffaloes) day after day. She warned us against any attempts to acquire their ancestral land ...

The second site near Emerald Lake was almost as attractive in terms of setting but the hill slope was deemed too small. Moreover, the site was much further away from Ooty ...

The third site happened to meet all our requirements. Fairlawn was a small forest reservation at the edge of Muthorai village. Bhabha, accompanied by Govind Swarup visited the site once again before the selection was finalised. On this visit, Bhabha was confronted by a very colourful delegation of Toda elders, men and women who came to demonstrate before him against the selection of Wenlock Downs site, led by Ms. Evan Weiderman Piljain. Piljain's mission was redundant, as we had already selected the Fairlawn site. This fact notwithstanding, Bhabha received the delegation in a manner appropriate to royalty and with eclat defused the issue ...

5.7 Cosmic-ray studies and their off shoots

We return now to the cosmic-ray programme initiated by Bhabha nearly half a century ago. It is convenient to discuss this under three heads: (i) Balloon flights, (ii) geochemistry and geochronology, and (iii) extensive air showers.

As already mentioned, the balloon flight programme of TIFR goes back to 1945 or so when Bhabha himself was involved in the experiments. Even prior to this, Millikan had visited India to conduct flights from Madras and Bangalore in the south to Agra and Peshawar in the north. In those days, one used rubber balloons, a cluster of them actually, which were used to lift a load of about 30 kg to a height of say 25km. During the war, the U.S. military gave contracts for the design of advanced plastic balloons which would carry higher loads to greater heights. After the war, U.S. scientists were able to use such improved balloons in their experiments. However, scientists outside America could neither buy the balloons, nor did they have the know-how to make it – the know-how was kept a secret by the U.S. till 1975. In 1955, Peters suggested to Bhabha that TIFR must immediately start a programme to develop large plastic balloons. In his note Peters wrote:

> Dr. Gokhale seems interested in undertaking such a program and I am strongly in favour of it because I believe the development of the plastic balloon technique will greatly benefit various branches of high-altitude research.

Bhabha immediately agreed.

It is worth digressing to briefly discuss the balloon design as it illustrates how one must intelligently combine common sense and physics to match the technical requirements of the experiment. Three principles provide the basic guidelines:

1. The surface to volume ratio should be as large as possible.
2. The tension in the fabric must be suitably distributed to avoid stress concentration in any region.
3. The balloon, especially the top, must withstand dynamic stress occurring during launch.

The TIFR balloons were made from polyethylene films 0.05 mm thick. The sheets purchased from the market were cut into strips of length ~50 metres and joined together by heatwelding – like the way plastic bags are sealed. At launch, the balloon shape is as in Fig. 5.1(a), the filling gas being hydrogen. The balloon then climbs to a predestined altitude (about 35km or so) where it coasts for a few hours as illustrated in Fig. 5.2. The balloon shape at this stage is as in Fig. 5.1 (b). This is called the natural shape (which is what is dictated by criteria 1 and 2 mentioned above). As the balloon rises, the gas expands and eventually the balloon attains the natural shape. When the balloon reaches this shape the excess gas is vented through ducts at the bottom.

As you know, the higher we go the cooler it is and at 35km it is colder than at the top of the Everest. At such low temperatures, the plastic becomes brittle which is bad for the balloons. The TIFR scientists used a clever idea to overcome this problem. Instead of using clear plastic they used black-tinted plastic which can absorb solar radiation and therefore get heated. The absorptivity must be just right – the plastic must not either get too hot or be insufficiently warm. If it gets too hot, then it would melt; if it is not sufficiently hot, the plastic would not be flexible enough.

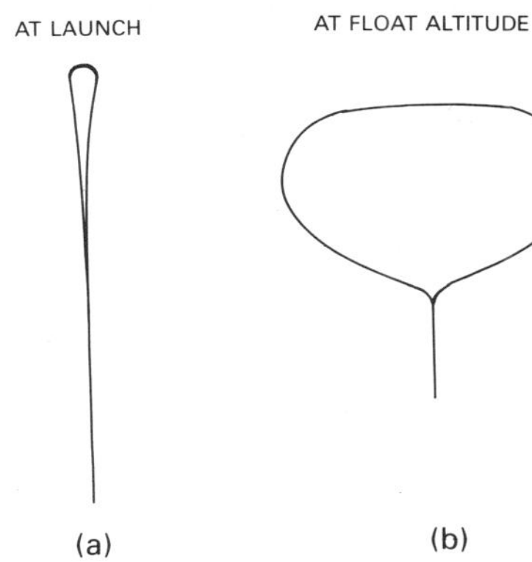

Fig.5.1 Balloon shape (a) at launch and (b) at ceiling.

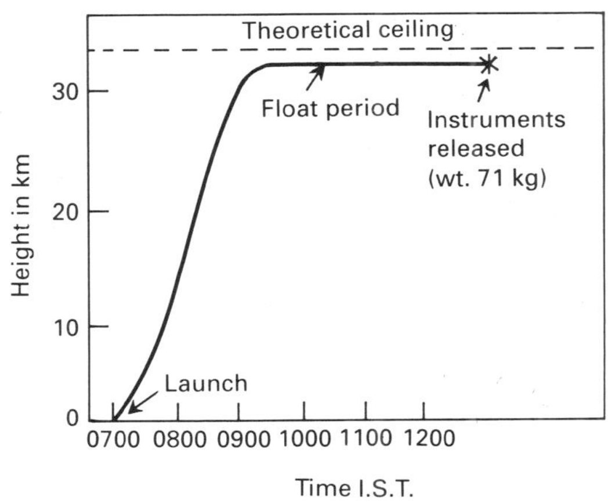

Fig.5.2 Height versus time curve for a typical balloon flight.

I don't want to get too deep into balloon design. All I want to mention is that when the tools for research were not readily available, Bhabha did not hesitate to support their development. This was always Bhabha's philosophy but unfortunately in recent years the country has largely forgotten this valuable advice.

Getting back to the balloon business, during the period 1959–1969, the balloon launches were made mainly from the campus of the

Osmania University in Hyderabad. In 1969, the Institute created a National Scientific Balloon Facility called Tata National Balloon Research Facility (TNBRF) on the outskirts of Hyderabad. From here much bigger balloons and much bigger payloads could be handled. To date over 400 flights have been made, nearly a hundred of them being with international collaboration involving scientists from various countries of Europe and North America. The studies have covered not only primary cosmic rays, but also X-ray, gamma ray and infrared astronomy.

Right from the early days of radioactivity, photographic plates have been used to detect radiation. It was natural that the photographic technique be tried in the cosmic rays. But these needed special techniques which were pioneered by Professor Powell of Bristol University, for which he later received the Nobel Prize. In fact the pion was discovered by the Bristol group using the emulsion technique. Peters had some experience in using emulsions in Rochester and here in India he now arranged for big stacks of photographic plates to be flown. An important event observed by TIFR scientists is sketched in Fig.5.3.

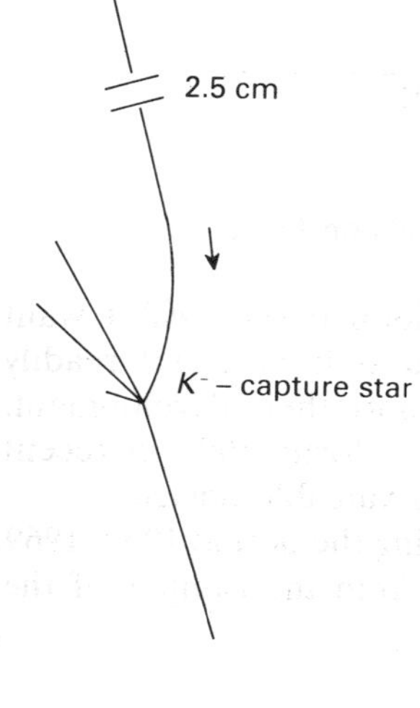

Fig.5.3 The first ever example of a negative K-meson ($m \sim 970m_e$) This event was recorded in 1953 in a multiplate emulsion stack flown by the TIFR group.

The emulsion work led to valuable information on the various reactions produced by the primaries. An important discovery was the radioactive nucleus Be^{10} which has a half-life of $\sim 1.5 \times 10^6$ years. Peters estimated that about 1000 Be^{10} nuclei are produced per square metre per second by cosmic-ray induced nuclear disintegrations in the atmosphere. He then remarked:

> The conditions for observing the resulting activity in rain water and in the various regions of the Earth are favourable and may be useful in measuring sedimentation rates and other geological surface rates during the Tertiary.

The idea of using long-lived radioactive nuclei for dating purposes was pioneered by Libby. He discovered and exploited C^{14} which has a half-life of 5730 years. The general idea is the following: Suppose a tree died two thousand years ago. Say we have a sample of wood from this tree. Wood contains carbon. The normal carbon isotope is C^{12} which is stable, i.e., is not radioactive. But there will also be present in the wood a certain amount of C^{14} produced by cosmic rays and which gets into the tree via the bio-cycle. Once the tree dies, there is no more fresh intake of C^{14} ; whatever was earlier accumulated now starts dwindling in number due to decay. By measuring the residue, one can estimate when the tree died because one knows the equilibrium C^{14}/C^{12} ratio in living organisms. This in brief is radio-carbon dating.

The long half-life of Be^{10} suggested to Peters its use in geological studies.

Briefly, the idea is as follows: Be^{10} produced in the atmosphere comes down during the rains and disappears along with the water into the ground. Suppose one digs and comes across a particular kind of rock layer. By studying the Be^{10} residue, one can estimate the age of the rock. But all this is building castles in the air. First one had to collect Be^{10} in reasonable quantity and demonstrate that it could be isolated. The isolation requires sensitive chemical techniques and very careful counting techniques. Peters tells us the collection story:

> Instead of launching balloons we now went on mountain expeditions [to Kashmir] ... Only two of the horses that carried our apparatus and equipment upto Khilanmarg were capable of going high enough. We extracted nuclei from thousands of litres of water [from molten snow].

Peter's student D. Lal was closely associated with this expedition. He recalls:

> I was married on 17 May 1955 and within a week left for Gulmarg, Kashmir, with my eighteen-year old bride, Aruna Lal. After acclimatisation at a lower altitude, we camped at Khilanmarg. We had four tents, one for the cook and helpers, one for Peters, one for P.S. Goel and B.S. Amin [collaborators], and one for Aruna Lal and myself. The experiment began soon enough, all as planned, but then within a week, Peters decided to leave alone for Bombay to catch the first rains ... We continued the Be^{10} extraction experiment from Khilanmarg snows.

And about the rain water collection Peters says:

> We began the work by collecting enormous quantities of rain water. Large plastic sheets were spread over the roofs of huts which served as temporary chemical laboratories at Colaba where later the modern laboratories of TIFR should arise. We even collected water on the large terrace of our apartment on Peddar Road. From there we channeled the monsoon waters through ion-exchange columns to extract the very small number of interesting atoms.

Soon, Be^{10} proved useful for geological studies exactly as Peters had forseen. Later Lal did excellent work in this area which received recognition through his election as a Fellow of the Royal Society.

In the last two chapters I told you about Bhabha's work on cosmic-ray showers. One of the effective ways of studying showers is through the use of cloud chambers. In Bangalore, Bhabha had a cloud chamber built similar in design to that used in the University of Manchester. When he moved to Bombay, Bhabha brought this chamber with him and in the early fifties, there was a cloud chamber group working in the OYC. At that time, the big accelerators had not yet made their appearance and cosmic-ray induced interactions were the only source of information about high-energy processes. Bhabha decided that TIFR should be in the forefront and two large multiplate cloud chambers were built for use at high altitudes. Ooty seemed a good spot and it was decided to have a permanent station there. Sreekantan recalls:

> When Dr. Bhabha approached the then Governor of Tamil Nadu, Sri Sriprakasa, for his help in securing a site at the highest elevation Dodda Betta, the Governor suggested that the activities could begin

> straightaway in some of the buildings belonging to the Raj Bhavan itself and that permanent laboratories could be built later. The two cloud chambers (which were named Rani and Maharani because of the location) were set up in these buildings in the Raj Bhavan estate overlooking the beautiful botanical gardens. The congenial atmosphere and the facilities provided by Raj Bhavan authorities and the Tamil Nadu Government at this location have been so good, that experimental work has gone on for 35 years without a break on a variety of aspects of cosmic radiation.

The arrival of the big accelerators in the early sixties did not quite drive the cosmic-ray physicists out of business. They simply redesigned their cloud chamber or whatever to make measurements beyond the reach of these machines. Staying one jump ahead now became the name of the game.

Figure 5.4 shows a rough schematic of the experimental arrangement used in Ooty in the early seventies to study high-energy interactions. I can't go into the details because that is outside our scope. But I should mention the following: (i) The purpose of the air Cerenkov counter [try to find out what is the Cerenkov effect] is to distinguish between pions and protons in the beam coming from above. (ii) The multiplate cloud chamber provides a photograph of the shower. (iii) The calorimeter at the bottom measures the energy released. Notice the size of the equipment! Experiments of this kind belong to what is often called NAPP (non-accelerator particle physics). India can't afford giant machines; instead it could and should concentrate on NAPP. Our scientists fully understand this.

Let me now turn to the underground experiments. These got off to a start in late 1950 when Bhabha told Sreekantan:

> Sreekantan, I suggest you take a cosmic-ray telescope down the Kolar Gold Mines and measure first the vertical intensity and then plan experiments to analyse the nature of the penetrating particles and verify whether they are all just muons.

The Kolar Gold Mines do not yield much gold (alas!) but the search for gold has been so intense that they have really dug deep, and we have the deepest mine in the world. For cosmic-ray workers, this is good news. (The only other comparable mine is in S. Africa). The first set of experiments conducted in 1950–1952 measured the intensity of muons as a function of depth down to 300 metres – see also Fig. 5.5.

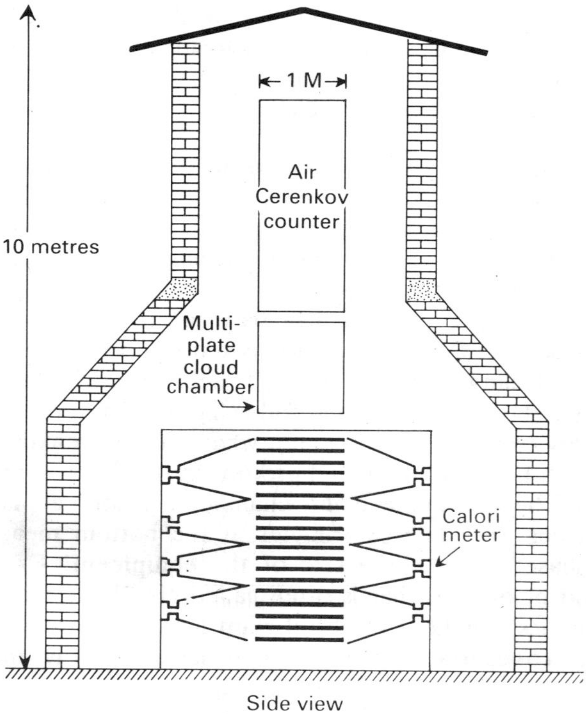

Fig.5.4 Sketch of the large experimental arrangement at Ooty. It has three parts: (i) An air Cerenkov counter at the top, (ii) a multiplate cloud chamber in the middle, and (iii) a total absorption calorimeter at the bottom.

Starting in 1960, the scope of these underground experiments was expanded by (i) having a collaboration with U.K. and Japan, (ii) going much deeper, and (iii) looking for exotic events with complex apparatus. Just a few years ago they were looking for the spontaneous decay of a proton which is what some theories of elementary particles suggest. (For a crude estimate of the lifetime of the proton,

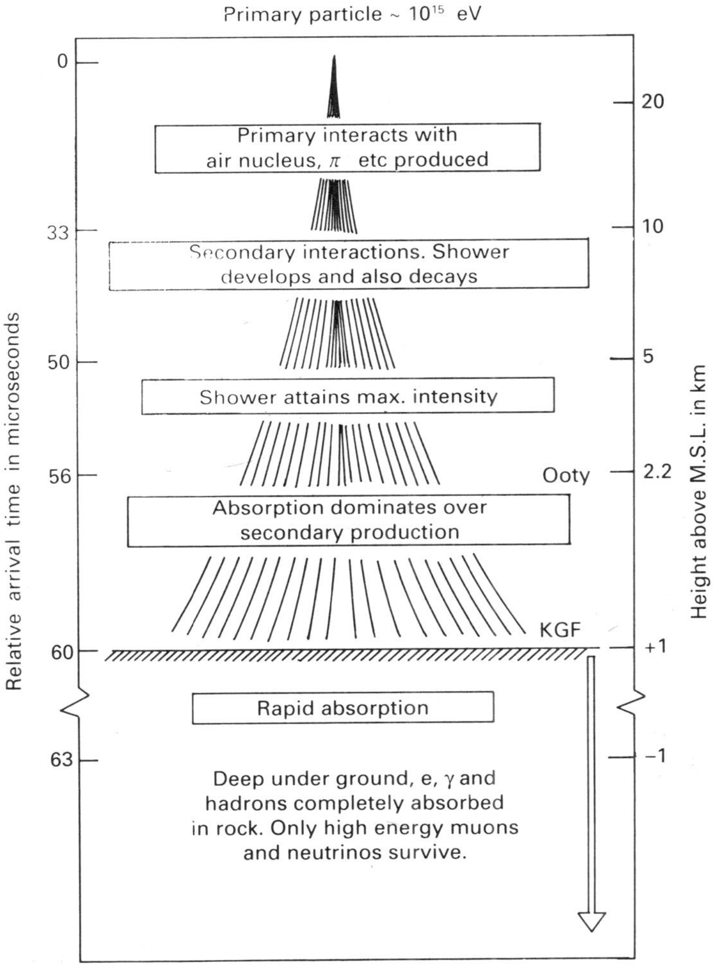

Fig.5.5 Schematic of how the shower attenuates as one comes from above.

see the last chapter of the companion volume, *Why Are Things the Way They Are?*). These experiments were being performed at a depth of 2.3km below the surface of the Earth, and the apparatus used weighed 140 tons. Imagine the problem of providing electric power air-conditioning, etc., at such a great depth. Such experiments are surely not easy but then, if only one catches the proton decaying ...! Meanwhile, the sad news is that the Kolar Mines are being shut down; a big blow to NAPP in India.

5.8 Bhabha and Chandrasekhar

I have already drawn attention to Bhabha's habit of first getting the best brains, and then organising scientific programmes around them. Buildings came last (but with Bhabha they were always worth waiting for!). This business of scouting for the best available talent goes back to 1944, as the following letters exchanged between Bhabha and Chandrasekhar show:

20th April 1944

Dear Chandrasekhar,

I was very pleased to hear of your well-deserved election to the Fellowship of the Royal Society. Please accept my warm congratulations.

The trustees of the Tata Trusts have decided to sponsor a scheme I put forward for an Institute for advanced research in Physics, both theoretical and experimental, to be located in Bombay. We hope to make it a centre of advanced research, especially of theoretical research in physics and mathematics in India. Your own line of research would certainly come within the scope of the scheme and if it were possible to create a Chair for you would you be prepared to consider it? The Professors grade will be the same as that in the Indian Institute of Science, Bangalore, namely Rs.1,000–Rs.1,250, though of course in special cases the starting salary may be anything above Rs.1,000. The duties of the Professors will be to carry on and direct research, to take part in colloquia and give say one course of lectures per term on some advanced subject in their own line. The leave and vacation rules will be more or less the same as in the Bombay University, enabling you to take 4 to 5 months vacation a year which you may use for visiting foreign countries like U.S.A. and maintain contact there. I think you will hardly get more favourable conditions for carrying on your research anywhere and especially in India. For example, as you are aware, a Professor in an Indian University even under the most favourable and special conditions is overlaiden with routine work and in the Government Research Institutions one would be the victim of the usual red tape with little understanding of the needs of scientific men.

I myself have up to recently felt that after the war I would accept some good job in some University in Europe or America, because a place like Cambridge has an atmosphere which no place in India has at the moment. But, I have recently come to the view that provided proper appreciation and financial support are forthcoming, it is the duty of people like us to stay in our own country and build up outstanding schools of research such as some other countries are fortunate enough to possess. It is for this reason that I put forward my scheme and I am very glad to say that it has met with understanding and liberal support. It is our intention to bring together as many outstanding scientists as possible in physics and allied lines so as to build up in time an intellectual atmosphere approaching what we knew in places like Cambridge and Paris. I am sure that if we do our work successfully, financial support on a liberal scale will not be lacking.

I should make it clear that this is only an informal approach on my own initiative, but if I hear from you that a Chair on the lines outlined above would be accepted by you, then I shall see what I can do to get such a Chair created.

With best wishes,

Yours sincerely,
Homi Bhabha

Dr. S. Chandrasekhar, F.R.S.
University of Chicago
Chicago

The University of Chicago
Yerkes Observatory
WILLIAMS BAY WIS

1944 May 22

Dear Bhabha,

Many thanks for your letter of April. It was kind of you to write the way you have.

I was very interested to know that on your recommendation, the Tata Trusts have decided to sponsor an Institute for advanced research in Physics to be located in Bombay. A professorship in the Institute under the circumstances you have described comes so very close to the ideal position I could have wished for myself that in the event of a Chair on the lines you have outlined being offered to me I would have no hesitation in accepting it. And may I add that I fully share your view that "it is the duty of people like us to stay in our own country and build up outstanding schools of research such as other countries are fortunate enough to possess."

There is only one condition I would require to be met before I accept such a position and that is that the travelling expenses of my wife and myself entailed in the transfer from Yerkes to Bombay be paid by the proper authorities.

May I wish you the best in your endeavours even if a position for me in the Institute should fail to materialize!

With kindest regards,

Yours sincerely,
S. Chandrasekhar

Bhabha and Chandrasekhar knew each other at Cambridge, and they also had the same supervisor for their respective Ph.D. programmes. Chandra's reply to Bhabha suggests that he was inclined to return to India. In a later letter (August 1945), however, Chandra expressed reservations about returning permanently, breaking all links in America. Instead he offered to come for a year and try things out. If everything worked fine, he was ready to accept a suitable permanent position. In a long reply written in October, Bhabha took Chandra on his offer and gave a detailed description of TIFR and its activities. This was followed by a formal offer from the Institute which included travel expenses for Chandra and his wife (to come to India). Chandra replied in April 1946 mentioning various immigration problems (in case he wanted to return to America) and also the reluctance of the University of Chicago to grant a year's leave. Nothing happened during the next few years until Bhabha met Chandra in Chicago in 1949. In February 1950, Bhabha reminded Chandra that a position had been specially created for him and that TIFR was waiting. Meanwhile, Chandra had become the Chairman of the Astronomy Department at Chicago and he felt he could not walk out at this juncture. There matters appeared to rest. However, the relations between Chandra and Bhabha did not cool off. Chandra always visited TIFR whenever he was in India, and I have myself attended a colloquium by Chandra in TIFR (on rotating fluids). On that occasion, Bhabha gave a wonderful introduction to the speaker.

Much later (in 1969 or '70), there was a passing reference to all this during the inauguration of the Homi Bhabha Auditorium of TIFR by Indira Gandhi. I was fortunate to be present on that occasion. Many distinguished speakers addressed the gathering, including Chandrasekhar who was then visiting India. The last speaker was Nawab Ali Yavar Jung, the then Governor of Maharashtra. The Governor took his own time to start his speech, wiping his glass in a leisurely fashion. He pleaded that he was forced to use delaying tactics because his speech had been stolen by Indira Gandhi! Everyone laughed, including Mrs. Gandhi. The Governor then went on to describe how years earlier when he was the Vice-Chancellor of Osmania University, he was trying to attract Chandrasekhar while Bhabha was trying to do the same. He then said, "But neither of us could catch him; he eluded us both!"

5.9 Concluding remarks

This book is about Bhabha and not TIFR. So I am afraid I can't tell you about all the exciting work going on there. And believe me, today TIFR is not just cosmic rays or mathematics or even molecular biology. There are so many things going on in so many areas – nuclear physics, condensed matter physics, chemical physics, astrophysics, semiconductor physics, computer science, why even dental research! Indeed there are several campuses of TIFR outside Bombay – in Pune, Hyderabad, Ooty, Pachmari, Bangalore and so on. And this is not all, because people who grew up in TIFR have gone out to seed research and development elsewhere and bring them upto a mature, independent status of their own. Thousands, literally thousands, owe their career to TIFR and it all happened because one man had the courage and the daring to dream. Bhabha's dream did not stop with TIFR; it was much bigger, as you will learn in the next chapter. But before going on to the next chapter, there is one lesson we must pause to absorb.

TIFR has been a success story not because of money or even facilities. Rather, it has been so because, thanks to its founder, the Institute has been *firmly committed to the pursuit of excellence.* All the Institute policies have derived from this one cardinal principle. Elsewhere in the world, this is the principle great schools (like that founded by Bohr in Copenhagen or Landau in Moscow, for example) swore by. In India, Raman followed this principle first in Calcutta and later in Bangalore. Bhabha proved that Raman's success was not due to magic but the result of adherence to sound principles and the pursuit of high goals. Others who have shown similar commitment have likewise succeeded, though perhaps not on the scale of Bhabha. If the pursuit of scientific excellence is neglected in the country today (except in pockets), we have only ourselves to blame.

6 *The Stuff Dreams Are Made Of*

Even from the last century, many patriots have dreamt of India becoming a strong industrial nation through the pursuit of science. It was such a dream that inspired Mahendralal Sircar to start the Indian Association for the Cultivation of Science in Calcutta in 1875 (for the full story, see *Raman and His Effect*). Jamshedji Tata, the Founder of Tata Steel and the I.I.Sc., had similar dreams but they differed in details. Scientists like Raman, Saha and others also strongly believed that India can progress only through the application of science and technology. Where Raman was concerned he confined himself to pure science, leaving it to others to take it from there. In marked contrast, Saha thought very deeply about the transition from science to technology and how the fruits should reach the people. This is not surprising because Saha had very strong socialist leanings and the Soviet Union was there as an excellent example to emulate. Saha expressed his views in a number of thoughtful and scholarly articles published over two to three decades. However, somehow he failed to go beyond just theoretical ideas. It is in this respect that Homi Bhabha was a marked contrast to those just mentioned.

6.1 The first step: formation of the AEC

In his original letter to the Sir Dorab Tata Trust, Bhabha had declared:

> When Nuclear Energy has been successfully applied for power production in say a couple of decades from now, India will not have to look abroad for its experts but will find them ready at hand.

While seeking grants, especially for basic research, it is quite usual for people to make all kinds of promises about fallouts, usefulness to society, etc. Bhabha also made such a promise but in his case it was not an idle one. We must appreciate that the year was 1944 and atomic energy was still a closely guarded secret. Nobody knew that America was close to building the atom bomb and that Germany was trying hard to do the same. Even so, already by 1939, the basic principle of the nuclear chain reaction (see Box 6.1) was known to all physicists. And since Cambridge was one of the principal centres of activity in Nuclear Physics, Bhabha was well aware of it. Based on this knowledge, Bhabha dared to predict in his letter to the Tata Trust that one day, nuclear energy or atomic energy (as it is often called) would become a reality. In passing, it is interesting that Lord Rutherford the great pioneer in Nuclear Physics himself did not believe that nuclear energy would ever become a practical proposition.

Box 6.1 Nuclear fission refers to the breakup of a nucleus into two sizeable fragments. Fission occurs only in heavy nuclei, and it can be induced as well as spontaneous (in some cases). The phenomenon was discovered in 1939 by Hahn and Strassman in Germany when they bombarded uranium with neutrons.

Uranium has two important isotopes ${}_{92}\mathrm{U}^{235}$ and ${}_{92}\mathrm{U}^{238}$. They are present in natural uranium roughly in the ratio 1 : 140. U^{235} is readily fissionable by slow neutrons (e.g., of energy $\sim$ 0.025 eV) whereas U^{238} is fissionable only by fast neutrons, i.e., of energy $\sim$ few MeV or more. A typical fission breakup is:

$$ {}_{92}\mathrm{U}^{235} + {}_{0}\mathrm{n}^{1} \rightarrow {}_{57}\mathrm{La}^{147} + {}_{35}\mathrm{Br}^{87} + 2\ {}_{0}n^{1}. $$

Notice that during the breakup, neutrons are liberated. Suppose one makes use of these neutrons to fission other uranium nuclei and then exploits the neutrons liberated to cause more fission and so on. One would then have a chain reaction as schematically shown in figure (a).

What is the big deal in having such a chain reaction? During each fission event, an energy of about 200 MeV is released. By contrast, in a chemical reaction like combustion reaction, for example, only a few eV of energy is released per event. Thanks to this factor of a million, a lot of energy can be released from a small quantity of uranium.

Where does this energy come from? Basically, when the uranium nucleus disintegrates some mass is destroyed which is what appears as energy (remember, $E = mc^2$).

Let us go back to figure (a). The neutrons released in fission are fast neutrons, most of them having energies between 1 and 2 MeV. If the chain reaction is propagated with fast neutrons, the reaction can multiply very rapidly. This is precisely what happens in an atomic bomb. The cross-section for fast neutron-induced fission is rather small whereas the cross-section for slow neutron fission is much larger. Neutrons with energies $\sim$ 0.025 eV are called thermal neutrons because 0.025 eV in

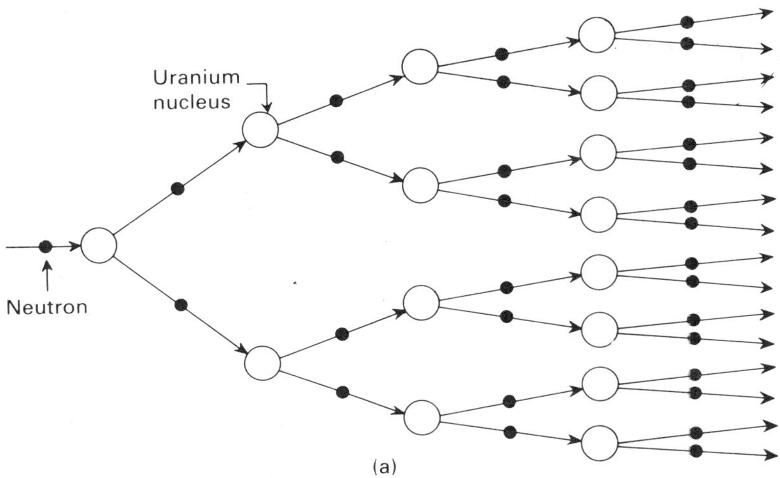

(a)

temperature units is $\sim 30°C$. The neutrons born in fission are fast neutrons. If we are to have a chain reaction with thermal neutrons, the fast neutrons must first be made to shed a lot of their energy. One uses for this purpose a moderator like water or heavy water. The fast neutrons emitted in fission collide with the hydrogen or deuterium nuclei and lose energy. Eventually they achieve thermal equilibrium with the atoms/molecules of the moderator and have a Maxwellian spectrum corresponding to $\sim 30°C$. One then says the neutrons are thermalised. They are now ready to cause fission. Thus, in this case, figure (a) becomes modified as in (b).

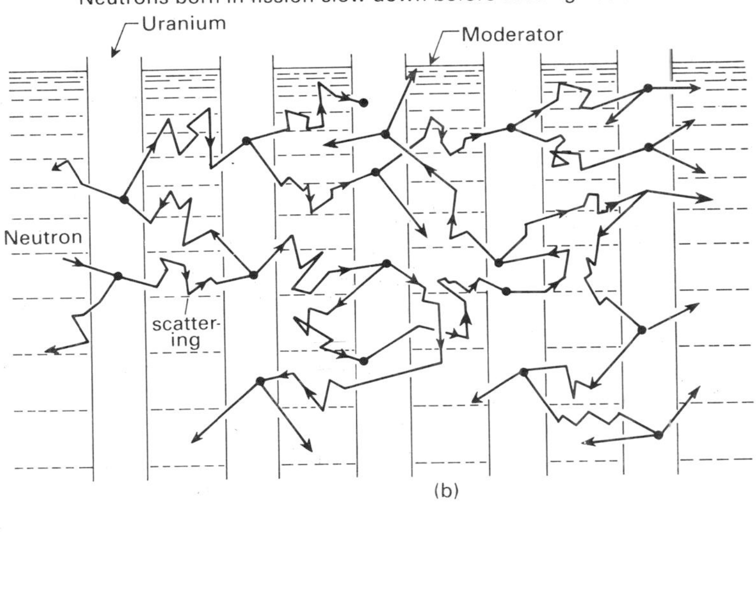

(b)

Scheme (b) leads to a controlled release of energy. The heat energy released can be used to generate steam which in turn can be used for generating electricity in the usual manner by driving a turbine. Scheme (a) is used in a bomb where as all the energy is released in a flash lasting a few microseconds.

The concept of Maxwellian spectrum is explained in the companion volume: *A Hot Story*.

Hiroshima and Nagasaki revealed to the world that atomic energy could be released for totally destructive purposes. But thanks to Enrico Fermi, one also knew that atomic energy could be controlled to release energy in a safe and useful manner; and, using the energy so released, electricity could be produced. In other words, atomic energy was a two-headed giant combining both evil and good. Though humanity was terrified by the evil face, there were also anxious glances towards the peaceful side. The peaceful use of atomic energy thus became at once a slogan and a promise.

Bhabha moved quickly. Even though the country was yet to achieve Independence, there was already in Delhi an Interim Government composed of national leaders. And talks were in full swing between these leaders and the British Government to make India free; Jawaharlal Nehru was the leader of this Interim Government cabinet. Bhabha promptly drew the attention of Nehru to the useful role atomic energy could play in independent India.

At the time, the science activities of the Government of India were mainly carried on through the Council for Scientific and Industrial Research (CSIR). The CSIR was created in 1942 by the British Government for supporting the war effort, and was patterned after a similar organisation in England. On the eve of the transfer of power, Nehru was preoccupied with a thousand things. It was not clear then whether there would be one India or the country would be split into two. The question of technological development came only after the country itself became free. Nevertheless, Nehru lent a sympathetic ear to Bhabha.

On August 15, 1947 India became free. Heralding the dawn of a new era, in a moving speech on the midnight of 14 August, Nehru said, "While the world sleeps, India awakens to freedom." True there was turmoil accompanying the birth of independent India. But there was also much hope and expectation. And though he was overburdened with numerous problems arising out of partition, Nehru began to give serious thought to the development of the country.

Where atomic energy was concerned, a Board of Research on Atomic Energy was constituted with Bhabha as the Chairman. This Board functioned as a part of CSIR. Meanwhile, there were plans afoot to create a Department of Scientific and Industrial Research (DSIR) as a full-fledged department of the Government. A proposal to this effect had been made by Sir S.S. Bhatnagar (the founding father of the chain of CSIR National Laboratories). In his proposal to Nehru, Bhatnagar had suggested that the Board of Research on Atomic Energy (which was then with the CSIR) should become a part of the newly proposed department. Bhabha did not like this one bit. Even earlier Bhabha had felt that the DSIR, when it came up, should not be under a Minister without Portfolio (as was being planned). In Bhabha's view, this department was too important to be treated that way; instead, it should be directly under the Prime Minister. Notwithstanding that, Bhabha wanted the atomic energy programme to be *outside* this new department.

It is easy to read Bhabha's intentions. If the DSIR came up, clearly Bhatnagar would be in-charge; and Bhabha did not want to be constrained by anybody in developing his ideas. Thus, on April 26, 1948, Bhabha prepared a note entitled *Organisation of Atomic Research in India* which he addressed to Prime Minister Nehru. The birth of the Indian atomic energy programme and indeed of all that followed can be traced to this one single note. In it Bhabha said:

> The development of atomic energy should be entrusted to a very small and high powered body composed of say, three people with executive power, and answerable directly to the Prime Minister without any intervening link. For brevity, this body may be referred to as the Atomic Energy Commission.

Bhabha also pointed out that the then-existing Board of Research on Atomic Energy could not be entrusted with this work since it (the Board) was an advisory body which reported to the Governing Body of the CSIR which in turn was composed of 28 members including officials, scientists and industrialists. Bhabha felt that the development of atomic energy would require a certain amount of confidentiality, especially where technical information derived from other countries was involved. Considering this, the CSIR, as it was set up, was ill-suited to deal with secrecy. As Bhabha put it, "secret matters cannot be dealt with under this organisation". He further stressed that the proposed Atomic Energy Commission should have "its own secretariat independent of the secretariat of any other ministry or department of the Government, including the envisaged Department of Scientific and Industrial Research." Bhabha also recommended that with the appointment of the Atomic Energy Commission, the existing Board of Research on Atomic Energy should be abolished.

Earlier, Bhabha on his own initiative, had already held discussions with British, French and Norwegian scientists on atomic energy matters and obtained assurances from the countries concerned that they would help India. Bhabha mentioned this also in his note to the PM.

Reading this document today, one is impressed not only by the brevity of the note but also the clear and precise manner in which all the points were spelt out. Bhabha knew that Nehru was a busy man and could not be burdened with a lot of trivial details; whatever was to be said had to be said clearly and briefly. Trained executives have this ability of preparing crisp notes. Bhabha was not trained as an executive but seems to have acquired this talent almost instinctively. Perhaps, moving closely with the Tata family helped.

To cut a long story short, within a few months the Government not only accepted Bhabha's proposal but actually piloted through Parliament the Atomic Energy Bill leading to the creation of the Atomic Energy Commission. Bhabha had crossed the first important milestone and also got ahead of his potential competitors (Bhatnagar and Saha). But there were other forces within the bureaucracy which tried to make the sailing rough. Essentially it all had to do with executive power. Some of that story is told separately in Box 6.2. Getting back to the history, the first Atomic Energy Commission had three members with Bhabha as its Chairman. The other two members were Sir S.S. Bhatnagar (head of CSIR) and Sir K.S. Krishnan (Founder-Director of the National Physical Laboratory, Delhi). Bhabha could now take steps to make his promise to the Tata Trust come true.

Box 6.2 Young people should not be taxed or frightened with description of bureaucracy and its devious ways. But since bureaucracy has been a major stumbling block in our development (science included) some remarks are needed to show how Bhabha skilfully manoeuvered.

In the text I have mentioned that the AEC started functioning in 1948 with three members. When the atomic energy programme grew, leading to the formation of the Department of Atomic Energy (DAE) etc., the Commission was expanded to accommodate full-time and part-time members upto a maximum of seven. Secretary DAE was to be the Chairman AEC – so Bhabha held these two positions. The Government order modifying the constitution of the AEC also said there would be a full-time member in charge of administration and finance. The order said: "No proposal with financial implications shall be sanctioned without his prior concurrence." Essentially, this made the Chairman AEC and the Secretary a toothless figure. Fully alive to the difficult attitude finance officers are generally prone to take, Bhabha reacted strongly. Nehru yielded and the constitution of the AEC was again amended. The idea of a full-time member for finance and administration was dropped. Secretary DAE was to look after administration and also exercise financial powers given to DAE. The Secretary of Finance Ministry was nominated (part-time) Member for Finance and his concurrence was needed only on financial matters for which DAE had no powers. Bhabha won because of Nehru; a lesser man simply would not have had his way.

6.2 Early days of the AEC

Initially, the Atomic Energy Commission concerned itself mainly with some exploration activities related to atomic minerals like uranium- and thorium-bearing minerals, and the processing of these minerals. In addition, the Commission also funded research on a small scale on various matters pertaining to atomic energy. Some of these research programmes were carried on at Kenilworth. And as a result, a small group of chemical engineers and metallurgists were able to produce the first gram of uranium metal in 1953.

The Atomic Energy Commission was essentially a policy-making body. A full-fledged atomic energy programme obviously could not be carried on and overseen on a day-to-day basis by such a body; for this, a regular department of the Government was necessary. Thus in 1954 Bhabha proposed to Nehru that a Department of Atomic Energy (DAE) be created within the Government of India which would be like the other departments in the Government. Among other things, the department would fund, create and operate all the facilities needed for the atomic energy programme. The activities pursued would range from mineral exploration at one end to technological research and development at the other.

6.3 Birth of DAE and AEET

It soon became clear that technology development could no longer be carried on within TIFR and that the time had come to start a new laboratory entirely devoted to this purpose. Bhabha proposed that this new laboratory be created at Trombay, near Bombay. He managed to acquire 1,200 acres of land for this purpose. The proposed laboratory was to be called the Atomic Energy Establishment, Trombay (AEET). Later, it would be renamed the Bhabha Atomic Research Centre (BARC) by Indira Gandhi; this is the name by which AEET is known today.

The DAE and AEET started functioning in 1954. Normally the departments of the Government are located in Delhi. However, Bhabha insisted that the DAE should have its secretariat in Bombay. While he wanted this arrangement so that it would suit his convenience (remember Bhabha was still Director, TIFR; in addition, he was also Director, AEET), it had the added advantage of being sufficiently far from the bureaucratic atmosphere of Delhi. Links needed with the Delhi machinery, were to be provided by a small branch office of the DAE in Delhi.

Having a department of the Government outside Delhi was a revolutionary step. It was unthinkable and yet Bhabha managed it because of his close links with Nehru. Decades later, Satish Dhawan followed this example and arranged for the Department of Space to be located in Bangalore, where, at that time, he was holding the post of Director I.I.Sc.

The manner in which Bhabha built up the scientific activities of the atomic energy programme is quite interesting. To start with he did not bother about having any structured organisation, divisions, groups or anything like that. In other words, he followed the same style as in the case of TIFR, i.e., he just picked people (physicists, chemists and metallurgists) based on their skills, talents and aptitudes. Some of these he had met during his travels abroad. Programmes were grown around these people; organisational structure came last – see also Box 6.3.

Box 6.3 In his famous ICSU lecture, Bhabha contrasted the way CSIR grew with the way he built up his institutions. About CSIR he said:

> The Council of Scientific and Industrial Research [CSIR] may be taken as the first planned attempt on the part of the Government to establish a broad base of scientific and technical

> research in the country ... In order to free it from the automatic application of all the Government rules and regulations, the Council of Scientific and Industrial Research was established from the beginning in the form of a society with a Governing Body nominated by the Government which included important ministers and officers ... The opportunity of framing an administrative structure and rules and procedures appropriate for a scientific organisation ... has, however, been lost to a large extent by the omnibus adoption of Government rules and regulations ...
>
> The Governing Body took early steps to establish a number of laboratories ... All these laboratories were brought into existence in the same way. A Planning Officer was appointed for planning the work and building of each laboratory. The plan was usually drawn up on the basis of the work of similar laboratories abroad, divided into divisions and sections, and an estimate of the staff required made on this basis. An attempt to fill the posts was then made on the basis of advertisement, and invitation also in the case of the seniormost appointments. While this method of setting up a laboratory might give reasonably satisfactory results in a developed country in which science is already an important activity and a large number of scientists already exist in the universities ... it has serious disadvantages in a country in which organised science is still in its infancy ... it [often] results in a mediocre one, satisfying the so-called minimum qualifications, being appointed to posts requiring originality, initiative and leadership ...

Bhabha clearly demonstrated the weakness of the traditional system and the superiority of hand-picking talent. Alas, while his formula still holds good, his views have been largely forgotten.

Till 1957, practically all of AEET's work was carried under the umbrella of TIFR. Scientists working on the atomic energy programme shared the Institute facilities including the workshop and the library. In fact, TIFR even managed some of the administrative matters, including purchase. At that time, one Mr. E.C. Allardice an Englishman who had earlier retired from the Indian Civil Service was the Deputy Director of TIFR. Allardice helped Bhabha with AEET administration also. Later he became the Controller (of administration) in AEET. In those days, there was no distinction between a member of TIFR and of AEET; the only difference was that their salaries came from different budgets.

In the early days, research activities associated with atomic energy could be accommodated in Kenilworth. But they expanded so rapidly that fresh space had to be found. Thus in 1953 or so the metallurgy programme was shifted to the Old Yacht Club while the chemistry, spectroscopy and allied activities were found room in the premises of an old defunct textile mill in Cadell Road (now Veer Savarkar Marg). The physics and electronics related activities were accommodated in the barracks in Colaba.

The physics part of the atomic energy programme was under the charge of Dr. Raja Ramanna who simultaneously held a position in TIFR. The electronics programme was headed by Dr. A.S. Rao who too had a dual position. Earlier, Rao had assisted Bhabha in developing electronic instruments needed for his cosmic-ray experiments. Years later Ramanna rose to become the Chairman of the Atomic Energy Commission and after retirement served (for a while) as Minister of State for Defence in Delhi. Rao moved to Hyderabad to become the first Managing Director of the Electronics Corporation of India Limited (ECIL).

Perhaps I could add a small personal note here which illustrates the style and informality of operations in those days. In March 1955, I applied to TIFR in response to an advertisement for appointment to the post of Research Assistant. In July, I was interviewed by a committee Chaired by Prof. Peters. Along with me, about half a dozen people were selected. Some of us were assigned by Dr. Bhabha to TIFR while the others were assigned to AEET; I was in the latter category. I was asked to report to Dr. Ramanna and assist him in research activities related to atomic energy. My place of work was the barracks in Colaba. Though I worked for AEET, for all practical purposes I was a member of TIFR and that is how H.L.N. Murthy of TIFR built some of my equipment (as described in the previous chapter). As the years rolled by, the links between AEET and TIFR weakened somewhat but where nuclear physics is concerned they still continue.

6.4 APSARA, the first milestone

In 1954, Bhabha decided that AEET must have a Swimming Pool Reactor (SPR) as a research facility. The control equipment for the reactor was built in A.S. Rao's group at Colaba while the mechanical equipment was fabricated in the TIFR workshop. The assembly of the systems commenced sometime in 1955 and the reactor itself went into operation in August 1956. Nehru dedicated the reactor to the Nation and gave it the name APSARA; it is still working. APSARA was a major milestone because the reactor had been designed and built in India. The fuel elements alone came from England, thanks to the close friendship between Bhabha and Sir John Cockroft, Director of the Atomic Research Establishment, Harwell, U.K.. Earlier Cockroft had worked under Rutherford and won the Nobel Prize. Bhabha and Cockroft knew each other from their Cambridge days.

Once APSARA became operational, there was little excuse for AEET physicists to hang around TIFR. They therefore packed up and left for Trombay, and I was a part of this migration. My description of the early years of AEET though brief nevertheless illustrates how Bhabha fulfilled his promise of using TIFR as the base for launching the atomic energy programme. Bhabha himself recalled all this in his address to ICSU. He said:

> I also pointed out in a letter dated March 12, 1944, that when Nuclear Energy has been successfully applied for power production in say a couple of decades from now, India will not have to look abroad for its experts but will find them ready at hand. The Trustees of the Sir Dorab Tata Trust decided to accept the proposal and financial responsibility for starting the institute (TIFR) in April 1944, more than a year before the explosion of the first atomic bomb on Hiroshima and before nuclear physics had become what might be called the 'bandwagon' of science. This was also before it had been made public that atomic piles [reactors] had been successfully operated and long before there was any talk of atomic power stations.

6.5 Triumph in Geneva

The year 1955 is a landmark in the life of Homi Bhabha. Responding to a suggestion from President Eisenhower of the United States, the United Nations decided to hold in August 1955, an international conference in Geneva on the peaceful uses of atomic energy. Such an international scientific conference had never been held before, especially under the umbrella of the United Nations (for whom this was a totally new experience). Also, never before in a conference had there been a discussion of such a wide range of topics: From nuclear physics, metallurgy and chemical engineering on the one hand to mineral exploration, effect of radiation on living matter and questions relating to international law on the other. As Bhabha stated in his report to the UN General Assembly, "it was attended by 1428 delegates from 73 nations, and 1334 observers. It was covered by over 900 correspondents." By popular acclaim, Homi Bhabha was elected the President of this conference (referred to as the First Geneva Conference). This was indeed a unique honour, considering that India's atomic energy programme was yet to establish itself in full measure. If Bhabha was unanimously chosen President, it was because of his immense stature and wide popularity. Though the superpowers US and the USSR were strong militarily as also in atomic energy, the honour of the Presidency did not go to them; nor did US and USSR grumble; rather, they supported Bhabha.

Bhabha's presidential address is a remarkable document and even today it is thrilling to read. Presidential addresses usually tend to be dull, boring and monotonous. Bhabha's address on the other hand was a brilliant essay on the history of mankind and its constant struggle to improve its control over the sources of energy in Nature. Understandably he made a strong case for atomic energy. We must remember that the year was 1955 when there were hardly any large, commercial nuclear power stations in the world; they all came later.

In his address, Bhabha made a very bold prediction. He said:

> The historical period we are just entering, in which atomic energy released by the fission process will supply some of the power requirements of the world may well be regarded one day as the primitive period of the atomic age. It is well-known that atomic energy can also be obtained by a fusion process as in the hydrogen bomb, and there is no basic scientific knowledge in our possession today to show that it is impossible for us to obtain this energy from the fusion process in a controlled manner. The technical problems are formidable, but one should remember that it is not yet fifteen years since atomic energy was released in an atomic pile [reactor] for the first time by Fermi. I venture to predict that a method will be found for liberating fusion energy in a controlled manner within the next two decades. When that happens, the energy problems of the world will truly have been solved for a while, for the fuel will be as plentiful as the heavy hydrogen in the oceans.

Bhabha was forecasting that fusion energy (see Box 6.4) would become possible. Two points must be mentioned. Firstly, fusion research at that time was a super hush-hush business, mainly because the hydrogen bomb was based on fusion. The US, Britain and the USSR were all engaged in research on the controlled release of thermo-nuclear energy but none of them talked much about it, including at Geneva. In fact, in the USSR such research was declared secret, i.e., classified. Bhabha's statement was therefore something like a jolt and had the beneficial effect of making these advanced countries come out in the open and say what they were doing in fusion research.

Box 6.4 In a nuclear fission reaction, a big nucleus breaks up into small fragments releasing energy. In a nuclear fusion reaction, small nuclei join up to make up a bigger nucleus, releasing energy in the process. Fission is dominant at the end of the periodic table while fusion is the favoured process at the beginning of the table.

The energy release in the Sun occurs via fusion (see *Chandrasekhar and His Limit*). The fusion reaction on which the hydrogen bomb is based is:

$$\underset{\text{(deuterium)}}{{}_1H^2} + \underset{\text{(tritium)}}{{}_1H^3} \rightarrow \underset{\text{(Alpha)}}{{}_2He^4} + \underset{\text{(neutron)}}{{}_0n^1} + \text{energy.}$$

For the reaction to proceed, both the deuterium and tritium nuclei must possess sufficient kinetic energy; otherwise they will fly away from each other due to electrostatic repulsion. To produce the required kinetic energy, the deuterium–tritium mixture must first be heated to $\sim 10^5$K or even more. In a H-bomb, this is done using an atomic bomb as a trigger! For the controlled release of fusion energy, one must form a deuterium–tritium plasma which is at this high temperature. Since the plasma is quite unstable, it is a problem to extract energy; it is like a fire that gets extinguished rapidly and is unable to propagate. Researchers the world over are still battling plasma instabilities. Since the fusion reaction is triggered by (intense) heat, it is sometimes referred to as *thermonuclear* reaction.

Bhabha's prediction has not come true. But then, in 1955 nobody knew that the plasma out of which fusion energy was to be squeezed was a wild beast and difficult to control. In fact, shortly after the Geneva Conference researchers at the Atomic Energy Research Establishment in UK reported success in their experiments and as being on the threshold of releasing fusion energy in a controlled manner. However, this proved to be a premature claim. Soon scientists everywhere realised that the plasma was extremely unstable and unless one learnt to control it, production of fusion energy in a controlled manner would not be possible. All research during the last few decades has been mainly to understand the instabilities of the plasma and how to overcome them. It appears now that at last one is close to achieving Bhabha's dream. Quite possibly, fusion energy may be available early in the next century.

Indian participation in the Geneva Conference was not confined to Bhabha alone. There was in fact a modest delegation, and papers were presented in various technical sessions. The most important of these undoubtedly was one by Bhabha arguing why nuclear power was essential for India. Considering the backwardness of the country, there was a widespread feeling both abroad as well as in India that nuclear energy was a luxury for India. With facts and figures, Bhabha strongly contested this opinion. Going by the experience of the developed countries, it was clear that a rise in the standard of living automatically increases the demand for electricity. India's population being rather large, the demand for energy in her case would be substantial. This demand cannot be fully met by our reserves of coal or water. Further, our coal is of somewhat inferior quality and to add to our problems, it is mostly located in Bihar. Thus, if one were to build coal-based power stations (arguing that they are cheaper than nuclear stations), then one would have the massive problem of transporting large amounts of coal everyday to power stations in distant states, e.g., Kerala, Rajasthan, Punjab, etc. In turn, this would mean huge investments on railways. Thus, the *overall* expenditure for the country would increase rather than decrease. I must mention that I am giving only the broad, qualitative aspects of Bhabha's arguments. In his paper, he presented detailed facts, figures and costs as would satisfy economists, bankers, managers and Government officials. Looking at this paper, it is difficult to believe that the author is the same as the one who wrote about orthochronous groups in the *Reviews of Modern Physics*! In brief, Bhabha argued that right in 1955, nuclear-power stations were cheaper than thermal-power stations in India, if their location was beyond 800km from the Bihar coal belt. One slogan of his which became popular was: "No power is costlier than no power!" Sounds confusing? Figure it out!

6.6 The Canada–India Reactor project – its genesis

The DAE and the AEET having been created, Bhabha stepped up technology development. While atomic energy could be used for peaceful purposes in many different ways, electric power generation was clearly the prime target. Britain had built the Calder Hall Power Station – a small one it is true, but it actually delivered electricity to the grid; and the Soviets also had a demonstration power station. India had to move quickly to catch up, and it was necessary to look far beyond APSARA even as it was nearing completion.

Bhabha now explored various reactor concepts that would suit power production in India. During the Geneva Conference, he had ample opportunities to discuss this matter with American, Canadian, British, French and Russian experts. At that time, there were three basic types of reactors which were candidates. Light-water (i.e., ordinary water) moderated reactors, heavy-water moderated reactors and graphite moderated reactors. Light-water reactors were popular in the US, having been developed earlier for the nuclear submarine programme. It was attractive in many ways but the catch was that it required enriched uranium (i.e., uranium with a higher content of U^{235} than natural uranium) as fuel. India already had experience in building a light-water reactor, namely APSARA. True, APSARA was not designed for generating steam and producing electricity but it highlighted the fact that the fuel had to be imported because it involved enriched uranium. Enrichment facilities are extremely expensive (even today, the fuel for APSARA comes from abroad). Light-water reactors therefore did not seem the best option, especially as India would then have to depend on imported fuel.

By contrast, heavy-water reactors needed only natural uranium. Of course, there was the problem of producing heavy water but that was easier to handle than producing enriched uranium. To show that India can do it, Bhabha quickly had a small plant set up in Nangal near the Bhakra Dam to produce D_2O by a simple electrolysis process. A lot of electricity was needed no doubt, which explains the location. (For over a quarter of a century, this old faithful has been making a modest but steady contribution to our reserves of heavy-water.)

Bhabha's old Cambridge friend W.B. Lewis was master-minding the Canadian atomic energy programme at that time, and Lewis had made building heavy-water reactors into a fine art. For India, the heavy-water reactor was in every way attractive. Firstly, it required only natural uranium which meant that India did not have to depend on any other country for fuel. Secondly, heavy-water production was manageable and India could do it (the Nangal plant had demonstrated that). Thirdly – and this was an important consideration – the heavy-water reactor had better neutron economy than the light-water reactor. In practical terms, plutonium could be produced more efficiently which was good news for launching our stage II (see Box 6.5).

Box 6.5 India has vast reserves of thorium (especially in the monazite sands in Kerala and Orissa), one of the largest in the world. By contrast, our reserves of uranium are small. Unfortunately, thorium is not directly fissionable but it has potentialities. Bhabha outlined a three-stage programme which India should follow in order to have a practically unlimited supply of energy for at least a thousand years! The three stages are as follows:

STAGE I

Build thermal reactors based on natural uranium and heavy water (the so-called CANDU-type reactor). Here energy release occurs due to fission of U^{235} However some of the more abundant U^{238} absorbs a neutron to become U^{239} which then transforms to ${}_{94}Pu^{239}$ (plutonium) by successive radioactive decay as shown in figure (a). Pu^{239} is fissionable just like U^{235} is.

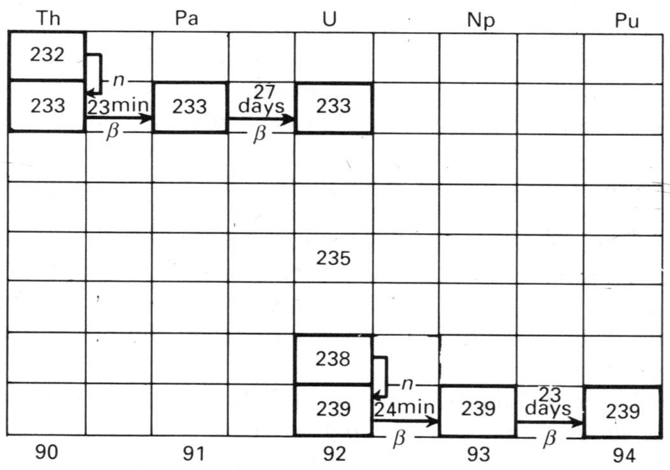

By reprocessing the spent fuel, Pu is extracted. This Pu is kept aside for stage II. Stage I ends when all the available U^{235} in the country is exhausted by fissioning.

STAGE II

Using the Pu stockpiled in stage I, one now builds a plutonium-based reactor called a fast breeder. Here, the fuel is plutonium. Into this reactor is also fed U^{238} lying around as waste from stage I. The U^{238} absorbs neutrons produced in fission and gets converted into Pu. Thus, a fast breeder consumes Pu but also produces *fresh* Pu by conversion of U^{238}. If the fuel produced is more than the fuel consumed, one has a *breeder*, also called a fast breeder or plutonium breeder. Imagine a diesel engine producing fuel and that too more fuel than it consumes! In the world of fission, this actually happens.

For countries which do not have thorium, the nuclear cycle ends when all the U^{238} in uranium is converted into Pu^{239} in fast breeders and is then used up. France, for example, has an ambitious programme of this kind. It was Bhabha's idea that India could stretch the nuclear cycle much farther with a stage III based on thorium.

STAGE III

Th^{232} can, by neutron absorption, become U^{233} as shown in (a). Like U^{235} and Pu^{239}, U^{233} is also fissionable and therefore usable as fuel in reactors.

Bhabha's idea was to "cook" some thorium in fast breeders to produce a starting stockpile of U^{233}. This then drives the $Th^{232}-U^{233}$ cycle via thorium breeder reactors. In this way, starting from uranium (our reserves of which are modest), the nuclear cycle can be extended considerably.

The three stages are illustrated in figure (b).

STRATEGY FOR NUCLEAR POWER IN INDIA

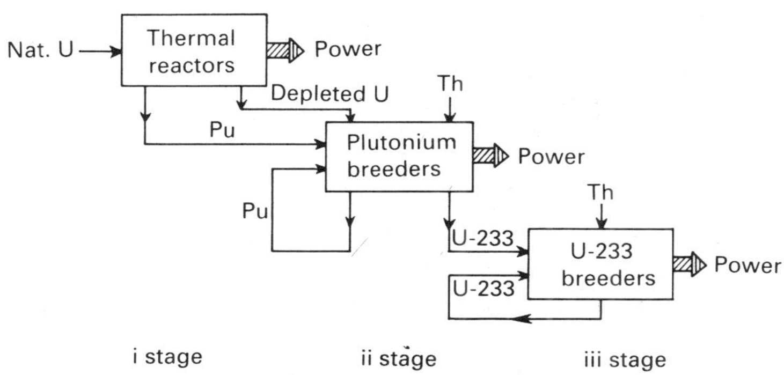

Bhabha paraphrased the three stages as follows:

> The total reserves of thorium in India amount to over 500,000 tons in the readily extractable form, while the total known reserves of uranium are less than a tenth of this. The aim of

> long-range atomic power programme in India must therefore be to base the nuclear power generation as soon as possible on thorium rather than uranium ... The first generation of atomic power stations based on natural uranium can only be used to start off an atomic power programme ... The plutonium produced by the first generation power stations can be used in a second generation of power stations designed to produce electric power and convert thorium into U^{233}, or depleted uranium into more plutonium with breeding gain ... The second generation of power stations may be regarded as an intermediate step for the breeder power stations of the third generation all of which would produce more U^{233} than they burn in the course of producing power.

Thus, even as the Geneva Conference was grinding to a close, Bhabha, based on his background discussions, zoomed in on the heavy-water reactor as the anchor for stage I. In fact, it now became clear to him how India should march ahead in three stages (as explained in Box 6.5). The next item of business was to get experience in heavy-water reactors. Here the Lewis connection helped.

Canada's involvement in atomic energy started during the war years. When the Hitler menace loomed large and the Germans were raining bombs on London, it was decided to shift the British atomic energy research across the Atlantic. Thus a research programme was started in Montreal, Canada. At the helm was Cockroft, with several other Cambridge colleagues including Lewis assisting him. Many Canadians also were involved. The British knew the Americans were on to achieving controlled chain reaction and while there was some cooperation, the British pursued an independent approach in Canada (which was then a British Dominion). After the war, Cockroft returned to UK to head the British atomic energy programme while Lewis remained in Canada to develop the Canadian programme.

The Canadians were not interested in the bomb but in electric power. Lewis made ambitious plans but the kind of research establishment it called for obviously could not be located in a big city like Montreal. So he shifted the scene to a place called Chalk River in the northern part of Ontario (the state in which the famous Niagara falls is located). And here he created a big research complex called the Atomic Energy of Canada Limited (AECL).

The residential area was some 25km away, in a small village called Deep River. In 1947, the Canadians built a 40MW heavy-water moderated, natural uranium thermal research reactor named NRX. At that time, and for nearly ten years after that, this was the most powerful research reactor in the world.

Bhabha decided that the way to get onto the heavy-water reactor route should be via a NRX-type reactor. And so while he was in Geneva in August 1955, he negotiated with Lewis (who was also attending the Conference) a cooperation agreement under which Canada would help India to build a similar reactor at Trombay. In addition, AECL would also train about forty engineers to operate and maintain the Canada–India Reactor (CIR).

For Bhabha this was a major step forward. He was not a fanatic who wanted every nut and bolt to be made in the country (although he did not hesitate to do so whenever there was a pinch; and there were many – recall the balloon development described in the previous chapter). On the other hand, wherever possible, he availed of foreign know-how to get a rapid start. As he himself put it (in his last address):

> The relative roles of indigenous science and technology and foreign collaboration can be highlighted through an analogy. Indigenous science and technology plays the part of an engine in an aircraft, while foreign collaboration can play the part of a booster. A booster in the form of foreign collaboration can give a plane an assisted take-off, but it will be incapable of independent flight unless it is powered by engines of its own. If Indian industry is to take off and be capable of independent flight, it *must* be powered by science and technology based in the country.

See also Box 6.6.

Box 6.6 Here is an example of how in the early days, science and technology helped each other and how we later closed our eyes to such symbiotic growth.

Our story starts in the mid-sixties, shortly after Bhabha's death. The Government was setting up a satellite receiving station at Arvi near Pune. Under the persuasion of Dr. Vikram Sarabhai, then Chairman AEC, the Government allowed BARC to build the control system for the receiver antenna. The man in charge was (late) S.N. Seshadri, later to become Head, Reactor Control Division, BARC. Seshadri had never built such a system before but he was not scared. He knew how to control a reactor and this did not look a more difficult problem. He delivered the goods and everyone was pleased. Govind Swarup heard of this, and immediately went to Seshadri to help him with controls for the Ooty telescope (see last chapter for that story). In a nutshell, know-how had been generated in the country (a) to build antennas and (b) to steer and control them. Some of this know-how was later passed on to ECIL which supplied satellite antenna systems to the defence services, railways, etc.

We now skip years and come to the late eighties, when the telecommunications department wanted a big antenna for some satellite link. Hearing that an order was to be placed with a Japanese company for the supply of this antenna, Swarup offered to build it in the country, for the same cost and within the stipulated time. But the import lobby was strong (as always), and the order went to a Japanese company. You might be shocked. What is more shocking is that preference for foreign technology over what is available in the country is pretty common, especially these days.

At that time there was what was called the Colombo Plan under which countries of the Commonwealth had various collaborations. The Canada–India Reactor project was conceived *outside* the Colombo Plan, even though both Canada as well as India belonged to the Commonwealth. The original idea of a collaboration between Canada and India arose during a conversation between Nehru and the Canadian PM. At that time Bhabha was toying with the idea of building in Trombay a heavy-water reactor similar to the British research reactor E-443 but when the suggestion for a collaboration with Canada emerged (from the discussion between the two Prime Ministers), Bhabha gave up the idea of building an E-443-type reactor in favour of one of the NRX-type "because this is a much more powerful tool." See also Fig. 6.1

The fact that the project would be outside the Colombo Plan was clearly understood by the Canadian Government, Prime Minister Nehru and of course by Bhabha. But the bureaucrats in the Department of Economic Affairs (DEA) in Delhi which was controlling the Indian side of the Colombo Plan activities thought that this reactor project was within their purview. And since DEA controlled the purse strings, promptly there was trouble. For Bhabha this was nothing unusual, and the way out was to use his standard *astra*, i.e., a note to Nehru. In it he said:

> Unless the action proposed above is taken [i.e., make it clear to the DEA that this project is outside the Colombo Plan], all inter-Governmental correspondence will have to be routed through the Department of Economic Affairs of the Ministry of Finance. The Canadian–Indian Reactor is a highly technical project, and this Department has been in continual touch with Atomic Energy of Canada Limited from the very beginning about a host of technical details regarding the design of the reactor, the cooling system [the Trombay reactor was to have a completely different cooling system compared to that in NRX], the choice and training of staff, etc. There is clearly no advantage in routing all this correspondence through the Department of Economic Affairs. Indeed it will only slow down the entire process.

Nehru responded immediately. It was tiresome for Bhabha to fight bureaucracy over every little point and it was equally taxing for Nehru to intervene every time on behalf of Bhabha. But that was the way it was.

Immediately after returning from Geneva, Bhabha swung into action. Lewis told him to send 40 engineers right away, who would be trained at NRX. They would return after a year or so to participate in the construction of CIR (subsequently, the name has been changed to CIRUS; by mistake, many refer to it as Circus!).

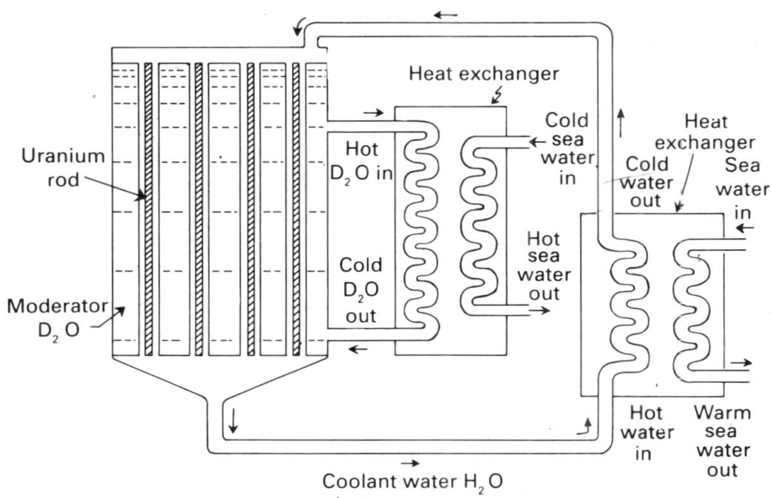

Fig.6.1 Schematic of the CIR reactor. The fuel is natural uranium, the moderator is heavy-water and the coolant is light water. In NRX, the secondary cooling is by river water; in CIR, sea water is used.

6.7 CIR launched

In August 1956, the north site of Trombay was a bush jungle. I visited it for the first time in late September, and by this time a tractor was beginning to clear the site proposed for CIR. Meanwhile, recruitment of engineers was in full swing and within a couple of months a group of about 40 young engineers were assembled under V. Surya Rao who earlier had experience working in power stations in England. Some of these recruits were sent to I.I.Sc., for a short course on power engineering. All this in preparation for sending the group to Canada for training at NRX.

Seldom before had such a big team been sent abroad for technical training – certainly not to Canada. Those were different days and few had any notion of what foreign countries were like; at best, one's impressions were based on Hollywood movies. To prepare the CIR team for a different style of living, etc., Allardice conducted orientation courses, including on how to handle knives and forks!

And in far away Deep River, there was keen expectancy. The Canadians knew about American Indians (many tribes live in Canada) but they knew little about Indian Indians. Whatever impressions they had of us were also based on Hollywood movies. In these movies, an Indian was always portrayed as wearing a turban like our maharajahs did (the AIR INDIA maharajah alone wears such a turban these days), and so they expected 40 maharajah-type Indians. And the ladies there wondered: "How are these fellows going to wash their turbans!" (One of the Canadian ladies later mentioned this to me.)

Canada was a different country, far away and awfully cold in winter but the locals in Deep River were warm and hospitable. The Indian group was accommodated in two apartments, one by the river side on a street called Beach and another a short distance away on Algonquin Street (named after a tribe of American Indians). These two groups therefore came to be known as Beach Indians and Algonquin Indians. Lewis' house also was on Beach Street.

The Canadians found the Indian names long and difficult to pronounce. So they contracted and "Canadianised" the names. Thus Sundaram became Sandy, Narahari became Harry and Lakshminarasayya became Lucky! After this renaming ceremony, two Indians were left for whom suitable names could not be found and they were simply called Tom and Jerry after the characters in the famous Cat and Mouse cartoon show! These names stuck and when the Indian engineers returned, they often used these nicknames while referring to their colleagues or in addressing each other.

Meanwhile, back in India the construction of CIR was in full swing. Bhabha saw to it that as many parts as possible were made in India. Unlike NRX, CIR was to have a circular steel containment building with an airlock. This also called for a revolving crane. Such items had never before been designed and built in India. The engineers trained in Canada were at the job, working with several Canadians who had come to Bombay to assist.

Bhabha decided that unlike APSARA, CIR should have Indian-made fuel elements. Based on the early experience in producing metallic uranium, our metallurgists had designed a plant to make uranium rods similar to those used in NRX. This plant was built next to APSARA. The Canadians were very skeptical about India making fuel elements. Bhabha then made a deal. He said (in effect): "I shall send you two Indian-made fuel elements. Use them in NRX for a year or so and see how they behave. If they are OK, then you must agree that half the fuel elements in the first charge for CIR will be Indian." The Canadians accepted. Soon two elements were flown to Canada and they performed exceedingly well – much to the surprise of the Canadians who now developed a healthy respect. (See also Box 6.7).

Box 6.7 In June 1959, Bhabha informed Nehru about the successful production of uranium rods. He wrote:

> At the end of January, the first ingots of atomically pure metallic uranium were cast. In order to turn this uranium ingot into a fuel element for a reactor, three essential steps have to be gone through. The ingot has to be melted and cast under a vacuum into a billet of the proper shape. The billet has then to be rolled into a rod. These two steps have now been satisfactorily accomplished. The final step is the cladding of the uranium billet in a can of aluminium or some other suitable metal.
>
> Although the building for the Fuel Element Facility is not yet ready, and even full supply of power has not been obtained, the scientific staff has worked with great enthusiasm and drive. On the last day the complicated rolling operations were started at 4p.m. and the scientific staff worked right through the night till the final bar emerged at about 11a.m. next morning.
>
> I have little doubt that we will be able to make satisfactorily fuel elements. There are hardly five countries in the world which make their own fuel elements today.

6.8 Research with CIRUS

Bhabha wanted CIRUS (CIR) for the following purposes:

1. As a training ground for reactor engineers, especially operators. Later they would operate our nuclear power stations.
2. As a powerful radiation source for producing various isotopes needed in medicine and industry.
3. As a source of plutonium. The irradiated uranium rods would contain quite a bit of plutonium. By suitable chemical processing, this could be extracted. (In fact, the plutonium for the FBTR reactor in Kalpakkam came from CIRUS. That story comes shortly.)
4. As a powerful neutron source for various experiments, particularly in physics.

A few words now about this last point.

Thermal neutrons have a de Broglie wavelength ($\lambda = h/mv$) of around 1A which is also the typical interatomic spacing. Besides, their energy $\sim$ 0.025 eV is also the typical kinetic energy of atoms in solids. Thus when a beam of thermal neutrons falls on a sample of a solid or liquid, the neutrons not only get diffracted but also exchange energy with the atoms. As a result, it is possible to perform experiments similar in scope to Raman scattering (see the volume *Raman and His Effect* for a description of Raman scattering). Such experiments call for a powerful neutron source and at NRX, many such experiments had been performed for the first time. Further, many techniques of neutron spectroscopy had also been developed. In NRX, the neutron beams were extremely crowded. Based on this experience, the CIRUS beams were laid out to make it more convenient for our experimenters.

Being a physicist, Bhabha always supported basic research. And while he saw the CIR as a valuable engineering tool, he did not overlook its importance to basic research. And thus it was that in 1957 P.K. Iyengar of AEET was sent by Bhabha to work with B.N. Brockhouse of Chalk River on problems of neutron spectroscopy (later, Iyengar rose to become the Chairman AEC). A year or so later I followed, and for the next few years there was a stream of visiting Indian physicists in Canada. (That is how I got a taste of cold Canadian winters, to which a reference is made in the volume *A Hot Story*.) On return, we teamed up and built various neutron spectrometers (and it is one of these that H.L.N. Murthy helped me to build).

Neutron spectrometers cannot operate without a neutron source – in our case, it was the CIRUS. In late 1960, the reactor became operational but soon there were problems. In their anxiety to leave for home before Christmas, the Canadians did not commission the cooling water system properly. As a result there was algae growth in the primary water system. The reactor had to be shut down and the entire charge of fuel scrapped. The Canadians had gone away and the problem was now ours! It took *two years* to solve the problem. Bhabha described it in a letter to Nehru which he wrote in January 1962. He said:

> I am glad to inform you that CIR operated for the first time for over ten hours at a power level of 30,000 kilowatts on the 4th and 5th of this month with a charge of 160 fuel rods only. Had we the full charge of 192 fuel rods, the operations would have corresponded to the maximum rated power of 40,000 kilowatts. When the Canadians handed over the reactor at the end of 1960 it could not be taken up to a power above 17 megawatts, and a number of difficulties, such as, growth of algae in the primary system, corrosion, pressure drop in the rods, rupturing of the rods, etc., impeded its operation even at a relatively low power level. Since then the reactor has been furnished with an entirely new charge fabricated at Trombay and apart from a thorough clean up of the primary system a great many improvements have been made on it. It was first taken up to a power level of 20,000 kilowatts several times during the first few days of this month, and its trouble free operation at 30,000 kilowatts now establishes that all problems connected with its operation have been overcome by our staff. In overcoming these difficulties, the staff of the Reactor Operations Division were helped in an important way by the staff of the other Divisions, as for example the Analytical Chemistry, Radiochemistry, Metallurgy and Biology Divisions. Unless the work of the Establishment covered all the other fields, we would not have been able to overcome the difficulties on our own. The scientific staff of the Establishment, and especially that of the Reactor Operations Division, have put up a very creditable performance.

Notice how having a multi-disciplinary research establishment helped in problem solving. With CIRUS in full swing, our hearts rose because this was the moment we were waiting for since the mid-fifties. Some of our spectrometers were ready and we could at last get busy with the experiments. At that time, there were very few countries with such facilities. Thanks to Bhabha we could now be in the forefront. Years later, during an international conference on neutron scattering held in BARC (on the occasion of P.K. Iyengar's sixtieth birthday), Trombay's record as a pioneer was appreciated by many a foreign scientist. I should also mention that just as we went to Canada for training, it was now our turn to train scientists from the countries of Asia. On return, many of them ordered neutron spectrometers from India as they were less expensive than western models. So BARC managed to pick up some business too and earn much-needed dollars!

6.9 The Training School

Trombay was now growing fast but the atomic energy programme was growing even faster. Also, it was beginning to spill outside of Trombay. All this growth required a large number of trained people. And so in 1958, Bhabha started the Atomic Energy Training School. Every year, over two hundred graduates drawn from all over India and belonging to a variety of scientific and engineering disciplines were recruited to the Training School. In a sense, this was like recruitment to the prestigious Indian Administrative Service (IAS) — except that unlike in the case of IAS, the recruitment here was via interviews by expert committees, rather than via written examinations. Bhabha also campaigned hard so that his trainees got reasonable salaries comparable to those offered in the IAS, besides similar promotion opportunities. Needless to say all this was far from easy, considering that IAS was (and is) the blue-eyed service, well protected in Delhi.

The Training School has been in operation for over 35 years and *thousands* have passed through it. It has remained the back bone of the atomic energy programme throughout India. In the early years, even TIFR took its entrants via the School but around the mid-sixties this stopped. Not all the graduates remained within the fold of the DAE. Apart from some who later migrated abroad, several found their way to other departments like Space, Electronics, Science and Technology, Defence Research, etc. Quite a few rose to positions of eminence, won national awards and international recognition. Many have criticised the Training School, but few can deny the catalysing role it has played in the development of technology. At least this much can be said of it: Its graduates did not take the first plane out of the country the day after graduation! (I am sure you follow what I mean.)

6.10 The power programme

In living systems, growth is invariably accompanied by differentiation. Analogously, when organisations grow, they diversify. This happened in the case of the atomic energy programme also. To start with, there was the atomic power programme, to pilot which a Power Plant Engineer Division (PPED) was created. Years later it transformed into the Nuclear Power Corporation (NPC). The PPED was charged with building and operating nuclear power stations all over the country. Today, there are several of them – at Tarapur (Maharashtra), Kota (Rajasthan), Kalpakkam (Tamil Nadu) and Narora (U.P.). Others are coming up at Kaiga (Karnataka) and Kakrapar (Gujarat). Except for the Tarapur power station, all are of the heavy-water type – the so-called CANDU-type reactor (the basic reactor design is Canadian). The first-generation reactors were capable of producing 235MW of electricity. In recent years, the engineers of NPC have evolved a design for 500MW reactors. Future power reactors will be of this type.

6.11 Off shoots from Trombay

With AEET going full steam, all the atomic energy activities scattered in various parts of Bombay city were now shifted to Trombay. There they multiplied, diversified and sometimes even resurfaced elsewhere as new centres. For example, the electronics production unit of TIFR which to start with made equipment for the early balloon flight experiments and for APSARA, moved to Trombay (south site). There it took on R & D as well. And from this team, a nucleus was taken by A.S. Rao to Hyderabad to found the ECIL which today is a Rs.100 crore company. In addition, a new division called Reactor Control Division was born from the Electronics Division. This was just the beginning. Over the years, the diversification continued and at present there are over forty divisions in BARC.

Just as I refrained from giving a catalogue of TIFR's activities, I shall here avoid a detailed description of Trombay's multifarious programmes; but a few points deserve mention. Besides ECIL, Trombay gave birth to several other plants like the Nuclear Fuel Complex in Hyderabad, the Beryllium Plant in Vashi (near Bombay), the entire Heavy-Water Programme with plants in Baroda (Gujarat), Kota (Rajasthan), Tuticorin (Tamil Nadu), Manuguru (A.P.), etc. Perhaps the best way of describing this spread of activities is via Fig. 6.2.

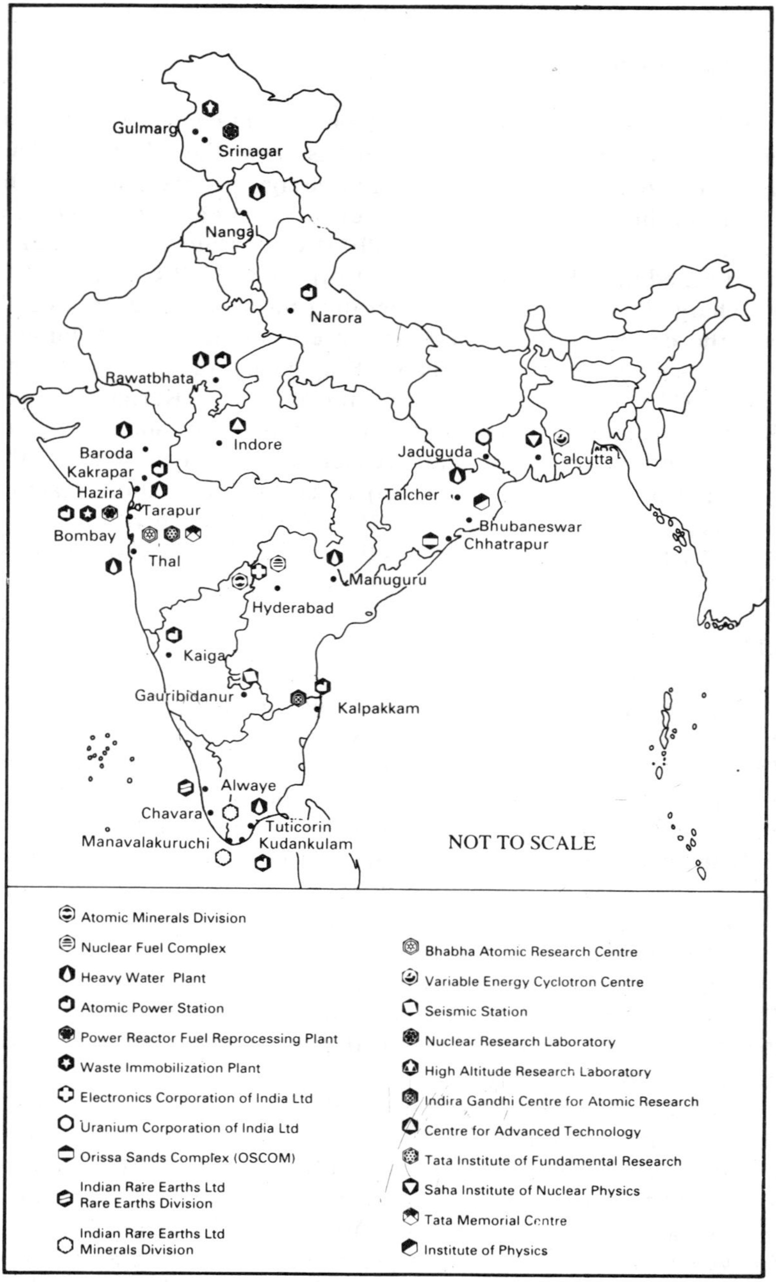

Fig.6.2 Map of India showing various DAE research centres, facilities, projects, plants, etc.

The year after Bhabha died, AEET was renamed Bhabha Atomic Research Centre (BARC). Since that time BARC has given birth to three major R & D centres: the Indira Gandhi Centre for Atomic Research (IGCAR), Kalpakkam, the Variable Energy Cyclotron Centre (VECC), Calcutta and the Centre for Advanced Technology (CAT), Indore. The IGCAR was set up for developing fast breeder technology and its major research tool is the FBTR reactor for which the plutonium came from CIRUS. VECC has a 100 MeV cyclotron for nuclear physics research while CAT is devoted to the development of synchrotron radiation sources and to laser research.

6.12 Atomic energy — a launching pad

Bhabha promoted atomic energy not merely because it was derived from nuclear physics (with which he was very familiar), not merely because it promised a steady source of energy for centuries (as should be clear from Box 6.5) but also because it was a new technology. He argued that the best way in which India could leapfrog in technology would be for her to get into a new area (like atomic energy) where the rest of the world was not too far ahead (may be only about 5–10 years) unlike in other areas where we were decades behind. Besides, it was a challenging technology and achievements if any would boost our confidence. Indeed this was so. If we made fuel elements we were one of the few countries to do so; the same was the case with the production of heavy water, plutonium, beryllium metal, zircalloy and a host of other things. Dr. Ramanna has summed it up as follows:

> I recall Homi Bhabha telling me that the introduction of atomic energy in India in the early 1950s was not purely for the sake of introducing atomic power, but essentially for the introduction of new technologies dependent on basic sciences generated within.

One can write a long chapter on this last point but I shall not do so. However, I should draw attention to one beneficial effect of our atomic energy programme on our manufacturing industry. Earlier, our industry was used to relatively "coarse" jobs as demanded by steel plants, cement factories, etc. In atomic reactors on the other hand, the quality requirements and the dimensional tolerances are quite stringent. Thirty years ago, our industry was totally unused to doing such jobs. Initially, they also shied away from them. But when persuaded, they took up the challenge and were pleasantly surprised to discover their own capabilities. Soon, manufacturers were proud to advertise that they had supplied equipment to DAE, meeting stringent standards.For the first time, quality consciousness and quality control was injected into our industry.

6.13 Into space

Bhabha did not stop with atomic energy. He recognised quite early that Space was becoming an important area of research. In 1958, the Russians launched SPUTNIK, the first ever artificial satellite, shocking the Americans and driving them into a space race. High altitudes were not unfamiliar to Bhabha but now rockets and satellites offered new opportunities for research. He therefore persuaded the Government of India (in 1961) to let DAE look after space research also. The Government promptly agreed. Inaugurating the first seminar on Space Physics in 1963, Bhabha said:

> [The second] reason for going into space research is that there are many areas in which it is likely to yield results of great practical interest and importance in the near future, and we would again be falling behind the advanced countries in practical technology if we were not to look ahead and prepare to take advantage of these new developments also ... If we do not do so now, we will have to depend later on buying know-how from other countries at much greater cost ...

Some of those who knew Bhabha have told me that he had ambitious plans in space research. Unfortunately, he did not live long enough to see space research grow but after he died, Sarabhai carried the torch forward admirably. Later, under Dhawan, an entire department for space research was created. Today, like the Department of Atomic Energy, the Department of Space (DoS) has a chain of labs and facilities across the country under the umbrella of the Indian Space Research Organisation (ISRO). Its programme and activities have expanded and exactly as Bhabha foresaw, the fruits of space technology are now reaching the people – just recall the Doordarshan relays and the satellite weather picture shown everyday during TV news; these are but two examples. Indeed, precisely as Satish Dhawan former Chairman of the Space Commission once predicted, ISRO is now seen as a "commercial threat" by the advanced countries; that is why ISRO has been included in the technology embargo imposed by the advanced countries and aimed at curbing India's progress in strategic areas (the ban started with DAE; now it is slowly spreading).

6.14 On technology import

Bhabha was always critical of our tendency to survive on constant "transfusions" of foreign technology. Citing the example of the steel industry, he once said:

> The steel industry had existed in India since the First World War, and one of the two steel plants was among the largest in the British Commonwealth in the early twenties. Yet when these steel plants had to be expanded, it was necessary to draw upon foreign consultants and engineering firms to plan and carry out the expansions. When the Government decided to establish a steel plant at Bhilai the same course was followed, this time with Russian technical collaboration. The third public sector steel plant at Durgapur had similarly to be set up with the help of British consortium ... Thus, the construction and operation of a number of steel plants has not automatically generated the ability to design and build new steel plants ...

Contrast this with the experience in the atomic energy programme. At Trombay, BARC decided to augment its research facilities with a 100MW research reactor. BARC engineers designed and built it themselves drawing upon previous training and experience. This reactor named DHRUVA is a successor to CIRUS (which by the way is still operating). Whereas foreign help was sought for CIRUS, none was taken for DHRUVA; Bhabha's principle was religiously followed. Indeed, in some cases like the design of the plutonium extraction plant, no foreign help was ever sought — it would not have been given anyway.

6.15 Bhabha and electronics

Right from his Bangalore days, Bhabha was well aware of the role of electronics not only in physics research but also in technology. Thus when AEET got going, he extended full support to R & D in electronics and also for limited production. And in TIFR he likewise encouraged various instrumentation projects as also the design and construction of the large digital computer named TIFRAC. In fact this was one of the earliest computers to be built in the country.

In 1962 the Chinese invaded India, exposing weakness in our defence preparedness. This sent shockwaves all across the country. Bhabha offered the services of AEET for whatever needed to be done in support of national security. Recognising the key role of electronics in defence systems, Bhabha recommended to the Government that an Electronics Committee be set up "to survey the needs of the country in electronics components and equipment and to recommend measures for planned development of electronics, so that the country as a whole may become self-sufficient in this field in the shortest possible time and in the most economical manner." The Government accepted Bhabha's advice and a Committee was formed with him as the chairman. The Committee drew up a detailed blue print for the development of electronics but unfortunately Bhabha died before the report was formally presented to the Government (in February 1966).

Little happened after that. The Government no doubt formed a Department of Electronics (DoE) but this did not blaze a trail like DAE and DoS had done earlier. Thanks to its Delhi base, DoE functioned like any other bureaucratic department while Bhabha's report gathered dust. Meanwhile, electronics developed at a fantastic pace elsewhere, and today we find ourselves in a sorry mess. Everyone knows there is a mess but we are so used to messy situations that few are really troubled or bothered!

6.16 In retrospect

The growth of technology (especially in India) is a subject close to my heart and usually I tend to get carried away while discussing the subject. Let me therefore apply brakes and focus now on Bhabha's philosophy before wrapping up this chapter.

Many in our society today think that Indian scientists and engineers are incompetent. Bhabha did not subscribe to this view. On the other hand, he firmly believed that Indians are as good as any anywhere. All they needed was (i) the challenge, (ii) the right leader, and (iii) firm backing. Where he was concerned, he created the challenges and himself assumed the leadership; and he was fortunate enough to receive the backing of Nehru (about which more will be said in the following chapter). In turn he identified leaders, posed them challenges (like making uranium rods or extracting plutonium) and gave them full backing.

Bhabha was fully alive to the difficulties and the handicaps of pursuing science and technology in India, especially if one was committed to excellence. He not only vigorously overcame obstacles that came in his way but repeatedly commented on the type of system we need. Where excellence was concerned, Bhabha was almost a fanatic (as you will learn in the last chapter).

Excellence is not new to this country. One has merely to go back in time to discover the pursuit of excellence by our ancestors in music, art, literature, philosophy and yes, even science and technology. Near Kutub Minar in Delhi, there stands an iron pillar going back to A.D.400 – it is still in perfect condition. They also knew the science of alloying and how to cast exquisite images of gods and goddesses.

In recent years, excellence has taken a back seat, having been replaced by what may be called the "lowest quotation" culture. Unfortunately, the Government which is the biggest buyer in the country has aided and abetted the growth of this obnoxious attitude. Whenever the Government buys, it selects the vendor who offers the lowest price. No one can quarrel with the idea for after all it is public money that the Government is spending. Unfortunately, when we buy at the lowest price, no one pays *real* or *serious* attention to the quality of the product (although there are lots of pretensions about it). Over the years this has often led to rackets of all sorts. No wonder then that buildings constructed on Government contracts are invariably substandard and often crack or even collapse, in sharp contrast to many of our ancient structures which have survived for centuries. Since Government has been extending unwitting support to such practices, shoddiness has now become almost a way of life for us.

There is an understandable passion in our bureaucracy to curb wasteful expenditure. No quarrel about that because we are after all a poor country. What is not acceptable, however, is the bureaucracy's unnecessary, unwarranted and unjustified rigid control over money released for developmental activities (although it turns a blind eye – perhaps it has no choice – to huge irregularities committed with political patronage). No wonder our scientists and engineers often feel frustrated and handicapped. If their performance is affected it is *NOT* entirely their fault. But everyone thinks they are to be blamed. Net result: There is not much faith or trust in Indian science and technology in Governmental circles, although a lot of lip service is paid. The press and the public also feel our science and technology have delivered little.

Few in our country understand how creativity or excellence is to be nursed. (This applies not only to science but equally so to sports.)

Where bureaucracy is concerned, it seems to think scientists and engineers are like machines which can be switched on and off at will. Any attempt to explain the conditions needed for creativity only produces the retort: "Oh you want to spend public money and not be accountable." Creativity flourishes only when human imagination is allowed free play; but this does not mean there should be no accountability. In fact, there must be a stiff demand for quality. And unless there is an environment where excellence can flourish, we have to depend on rare "accidents" like Ramanujan who anyway happen only once in a few centuries.

The recipe for nursing excellence is not all that complicated – pick the right people, give them some money to have the desired facilities and then leave them alone. Today, money for science *has* to come from the Government – it is so in *all* countries. But in India accepting Government money also means accepting unhelpful Government rules *lock, stock and barrel*. Bureaucrats think this is the only way of ensuing "accountability." Unfortunately, they are mostly concerned with rules and procedural "irregularities" rather than with reaching the goal. They fail to appreciate that thousands of Indians abroad are doing well simply because the environment there is better. And it is not as if there is no accountability abroad. In fact, there is lots of it but of the right kind. In India we are not able to function well because of too many irrational checks, controls and regulations.

Bhabha stoutly resisted all such shackles. Where TIFR was concerned, he was largely successful in preventing the omnibus application of Government rules but where the DAE was concerned, he had to yield somewhat since it was a Government Department. But as long as he was around, he did shield his department from rigid external control. Today, all the examples he set have been largely forgotten. By and large as a Nation we tend to think too much like accountants and lawyers. Everyone, the press, the public and the parliament, is excessively attached to rules, procedure and audit.

Dear young reader, I won't tax you anymore with this sad story for at your age you must dream, let your imagination soar and be inspired by towering achievements. If I have told you a bit of this sad story, it is in the hope that at least you and your generation will correct the mistakes of our generations. From the famous Indus Valley Civilization onwards, no great civilization anywhere has been built by accountants and lawyers. But we desperately seem to be trying to do precisely that!

There is a lot of mess around and if bureaucracy (about which I have been critical) appears to be behaving in a certain way, perhaps it is merely mirroring society. Maybe it cannot be blamed too much. Meanwhile, where science and technology are concerned, bureaucracy unfortunately remains our checkpost and much of Bhabha's battles were fought there. Significantly, the last part of his last ever speech dealt precisely with this problem. He said:

> There is one final point I would like to touch on and that is the role of administration in science. It is thought by many that we are reasonably advanced in administration but backward in technology. This statement is misleading. We have fortunately inherited extremely competent administrative services capable of dealing with all the types of administration which had to be dealt with before Independence in what was intended to be a static and underdeveloped economy. Consequently, experience of the type of administration needed for industry and for science and technology has been lacking. [In recent years the Government has woken up to this need but bureaucracy, especially at the lower level, is still in slumber.] The type of administration required for the growth of science and technology is quite different from the type of administration required for the operation of industrial enterprises and both of these are again quite different from the type of administration required for such matters as the preservation of law and order, administration of justice, finance and so on. It is my personal view ... that the general absence of the proper administrative set up for science is a bigger obstacle to the rapid growth of science and technology than the paucity of scientists and technologists because a majority of the scientists and technologists are made less effective through the lack of the right type of administrative support. The administration of scientific research and development is an even more subtle matter than the administration of industrial enterprises, and I am convinced that it cannot be done on the basis of borrowed knowledge. It must necessarily be done, as in the technologically advanced countries by scientists and technologists themselves.

Today, one would perhaps slightly modify the last sentence by adding: "By a cadre of specially trained people tuned to the needs and aspirations of R & D personnel." In the advanced countries, scientific research has not only become a billion dollar affair (e.g., at CERN) but also international (e.g., at CERN and at the European Synchrotron Facility in Grenoble, France). Projects go through smoothly in all these places — they are finished in time and within the budgets sanctioned. There is no reason why we too can't do likewise – only, we must be permitted *and* enabled. Bhabha was, and he produced results. Somehow, after his death things slid back to "normal". Why so, and who is responsible? Answers not here please, for that would require a book of its own!

7 *Bhabha and Nehru*

The close relationship between Bhabha and Nehru played a vital role in accelerating the growth of science and technology in the country. Barring perhaps the example of the Lord Cherwell–Winston Churchill pair (in UK), I cannot think of any other parallel. Indeed, even Cherwell and Churchill did not bring about a revolutionary change like the Bhabha–Nehru team did.

Like Bhabha, Nehru also went to Cambridge, years earlier of course. Nehru was personally attracted to science but had to settle for a study of law for various reasons. Later he said:

> I haunted the laboratories of that home of science, Cambridge. Though circumstances made me part company with science, I turned to it with longing ...
>
> In later years I arrived again at science when I realised that science was not only a pleasant diversion and abstraction, but was the very texture of life, without which our modern world would vanish away. Politics led me to economics, and this led inevitably to the scientific approach to all our problems and to science itself.

In the mid-thirties, Nehru visited the Soviet Union (now extinct!) and was tremendously impressed by the rapid progress made there through large-scale industrialisation. This made him declare:

> It was science alone that could solve the problems of hunger and poverty, of insanitation and illiteracy, of superstition and deadening custom ...

As an intellectual, Nehru was greatly attracted by the aesthetic beauty of science but as a man of the masses, he was equally if not more attracted to technology and the promise it held. From the year of Independence, he made a "pilgrimage" every year to the annual session of the Indian Science Congress. And on every occasion, he delivered, always extempore, a stirring address. As early as 1947 he declared:

> Surely, science is not merely an individual's search for truth. It is

> something infinitely more than that if it worked for the community. It must have a social objective before it. For a hungry man or woman, truth has little meaning. He wants food. For a hungry man, God has no meaning. He wants food. And India is a hungry, starving country ...

Alas, it continues to be so, at least where the four hundred or so millions who live below the poverty line are concerned.

After his visit to the Soviet Union, Nehru was greatly attracted to socialism, state planning and massive industrialisation, all of which the Soviet Union swore by. Understandably, he joined a society called *The Friends of the Soviet Union*. Bhabha too had socialist leanings, and he too was a member of this society. This was one of the bonds that existed between Bhabha and Nehru – shared ideals. But this was not all for they also shared similar tastes in art, culture and literature. Added to all of this, was that they both had a liberal, international outlook, definitely not common in India then and not too common even now, nearly fifty years later. And to cap it all, they had both studied in Cambridge.

The personal contact between Bhabha and Nehru began in 1937 when Bhabha and Nehru and his daughter were travelling by the same ship. This was revealed by Indira Gandhi while inaugurating the Homi Bhabha auditorium of TIFR in 1968. During the early forties, there was hardly any contact between the two; Bhabha was immersed in research in Bangalore while Nehru was in jail, "discovering India". It was only in the late forties, especially after Bhabha got involved with atomic energy, that their relationship blossomed.

Earlier I mentioned Nehru's unfailing appearance at the annual sessions of the Science Congress. In 1951, the Science Congress met in Bangalore with Bhabha as the General President. Welcoming Nehru, Bhabha said:

> I also wish to express on behalf of all of you, and myself, our great appreciation of the fact that our Prime Minister has decided to be present with us on this occasion. That he flew to Bangalore yesterday, and will fly immediately after this meeting to Bombay and thence to England on a mission of prime importance, is a measure of his great personal interest in the development of science in India. Were it not for this, scientific development would receive much less encouragement and support than it does, in spite of the fact that only science and technology can solve the immense problems facing the country, the problem of food shortage, low standard of living and illiteracy.

Bhabha then went on to describe what he called the *Present concept of the physical world.* Remember, at that time he was busy studying the Bhabha equation (that is, whenever he could spare time for research). When it came to Nehru's turn, he said:

> You have just been listening to Dr. Homi Bhabha's address and no doubt all of you found it very interesting, as I did. All these are very fascinating subjects and yet I was trying to correlate what he said and the subject to the kind of problems we have to face. I am quite certain that these things are not unrelated to each other, although their relation may not be obvious. But then, today, when we have to face all kinds of rather urgent and immediate problems, how exactly do we bring about this relation ...
>
> Inevitably, a person like me who is concerned with day-to-day problems of great importance has always to think a little less of pure research but more of the application of research to the problem of human society ...

As we saw in an earlier chapter, Bhabha was not the "ivory tower" scientist whom politicians abhor. On the contrary, he gave equal if not even greater emphasis to technology, a fact which greatly endeared him to Nehru.

Let me now illustrate the unusual relationship that existed between these two great men with annotated excerpts from some of the correspondence they exchanged, both personal as well as official.

I shall start with a letter of Nehru in which he recommended to Bhabha to add one more country in his tour of Europe. To me this is absolutely incredible because as a rule, Government frowns on foreign trips and to think of the Government proposing additions is almost to think of the impossible. Are you wondering then how so many of our bureaucrats are constantly junketing? Ah, I leave you to figure that one!! Let us get back to Nehru's letter.

New Delhi
July 29, 1956

My dear Homi,

I met your Atomic Energy guests from Burma [now Myanmar], Egypt, Ceylon [now Sri Lanka] and Indonesia yesterday and had a talk with them. They appeared to be satisfied with their visit and the work they had done at your Conference.

I have just received a paper containing your programme for your visit abroad. This shows that you will be in Austria on the 9th to the 11th and then for some weeks on leave. Would it not be possible or desirable for you to pay a brief visit to Yugoslavia from Austria? You will be quite near and it will be easy to go there. You have wanted to visit Yugoslavia for some time past ...

Perhaps I might be seeing you again on the 1st August in Poona [Pune]. That will have to be rather late at night, because I am engaged the whole day.

Yours sincerely,
Jawaharlal Nehru.

Fat volumes can be written on the rigidity and the stupidity of many of the rules of Government, some of which appear to go back to the days of the East India Company. Bureaucracy has its own axe to grind and is least bothered about the inconvenience caused or even the obstruction to progress. In 1956, the construction of India's first reactor APSARA was in feverish progress at Trombay. Prodded by Bhabha, scientists and engineers were working round the clock. Trombay is somewhat distant from the city (in those days, Trombay was quite isolated, and all the crowded suburbs that have now sprung up did not exist), and there was a problem in shuttling people back and forth from the city at odd hours. Bhabha then sent a note to the Prime Minister:

During the last few days they [scientists] have invariably worked till late at night, and on several occasions right throughout the night. Trombay is about an hour's drive from the Fort [centre of the city], and our canteen at Trombay has not commenced operation. The loading of the reactor is a difficult operation, and a mistake may seriously set the project back. It is clear that in the circumstances, everything should be done which should relieve the physical strain. I have, therefore, ordered:

(a) that two cars should be put at their disposal on a 24-hour basis, which will take them from their residence to the place of work at Trombay and back at any time they consider best from the point of their work, and
(b) that lunch and dinner supplied by an appropriate restaurant shall be provided for them at Trombay in the reactor building.

Both (a) and (b) are not permitted by Government regulations, and I therefore wish to have the Prime Minister's approval for the action taken. Incidentally, this provides an example of the way in which the present rules and regulations of Government are not really suited for executive work which is to be done at speed and pressure ...

Since the above was written, the group worked upto 3 a.m. on Tuesday morning. Our group of scientists concerned, Mr. Allardice and I started again at noon on Tuesday (yesterday) and worked continuously through the night till 7 a.m. this morning. It would be unreasonable to try and apply Government rules to groups and departments which work like this. The result will only be to reduce output and enthusiasm.

H.J. Bhabha
1.8.56

The note seems to have been rushed to Delhi, for Nehru approved it on the same day with the words: "I agree." Such wonders don't happen easily, especially nowadays. A so-called note to the Government winds its way through a long channel of officials starting with lowly ones, all of whom are well trained in stonewalling. In short, such a note normally has "less chance than a snowflake in hell" as the popular saying goes. Bhabha could have his way because of his strong personal rapport with Nehru. The bureaucracy was well aware of that; even so, it always tried hard to block Bhabha, and seldom gave up without a fight.

At 3.45 p.m. on August 4, 1956, India's first reactor SPR went into operation. The Department of Atomic Energy released a press note, and the news was flashed by the radio (in those days, we had no TV). Nehru obviously was the first to be informed (on the phone). Bhabha also wrote to Nehru as follows:

August 4, 1956.

My Dear Bhai,

I send you with this letter a copy of the press note which I released this evening, with the photograph of the reactor. You saw it the other day.

When I got home at seven this evening, my mother told me that there was an announcement on the subject from you.

I conveyed your congratulations to our young men. They richly deserved them, as they worked with real devotion and enthusiasm.

I had to delay my departure by a day, due to the starting up of the reactor. I am now leaving on the evening of Monday the 6th August. Au revoir,

Yours ever,
Homi Bhabha

Pandit Jawaharlal Nehru
Prime Minister
Government of India
NEW DELHI.

P.S. After the above was dictated, I received your telegram yesterday evening. Thank you very much for it. I am circulating it to our young men. I am sure it will spur them to greater efforts.

Notice how Bhabha addresses Nehru. No "Dear Sir" or "Dear Prime Minister" but as Bhai.

These days, we are facing a resource crunch. Actually, there has rarely been a time when we did not face such a squeeze! On such occasions, there is an inevitable tussle between those who dream of development and those who control money. Nehru wrote to Bhabha in the late fifties on the subject. This is what he said in part:

> We are, as you know, in a terrible fix about our foreign exchange and to some extent even our internal resources. We are trying to raise very large sums of money as loans in countries abroad. This is difficult enough, and I do not know if we shall get them. Even if we get them, we have to pay a heavy interest on them for many years. Thus we shall have to carry a great burden for the next seven to ten years ...
>
> It has been a frustrating experience to go and ask for money from other countries. They enquire: Are you going to be equally ambitious in your third Five Year Plan and then come again for loans in a big way? It is clear that we cannot repeat this performance of asking for big loans ...

Interestingly, we have not stopped asking for big loans; only, they are getting bigger all the time. But that does not concern us here. What I would like you to notice is the courteous and personal explanation the PM is offering about the resource crunch; in short, Nehru is trying to soften the blow. Such gentle explanations disappeared with Nehru.

A view of TIFR

Aerial view of the laboratory complex in Trombay.

View of the CIRUS (R) and DHRUVA (L) reactors at Trombay.

Cartoon by R.K. Laxman showing Nehru piloting India into the Atomic age.

Another cartoon by R.K. Laxman. The person with wings and holding leaves is Lal Bahadur Shastri, then Prime Minister of India.

Stage set designed by Bhabha for Calderon's play "Life is a Dream

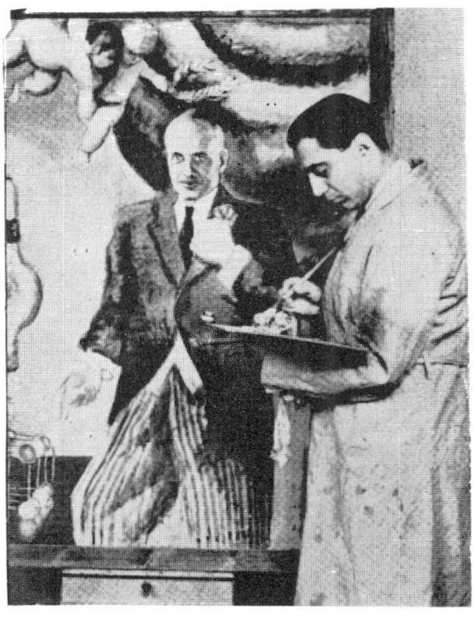

Bhabha engaged in painting.

Sketch of artist M.F. Hussain by Bhabha.

RUTHERFORDIUS NOSTER, cum Praeses Societatis Britannicae ad Indiam profecturus orationem pararet, nullius nominatim nisi huius viri mentionem facere decrevit; adeo iam tunc excellebat. Qui patre natus Oxonii alumno et in India sua eruditus Cantabrigiam pervenerat, ubi studia exercuit primum machinalia, deinde physica, stipendiumque ex nomine Isaaci Newton nuncupatum promeritus est. Redux postea in patriam et naturae rationes a vulgari intellegentia remotiores subtiliter scrutatus, meditatus, commentatus, doctrinae physicae in Instituto Tatano Professor evasit. Umbraticus tamen minime est, ut qui domi sit eiusdem Instituti Rector, consiliique Indici Praeses potentiae in atomis latentis regendae causa constituti, foris tanto in honore habeatur ut, cum nuper e multis gentibus legati Genavam convenissent qui de eadem potentia quaererent quomodo ad innoxios usus verteretur, hunc consilii magistrum delegerint.

Sed ad studia ita semper accubuit ut convictui humano et societati vacaverit, linguarum complurium peritus ubique peregrinetur, picturae et musicae artibus ipse exercitatus cum talibus viris libentissime versetur. Quid enim? Traditur idem in Collegio suo quinti remigii gubernator olim fuisse.

Duco ad vos Regiae Societatis Sodalem, Collegii Gonvillii et Caii Socium honoris causa creatum

HORMASJI JEHANGIR BHABHA

When Lord Rutherford was composing his speech before setting out for India to preside over the meeting there of the British Association, this was the only man whom he found occasion to mention by name; such was his eminence already. His father was an Oxford man. He himself, after education in India, had come to Cambridge, where he studied first engineering and then physics, and was awarded the Isaac Newton Studentship. On his return to his own country, after subtle research, thought and observation on the more recondite laws of nature, he became Professor of Theoretical Physics in the Tata Institute. But he is by no means a scholarly recluse, being at home Director of the same Institute and Chairman of the Indian Atomic Energy Commission, while abroad he is held in such esteem that he was elected Chairman of the International 'Atoms for Peace' conference held recently at Geneva.

But concentration on his studies has never prevented him from finding time for social intercourse and relationships: he is a good linguist, and travels widely; and being himself an exponent of the arts of music and painting, he eagerly seeks the society of such men. Should I add that he is also remembered in his College as cox of the fifth boat?

I present to you

HORMASJI JEHANGIR BHABHA, F.R.S.
Honorary Fellow of Gonville and Caius College

Citation read out in Latin and English when an Honorary Degree was conferred by Cambridge University on Bhabha. See Bhabha's letter to Nehru on the subject. (Chapter 7)

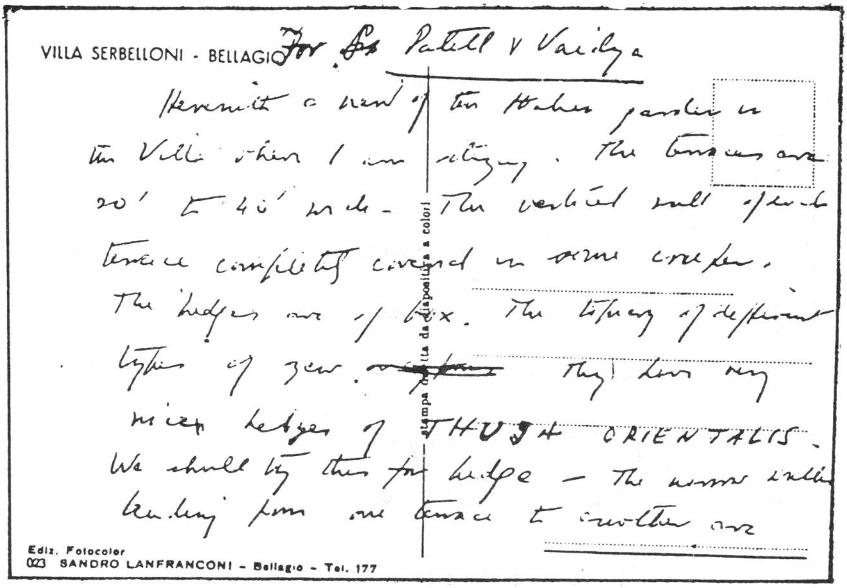

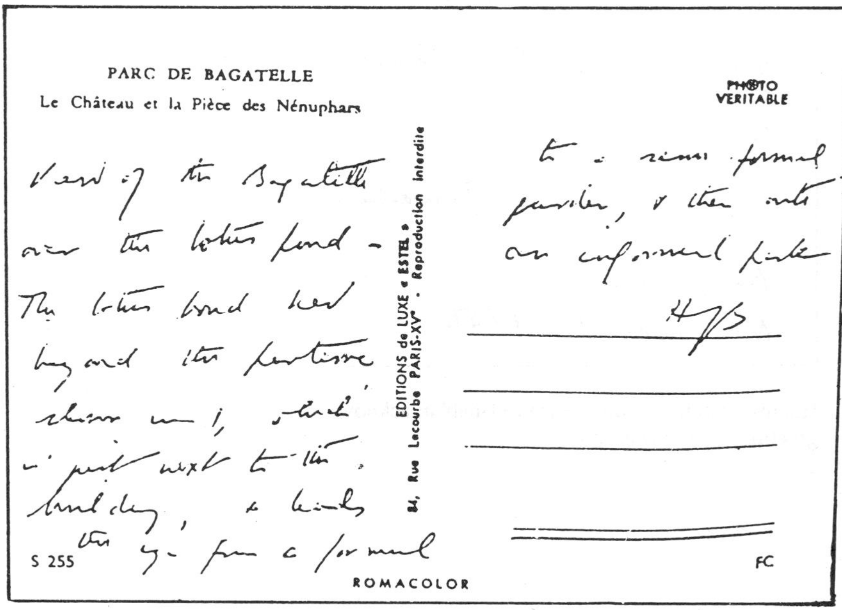

Samples of postcards sent by Bhabha to Mr. Vaidya of BARC concerning gardens in Europe—see Chapter 8.

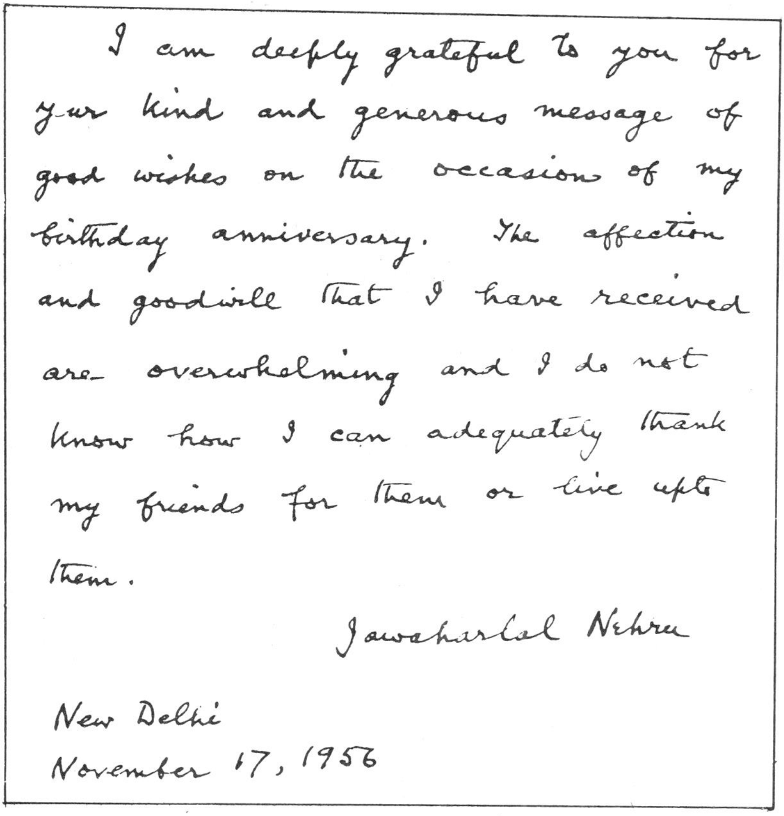

I am deeply grateful to you for your kind and generous message of good wishes on the occasion of my birthday anniversary. The affection and goodwill that I have received are overwhelming and I do not know how I can adequately thank my friends for them or live upto them.

Jawaharlal Nehru

New Delhi
November 17, 1956

Handwritten note from Nehru to Bhabha, acknowledging birthday greetings—see Chapter 7.

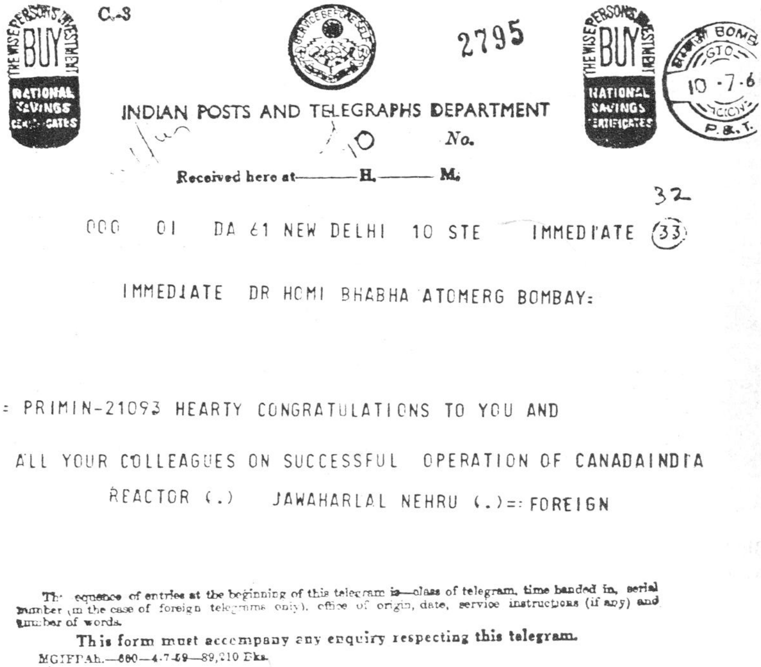

C.-3

2795

INDIAN POSTS AND TELEGRAPHS DEPARTMENT

No.

Received here at———H.———M.

32

000 01 DA 61 NEW DELHI 10 STE IMMEDIATE (33)

IMMEDIATE DR HOMI BHABHA ATOMERG BOMBAY:

= PRIMIN-21093 HEARTY CONGRATULATIONS TO YOU AND ALL YOUR COLLEAGUES ON SUCCESSFUL OPERATION OF CANADAINDIA REACTOR (.) JAWAHARLAL NEHRU (.)=: FOREIGN

The sequence of entries at the beginning of this telegram is—class of telegram, time handed in, serial number (in the case of foreign telegrams only), office of origin, date, service instructions (if any) and number of words.

This form must accompany any enquiry respecting this telegram.

MGIPPAh.—660—4-7-59—89,210 Bks.

Nehru's congratulatory telegram sent when CIR achieved first criticality—see Chapter 6.

First day cover issued after Bhabha's death. The musical score below Bhabha's photograph is from Beethoven's ninth symphony.

Bhabha, chairing the First UN International Conference on the Peaceful Uses of Atomic Energy, Geneva, 1955.

Homi Bhabha in conversation with Professor Neils Bohr during the International Colloquium on Function Theory at TIFR, 1960.

Bhabha at the control room in Trombay with Pandit Jawaharlal Nehru.

Queen Elizabeth II and Homi Bhabha in the foyer at Trombay.

Bhabha frequently travelled abroad and after a visit in 1959, he wrote to Nehru as follows (in part):

> I enjoyed the two days I spent in Cambridge in connection with the conferment of an honorary degree of Doctor of Science on me. The ceremony was as usual. Among the other recipients of honorary degrees (of Law, Literature, Science, and Music) were Dr.Vivian Fuchs who led the recent expedition across the Pole, Le Corbusier [to whom we owe the planning of Chandigarh], the sculptor Henry Moore, the composer Mr. Benjamin Brittan, and Mr. Louis Clarke, one time Curator of the Fitz William Museum. The citations were as usual read out in Latin by the Public Orator, but for the first time a crib with the English translation was distributed to the audience. There was a very large luncheon in the hall of Trinity College immediately after conferment, at the end of which Lord Tedder, Chancellor of the University, made a speech referring to all those on whom a degree had been conferred. I had been asked to reply to his speech on behalf of all the recipients of honorary degrees, and I enclose herewith a copy of my speech. (The text published in the India House bulletin had some mistakes and omissions in it.) Being an after-lunch speech, it included a certain number of humourous topical references which may be lost if one is not aware of the local incidents to which they allude. For example, the last paragraph refers to an undergraduate prank which was narrated to me by the Vice-Chancellor, Lord Adrian. One morning the authorities of the University found to their surprise an entire automobile on the roof of the Senate House. How it had been put there overnight is still something of a mystery, in view of the enormous trouble which had to be taken to get it down again without damaging the Senate House.
>
> I stayed in Cambridge at the Master's Lodge in Trinity as the guest of Lord Adrian. This was evidently a particularly good year for roses. I have never seen such profusion of beautiful roses, as was to be found in his garden at the back adjoining the river. The two days in Cambridge, although very hectic, were most refreshing. I sometimes wish I could spend 3 to 4 months there in quiet study and contemplation. I hope some of the scientific laboratories and establishments we are building today will have a beauty of their own, which will have its due effect on those who work there. I think both Trombay and the Tata Institute of Fundamental Research will be architecturally, and botanically beautiful, when they are completed.

Bhabha wrote this letter from Bangalore where he was holidaying for a few weeks, trying among other things, to revise the last chapter of his book on *Algebra for the Theory of the Elementary Particles* (the book remains unpublished). Nehru's reply is brief but warm and in it he says: "So you are back after collecting more honours!" In passing I should mention that almost every year, Bhabha spent a month or so on holiday in Bangalore, Ooty and places like that. In the late fifties, TIFR started organising Summer Schools on topics in Physics. In those days they were always held in Bangalore. Bhabha often dropped in. One year, Gell Mann was the star lecturer and in his presentations, he gave his audience a preview of his yet-to-be-published famous quark model. Bhabha attended Gell Mann's lectures and also a party in his honour.

There was another occasion when Bhabha wrote to Nehru in a similar vein; that was after attending the Tercentenary Celebrations of the Royal Society. During this trip, Bhabha, along with six others was honoured by the University of London with an honorary degree.

And now for a sample of the cordial informality that prevailed in the relations between these two giants.

January 28, 1961

My dear Bhai,

This is to remind you that you have agreed to attend the buffet supper which I am giving as Chairman of the Atomic Energy Commission for the representatives of foreign Governments attending the inauguration at Trombay. The supper is at the Ashoka Hotel at 8.45 p.m. on Sunday, the 29th January (tomorrow). [Bhabha writes this from the Ashoka Hotel in Delhi.] There will be roughly 35 foreign representatives present, plus about an equal number of Indian invitees.

I have also sent separate invitations to Nan [Nehru's sister Vijayalakshmi Pandit], Indu [Indira Gandhi] and Betty. I am merely mentioning this, in case they have gone astray.

Yours affectionately,
Homi Bhabha

There is an immediate reply from Nehru.

Prime Minister's House
New Delhi
January 28, 1961

My dear Homi,

Your letter. I shall come to Supper tomorrow at the Ashoka Hotel. So I think will Indu. Nan will not be here as she is accompanying

Queen Elizabeth to Agra. About Betty, I am not sure. She has not been too well. I suppose she will come if she is well enough.

Yours sincerely,
Jawaharlal Nehru.

The Government regularly appoints many committees, councils, etc., but seldom does it bother to seek the consent of those appointed. The appointments are almost like an order, it being taken for granted that those appointed would jump with joy and be eager to comply. In the case of Government servants, there is no consultation – they are just told. See how different it was between Nehru and Bhabha.

October 21, 1961

My dear Homi,

You must know that we held a National Integration Conference at the end of last month. You had been invited to this also, but of course, you could not come. This conference decided to have a Council consisting of the Prime Minister, the Union Home Minister, all Chief Ministers of States and a number of other people. Among these are supposed to be three scientists and educationists. Kothari, as Chairman of the University Grants Commission, is one of the persons selected. I should like you to join this Council.

I do not know if it is possible for you to send me an answer soon. I shall presume your agreement and announce your name after three or four days.

Yours sincerely,
Jawaharlal Nehru.

These are but glimpses of the warm friendship that transcended official limits. Nehru died in May 1964 and Bhabha offered him a stirring tribute – see Box 7.1. Roughly twenty months later Bhabha died and in a tribute to him, Indira Gandhi observed: "He demonstrated that even in India it is possible to cut through the pervading red tape and to adopt bold methods." Needless to say that this was possible largely because of the special relationship that existed between Bhabha and Nehru. Describing that special bond, Indira Gandhi said:

> The life of a politician lacks many of those warm moments of sensitivity that other people take for granted in their everyday life ...

I know that Homi Bhabha opened one such 'window' for my father. No matter how tired my father was, no matter how late it was in the night, he always found time for Dr.Bhabha, not only because the problems which Dr.Bhabha brought were important and he wanted to give them urgent attention, but because he found at the same time it was relaxing and it was an entirely new world.

Box 7.1 On June 1, 1964, Homi Bhabha broadcast a talk entitled *Jawaharlal Nehru and Science* over All India Radio. Some excerpts:

> For Jawaharlal Nehru the supreme task of the age was to lift mankind from its age-old state of bare subsistence to a social level which provided security, material plenty and above all the opportunities for fulfilment and a higher life to all. He knew that this aim could be achieved through, and only through, science and its application ...
>
> He [Nehru] felt, quite rightly, that operating a steel mill or a chemical plant set up by foreign assistance hardly made the country an advanced and industrialised nation, any more than using a car or flying an aeroplane purchased from abroad. It is only when India has acquired the ability to *design, fabricate and erect* its own plants without foreign assistance will it have become a truly advanced and industrialised country, and for this a much greater development of science and technology is still necessary. "We have to produce not only machines that are to be used"; he said "we want men who will *design* machines and improve them. There must be *creativeness*." [Alas, the pleas of Bhabha and Nehru lie forgotten.] ...
>
> When the new Department of Atomic Energy was created in 1954, and I was asked to take charge as Secretary to Government in the new department, I made it clear that I did not wish to be divorced from direct participation in the scientific work and that it was in the interest of the work that the department should be located in Bombay, near the centre of our scientific activities. The Prime Minister accepted this unorthodox proposal immediately, though it might have appeared at first to be a personal inconvenience to him ...
>
> He [Nehru] indicated at the beginning the matters on which he would like to have papers put up to him. The list became shorter and shorter as time went on [these days, bureaucracy

makes such lists longer and longer!]. He gave a few broad directives with regard to policy, and his immediate decision when any policy matter was put up to him. But he never interfered in the running of the department .

Although not a practising scientist, Jawaharlal Nehru's personality revealed throughout the essential attributes of the real man of science – "his unquenched thirst for truth, his questing mind that admitted no man-made barriers, his essential humility, his constant willingness to learn and to teach" [quote from the resolution passed by the Science Advisory Committee to the Cabinet, of which Bhabha was the head].

The Nehru–Bhabha partnership was like a dream opening wicket partnership, if one were to use a cricketing analogy. It would be a long time before we see another such example, especially in today's climate.

One last word about Nehru. While inaugurating the new buildings of the Tata Institute of Fundamental Research, he [Nehru] said:

> It is really meeting these young people, who have already distinguished themselves and who I am quite sure will distinguish themselves still more in future, it is in meeting them and finding out what they have been doing, that I have felt so hopeful, so optimistic about the future of science in India ...

It is now for the scientists in India, particularly for the younger generation of scientists (and that means *YOU* dear reader!) to justify the trust he (Nehru) placed in them.

8 *The Lesser Known Bhabha*

A passing mention was made earlier that Homi Bhabha had strong interests in art and music. Those who knew Bhabha are well aware of this aspect but the world at large knows little about this.

Homi Bhabha's interest in art, literature and music began at an early age. The environment in which he grew up had a lot to do with this. At home there was his father's large collection of books, especially on music and on art. In addition, there was a good supply of gramophone records of classical music, particularly Western music. All this, and the cultural milieu so often associated with wealthy Parsis greatly increased young Homi's exposure to Western art, culture and music. Brother Jamshed Bhabha remarks:

> For Homi Bhabha, the arts were not just a form of recreation or pleasant relaxation; they were among the most serious pursuits of life and he attached just as much importance to them as to his work in mathematics and physics. For him, the arts were, in his own words, "what made life worth living".

8.1 Bhabha and music

I have already narrated in Chapter 1 the incident about music and the crying child which drew the attention of Homi's mother to her son's natural musical instincts. As a young boy Homi often went to the house of his aunt, Ms.Coover Panday who had a large collection of Western music. There, in the company of his brother (Jamshed), his cousin Dinsha Panday and Ms.Coover Panday, young Homi would listen for hours to the music of Beethoven, Mozart and the like. Lights would be dimmed and there would be total silence during the entire listening period. These sessions greatly helped him to cultivate a deep and profound taste for Western music. By the time he was sixteen, "he was familiar with many of the major symphonies, concerti and chamber music of Beethoven, Mozart, Bach, Heydn and Schubert, as well as a wide range of popular classical music by Chopin, Mendelssohn, Wagner, Dovrak, Tschaikovsky and others".

Bhabha also started taking violin lessons at the age of sixteen. But before he could make much progress he had to leave for Cambridge, and music lessons seem to have ended right there. However, in Europe, Homi got the opportunity to attend real concerts instead of merely listening to gramophone records. Within a few weeks of landing, he heard the London Symphony Orchestra perform Beethoven's "Eroica" the symphony and described it in a letter home as "colossal, magnificent, superb and tremendous". A year later, after listening to Beethoven's Ninth Symphony, he wrote to his brother:

> It is now almost one o'clock, but I cannot help writing to you. I came back from the Concert at about eleven or earlier and have been thinking of the Ninth Symphony all the time. I am so overwhelmed by it that I can neither talk nor think of anything else. Never before have I been so moved. The performance was by no means faultless and Henry Wood is not the best conductor for Beethoven. But all the faults of execution are forgotten in the greatness of the work. I was drawn out of myself and raised to sublime heights and my mind hardly got back to work till a long time after the end. I walked back in a dream, and, now that I think of it, I am surprised that I got back at all. It is the sublimest and happiest time I have *ever* had in my life. Happy is hardly the term, it is something greater. Truly, this Symphony is the greatest piece of music ever written. In all Beethoven's works, particularly of the later second and third periods, one feels his immense genius, his colossal feeling and the perfection of his music. The Ninth Symphony is sheer greatness, the sublimest and most colossal achievement of the human mind. Composed when he was totally deaf, it represents all he had to say to men, the result of his own life.

Young Homi is still not out of his teens but notice the depth of his perception, his understanding and the way he is *moved* by music.

It was not concerts all the time (for attending which one often had to go to London) and Homi continued listening to gramophone records, but this time with a difference. He followed the music by having before him the score, trying to absorb the composition, the style and the various nuances. He even attempted a few compositions, one of them a symphony in the style of Mozart. Thanks to the presence of various Indian friends, he also took to serious listening of classical Indian music. And after his return to India, he made it a point to attend concerts of Indian classical music – both Hindustani and Carnatic – as often as he could manage. Thus it was that he developed admiration for eminent Carnatic music vocalists like Ariyakudi Ramanuja Ayyangar, M.S.Subbalakshmi, Madurai Mani

Iyer, Musiri Subramania Iyer, Semmangudi Srinivasa Iyer and many others. As his brother Jamshed remarks, "In this respect, he shared with his admired friend, Yehudi Menuhin, a love of both Indian and Western classical music".

Even while he was at Cambridge busy with exciting research, Bhabha found that he could not concentrate on mathematics and physics for more than about five hours a day. After exhausting himself with science, he would seek relaxation through painting, music and the other arts. And this continued throughout his life. Brother Jamshed says:

> Even in his last fifteen years, when he became increasingly immersed in his organisational and administrative tasks of building and developing the Tata Institute of Fundamental Research and the Atomic Energy Centre at Trombay ... he would find relief from tension and fresh stimulus in listening to music at night. In fact, there was hardly a single free evening at home when he would not be listening to music after dinner and before taking up again his mathematical work till late at night.

8.2 Bhabha, painting and literature

Bhabha's fascination for the fine arts was all-round. He was not only drawn to music but equally so to painting, literature, architecture and landscaping. Bhabha was a born artist. While young he received training in painting from one Mr. Jehangir Lalkaka, in the classical style. And pretty soon, young Homi started winning prizes at the Annual Exhibitions of the Bombay Art Society.

Europe opened up Bhabha's horizon and he "changed his drawing and painting from the dull academic manner learnt in Bombay to a more vigorous individual style". In Cambridge, Bhabha came under the notice of Roger Fry, Slade Professor of Fine Art. Fry noted that Homi definitely had a talent for art but qualified his praise with the remark that he [Bhabha] lacked a "certain sensitiveness". Bhabha was naturally a bit disappointed, especially because he was still evolving. He conveyed his feelings a few years later in a letter he wrote to his parents after exhibiting some of his works at Cambridge. He said: "I wish Roger Fry could have seen the latest stuff".

While at Cambridge, Bhabha designed a new cover for the College magazine: A head with long flowing hair with the College "Gate of Virtue" behind and above. But the students found this too radical a design.

About his painting style, Bhabha's artist friend Leyden writes:

> Dr. Bhabha's style is best described by "judicious and learned naturalism" in which the usual maligned term "naturalism" is meant to convey an understanding of Nature and not its servile imitation. This naturalism has romantic overtones caused by the artist's personal attitude to his subject. What makes his drawings so appealing is that his personal attitude is one of modesty and humility, a kind of wooing his subject, a penetrating struggle to understand and reveal.

Bhabha's interest in the fine arts was not compartmentalised but an integrated one. At Cambridge, Bhabha not only produced several paintings for which he drew inspiration from music, but also designed the decor and the sets for various operas and plays.

During this period, Bhabha began to read Shelly, Keats and Shakespeare. And his letters home contained descriptions of the powerful impressions made by these writers. About Shakespeare he wrote:

> I am more and more impressed with his towering greatness. He leaves all others far behind in the literary world. I have just finished *Anthony and Cleopatra*. Without reading it, you can get no idea of the heroic glamour of the style of this play. He made me weep with the intensity of the consciousness he has given me.

Besides painting, Bhabha also indulged in sketching which he did quite well. After he died, AIR INDIA brought out a calendar using his sketches as illustrations.

Bhabha supported Indian artists in a big way. Noted art critic Karl Khandalawala writes:

> Bhabha's appreciation of art was not only marked by unusual insight, but the courage to express his opinion freely disregarding other informed opinions if he was not in agreement with them. Even in the days when the now famous Indian artist Amrita Sher Gil was neglected and scoffed at, he proclaimed that she would some day be hailed as one of the great painters of all times. How true this prophecy proved to be after her death.

For TIFR, Bhabha acquired the paintings of leading painters and had them tastefully displayed. He also commissioned the celebrated artist M.F. Hussain to paint a large mural in the lobby. In such matters, Bhabha was a trailblazer in India. Thanks to his initiative, even Government rules were modified to permit spending a few percent of project costs for artistic acquisitions. In practice, however, outside of the DAE, bureaucrats refuse to recognise this enabling provision. Indeed, even in the DAE such purchases appear to have considerably dwindled after Bhabha's demise.

8.3 Bhabha and architecture

Painting, plays, poems, sculptures and musical compositions are expressions of creativity. But so also are buildings and monuments. Every great civilisation of the past has left its relics of temples and monuments, and we have a good collection of them here in India too. Bhabha was attracted to all these. When he was in Europe, he closely observed the great buildings there, be they museums, opera houses or palaces. He not only paid attention to their geometric forms but also how these buildings were conceived in relation to the purpose for which they were built, and how they were balanced by the surrounding landscape. About such interests, Leyden comments:

> He [Bhabha] was deeply conscious of the beauties of the cities of Delhi and whenever he could steal an hour, he would relax at Haus Khas or in sight of the Lodi Tombs or in front of the magnificient facade of Shersha's mosque at Purana Kila. Once we stood together on those ramparts and looked at the wide panorama stretching before our eyes, and I remember how he spoke, in great anger, of the rape of this beautiful city by sterile PWD [Public Works Department] architects, by the tastelessness of bureaucrats and politicians, by the avarice of land speculators and by the complete lack of culture here, in this city, where a half-ruined chhattri at the end of a broken down wall has more significance than all the post-1947 Bhavans put together. And what he regretted most was the loss of such tremendous and challenging opportunities.

When Bhabha turned institution builder, he had the opportunity to give expression to his ideas. While he did not hesitate to start scientific work in whatever space was available (recall that the Chemistry and the Spectroscopy Divisions of BARC functioned for years in abandoned mills), he was equally emphatic that the final building must be properly planned, and also aesthetically appealing. If it was not so, Bhabha held that the building was also functionally wrong. He strongly felt that if the scientist did not have a harmonious setting to work in, he would develop a split personality. Equipment, computers and other facilities can make up only a part of what the creative mind needs. Besides these, it also requires a congenial environment.

Ancient Indians understood the spiritual significance of architecture. So did the great pioneers of the renaissance when they went about building churches, etc. The Moghuls too had the right outlook. And indeed the creator of the city of New Delhi paid loving attention to the architectural concept of the city though most of the buildings were meant for bureaucrats. But the post-Independence era saw a rash of ugly match box like monstrosities often painted in a depressing "Government yellow". The routine argument for creating such substandard and offending buildings was that one could not "afford" anything better. Bhabha disdainfully rejected such nonsense. Even from the point of view of finance, in the long run one actually ended up spending more on the maintenance of such cheap constructions.

The first chance that Bhabha had for breaking away from this dull approach was with the TIFR building. He got the eminent American architect Helmuth Bartsch to design it. Later Bartsch said:

> In this development the architect worked *with* a client rather than *for* a client. The client displayed unending interest and encouragement and constantly added intelligent suggestions and advice.

Nehru laid the foundation stone of TIFR in 1954 and eight years later he inaugurated it. Speaking on that occasion he said:

> You had been told that a little more than eight years ago I was invited here to lay the foundation stone or the cornerstone of this structure. It is so long ago that I had almost forgotten that I had done it. And I began to think of another instance which happened in Delhi when the foundation stone was laid and after a few months people discovered that someone had stolen it. (Laughter). Normally speaking, a delay of eight years in completing this structure seems rather excessive. But coming here once in-between and today, going around partly over this building, my original impulse to criticise the delay was considerably modified because it has been a great effort to put this up as it has been done. There have been difficulties and anyhow the result achieved is something very much worthwhile.

The Trombay campus was much larger than the TIFR campus, and the complex of laboratories, reactors and other facilities that Bhabha wanted to create there (similar to what existed in the other atomic energy research establishments), offered an altogether new challenge as well as opportunity to Bhabha. Here he could dream not only of beautiful buildings, but also of exquisite gardens, pools, avenues, and a whole landscaped hill!

To translate dreams into reality, Bhabha created a civil engineering division and attached to it a cell consisting of very competent architects – see also Box 8.1. Of course, the dreams were always that of Bhabha but the architects and the civil engineers helped to translate them into reality.

Box 8.1 Here is one example of Bhabha's running battle with the bureaucracy in Delhi. He had problems in appointing private architects as consultants, and on June 18, 1956, he sent a note to Nehru on the subject. He says:

1. A site of some 1200 acres has been acquired for the Atomic Energy Establishment, Trombay, which is bounded on one side by Trombay Hill and on the other by the waters of Bombay Harbour. The main site is virgin and has no buildings on it. [I recall my first visit to this site around September, 1955.] The Establishment will have 23 large and small buildings on it for laboratories, library, administration, workshops etc. ... (this does not include atomic reactors) ... The above unique circumstances present an opportunity for developing an architectural project which is not only functional and efficient but of architectural significance, reflecting the developments of the age we live in. There is indeed an obligation on the Department to do the best it can and see that this opportunity is not missed.
2. Accordingly, this Department put up the proposal that the following five well-known architectural firms be invited to prepare a site plan ...

    1. Mr. D.S. Bajpai
    2. Messrs Bhuta and Associates
    3. Messrs Kavinde and Rai
    4. Mr. Rustom B.J. Patel
    5. Messrs Polk and Stein ...

3. The Ministry of Finance have turned down the proposal (without it being seen by the Finance Secretary, who is on leave) on the following grounds:

    "We have not hitherto dealt with such a proposal ... Generally the procedure followed is that a number of architects are called upon to submit plans, designs etc. ... From the plans, designs etc., submitted by different architects, the Department chooses the best. Just as no honorarium is paid to a tenderer, no honorarium is paid to an architect also ..."

> The comparison between asking a number of architects to submit designs with a calling for tenders by contractors is clearly misconceived ... Anyone who has any experience of intellectual activity knows that the conception of an architectural project is the most important part of it in which the architect's real merit is shown ... I consider it wrong to exploit or compel professional men to do work without legitimate payment ... It is said in the Finance Ministry's note that no such honorarium is paid by CPWD [Central Public Works Department]. This may be one of the reasons why CPWD work is architecturally so insignificant. The general tendency in India today to employ civil engineers instead of architects is also probably one of the causes why architecture, which was one of the glories of Indian civilization in the past, has now sunk into complete insignificance...

Nehru responded the very next day, quite sympathetically. He knew precisely what Bhabha was saying and how he [Bhabha] felt. Besides, Nehru himself had commissioned the world famous architect Le Corbusier to prepare plans for Chandigarh. So he wrote in the file:

> I have read this [Bhabha's] note. I think there is much truth in what Dr. Bhabha says. If we are to have any improvement in our present low level of architecture, we shall have to adopt other methods than those of the Central Public Works Department ...
>
> I do not think that the proposal of Dr. Bhabha involves any marked additional expenditure considering the size of the project. It is likely to result in much better buildings. I would, therefore, approve of it.

It is not easy to win battles against the officials of the Ministry of Finance, however short-sighted or incorrect they might be. That Bhabha succeeded was entirely due to his special rapport with Nehru, who was equally sensitive on matters involving taste.

Rustom Patel, an architect who closely worked with Bhabha says:

> As one of the few architects who had the privilege of close association in this field of work with Dr. Bhabha – I witnessed as much of architecture taking root in a Man of Science, as of his scientific philosophy guiding his own architectural thinking. His interest in this subject took him beyond the limits of a "client-architect" relationship

> on any project that he guided; it amounted to an intensive participation some (might have even said interference) but he had the uncanny knack of being right more often than not in matters of conceiving and the frankness to be self-critical of his own design decisions when proved wrong. Of the powerful driving forces that made up the highly creative entity that he was, the Ego was understandably dominant: However, in frequent cases of disagreement on architectural ideas, formidable though he was to convince and relentless in putting through his own point of view, he disapproved of mere concurrence from others when it was without true conviction.

The master plan for Trombay took over ten years to take shape. Whenever he travelled abroad (which was quite often), Bhabha was always on the lookout for ideas, not necessarily from other equivalent laboratories. And on occasions, he had his architect on tow as he toured other countries. Back in India, he would take to the drawing board he had at home where he would spend hours sketching and trying out ideas, in the evenings, at nights and on holidays. Suddenly after dinner, Patel would get a phone call: "Doing anything tonight?", which meant "Drop everything and come over to my house at once!" And when he came, the latest ideas would be unveiled with the remark: "Well, what do you think of it?"

Bhabha wanted to make Trombay the VERSAILLES of the scientific world — so tremendously was he impressed with Versailles, its buildings, its gardens and its general landscape. As one who worked in Trombay while this fantastic dream was coming true, I can not only say that I actually saw it happen but also how it happened.

No detail was too small for Bhabha's eyes. If a wall had to be painted, small patches of sample colours (suggested by the architects) would be painted on a wall for the big man to see and select. Sometimes it would be months before a selection was made because Dr. Bhabha was not available as he was on tour. But *he* had to approve before the full painting operations could commence. If a washbasin was to be fitted in the bathroom, different models available in the market would be procured and arranged in a display till a selection was made by Bhabha. And so it was with every choice. In the case of the Modular Laboratory, often called the longest building in Asia, the support pillars went through many iterations. Architect Patel recalls:

> For us it was very often a challenge to our skill and endurance to keep up to the pace he would set, particularly on a scheme such as the Modular Laboratory at Trombay, the only single building (besides

> the Tata Institute of Fundamental Research) to which he gave his special care and attention. In its innumerable design details that had to go through his surveillance, every season had its major architectural hurdle to cross before he could be convinced and give his final consent. For example, I remember 1964 as the "the year of Concrete Facia" or 1965 as "the year of the Jalli", there was hardly any compromise – only *THE* Solution.

Bhabha did not view individual buildings in isolation. To him they formed an integrated complex which meant that he paid careful attention to how the various buildings would be located with respect to each other, how they appeared when approached from along the different routes, etc. In turn, this meant laying out the roads in the most effective manner and filling the spaces in between so as to achieve the correct artistic balance. Sometimes he used technical requirements to his advantage. The CIRUS reactor required a cooling system which called for sprays. Inspired by the pools of the Rashtrapathi Bhavan, Bhabha designed a circular pool containing fountains which produce a most pleasing effect when in operation.

In India we seem to be content, at least these days, in doing things in a most casual manner. We are in the grip of what is popularly referred to as a *chalta-hai* attitude. Bhabha never tolerated this. Those who worked with him learnt this lesson (sometimes the hard way! – see Box 8.2), and thanks to that, today the Department of Atomic Energy continues to insist on well-designed and properly built buildings and civil structures in marked contrast to the shoddy "PWD culture" that Bhabha detested.

8.4 Bhabha – trees and gardens

I come now to yet another dimension of Bhabha's personality – his love for gardens and his passion for trees. Let me introduce the subject by quoting Leyden, who says:

> It must have been the last time that I spent an evening with Homi at his beautiful house. As always, the conversation was stimulating and far-ranging, from politics to architecture, from science to art, from food and good cooking to gardening, and there stood, near his desk, an enormous drawing board with huge printed plans, pinned to it. It appeared they were the first layouts for the afforestation schemes and suggested gardens at Trombay ... He spent many hours at night poring over these plans, trying to visualise in his mind's eye the setting of this new city, which he had founded and built nestling

> below the tree-grown flanks of the Trombay Hill and within a vast arrangement of gardens.
>
> The planning, design and the style of these gardens fascinated him. By the side of the drawing board were fine illustrated volumes on the gardens of Versailles, on the English Gardens of the 18th century, on Italian, Japanese and on Persian Gardens ... We talked about the apotheosis of water, which is the central theme of the Persian and the Indian Moghul Garden. His detailed knowledge was tremendous. He could describe the essential points of a garden design, whether he had seen it in Vienna, Paris, Rome, Yorkshire or Kyoto. He knew instinctively the intentions of garden architects, what they were aiming at and what was their underlying idea.

Bhabha never considered landscaping a luxury. A good garden not only lent beauty to the surroundings and enhanced the appearance of the building itself, but more important, it brought cheer to the people working there. In fact, during intense spells of working, Bhabha himself used to get out for a while, stroll in the garden and return to work refreshed and relaxed.

When the Trombay site was chosen, the long hill there formed more or less the western boundary of the site. On the other side of the hill were several industries, including an oil refinery. The hill was barren, having been stripped over the years of all vegetation by people in search of firewood. Bhabha's first item of priority was to afforest the atomic energy side of the hill. S.D. Vaidya who closely worked with Bhabha and later served as the Head, Landscape Architecture Division of BARC recalls:

> A plan for planting over a million and a half trees was drawn up to cover all the barren portions of the hill ... The work of tree planting was carried out before the erection of the main laboratories and for that Dr. Bhabha was criticised for giving priorities to aesthetics. But his explanation was that trees take their own time to grow... Early planting was done only to gain time.

The result of Bhabha's far reaching vision can be best appreciated today by viewing the Trombay Hill from a boat in the adjacent bay. Visitors to the Elephanta Island probably can get such a view while crossing the bay. Seen from that angle (and I have done that many times), the contrast between the two sides of the hill must be seen to be believed. While the refinery side remains to this day absolutely brown and barren, the BARC side is lush green even during the non-monsoon season.

Bhabha recognised that gardens had a functional utility also. The labs required clean atmosphere inside and it helped to control the dust levels in the environment. Trees greatly helped in this matter. In addition, they helped in lowering the local temperature, thereby reducing the load on airconditioners.

Bhabha was a lover not merely of manicured gardens but of plants and trees in general. His observation of trees was sharp. Once when he was in Bangalore he saw a casuarina tree with a foliage that looked different from the usual.He immediately called Vaidya on the phone to check whether this was indeed a different species. Vaidya said that this was possible. Bhabha then asked whether he could bring some cones with him to Bombay for trying out the new species at Trombay. Vaidya replied that fallen cones would not have seeds in them whereupon Bhabha had seeds collected from cones still hanging on the trees and despatched them to Bombay by a courier. The trees grown from such seeds are to be seen in Trombay even today. Bhabha's love for trees is best described by Vaidya himself:

> While planning roads in Trombay he observed from the landscape plan that an old mango tree came in the way of one of the roads. The civil engineers had recommended complete removal of the tree to have a straight road. Dr. Bhabha was very unhappy with this proposal. He felt that the tree which had lived there for over a hundred years had every right to continue to stay in the same spot. As there was enough space around the tree to modify the road layout, he suggested realignment of the road to save the tree. The tree had given character to the whole area for over a century and is still happily standing there as a living sculpture. Also, along the approach road to the Tata Institute of Fundamental Research there was a huge rain tree which came in the way of the road construction. As this road alignment could not be changed, because the local conditions could not permit it, he had the tree transplanted in the adjoining locality.
>
> Once while coming from his house to the Trombay Establishment he saw a few people cutting a rain tree along Peddar Road. He stopped to inquire why they were cutting the tree and whether they had legal sanction to do so. He was told that the tree had been disposed off by the Municipal Corporation as it fell in the road-widening line and that they had purchased the tree for the highest bid. He requested the workers to stop cutting it further till he found out whether the tree could be saved. As soon as he reached Trombay he told me to examine whether it was possible to transplant and save

> the tree. When I inspected the site I found the tree was completely mutilated. I reported to him that it would not be wise to spend a large sum of money on the transplantation of the tree which had lost its aesthetic value. He immediately asked me, "if you were a doctor would you not try to save a patient who had third-degree burns which made his face disfigured?" He also told me that scientists and artists should not waste their talents on bothering about the monetary involvements of the projects. Their duty is to come out with their best in the larger interests of mankind. Financial wizards and administrators are paid for finding out ways and means for making the funds available for any good cause.

How I wish our finance officers and administrators view their duties in this fashion! To get back to the story of this poor rain tree, Vaidya had it transplanted in a neighbouring compound, and it is doing well even today, quarter of a century later.

This incident set a new trend and trees began to be transplanted all over the place, including in Trombay and in TIFR. As Vaidya says:

> It is difficult to believe that the majority of the large trees in the gardens of the Tata Institute of Fundamental Research are the ones which were given a new lease of life at the instance of Dr. Bhabha.

Bhabha was a true friend of trees and did everything he could to save them whenever they faced the axe. Once he saw many trees being removed in Malabar Hill to make way for a housing complex. On this occasion, Bhabha went to the very top, meaning he got in touch with Nehru to stop the massacre; it worked. Years later, responding again to a request from a lover of trees, Indira Gandhi intervened to stop a large scale deforestation near Bombay, just a couple of days before her brutal assassination.

8.5 Looking back

And so we come to the end of this story about a remarkable man. As we look back, we see many Bhabhas — brilliant scientist, imaginative visionary, shrewd planner and organiser, able administrator, sensitive artist, devotee of music and literature, and a passionate lover of trees and gardens. Many are the examples of people who have achieved excellence in one or two areas but seldom does one come across a person so versatile as this.

Let us start with Bhabha the scientist. The contrasts between him and Raman, Saha and Bose on the one hand and with Chandrasekhar on the other are quite striking. Raman, Saha and Bose were all products of the Indian "backwaters". They were essentially self-taught and lacked the discipline of a formal training such as one gets in a place like Cambridge. And they were all products of a prevalent feeling of national revival. While they could not always keep pace with the times and produce papers of uniformly high quality and significance, they made up with brilliant flashes of intense creativity which won for each of them a special niche in science. Bhabha with his Cambridge exposure was very different. He maintained throughout an extremely high standard in his papers and while he did perhaps foresee many a later development, none of his discoveries has the same eternal quality as Bose statistics, for example.

The contrasts between Bhabha and Chandrasekhar are equally interesting. Homi Bhabha received his basic training in the West and later showed that he could be quite successful staying and working in the so-called "backwaters". Let us remember that Bhabha won the Adams Prize for an essay written in India and that his work on the Bhabha equation also was done in India. Chandra went the other way – college education in India, followed by rounding off in Cambridge after which came a most successful career, carved out entirely in the West. Would Chandra have sparkled equally if he had returned to India? Nobody can say; he himself thinks not – at least that is what he once said to his father. What about Bhabha? Would he have done better as a scientist if he had gone back to the West after the war? Judging by the experience of Chandrasekhar and Abdus Salam, Bhabha might well have attained even greater heights in pure science. In that sense, Bhabha did make a *tremendous sacrifice* by deciding to stay on in India. At the same time, by skilfully turning to institution-building he made sure that his Indian experience did not become a sour one.

As an organiser and an institution builder, Bhabha has few comparisons in India. Among the trio mentioned earlier, only Saha attempted something but he was not in Bhabha's class. True Saha did not command the influence that Bhabha did or the money. But as against this, we must remember that when Bhabha received his very first grant to start on cosmic-ray research in Bangalore, Saha too received money from the Dorab Tata Trust for building a cyclotron (it took many years before the cyclotron could be got working and by that time it had become obsolete). And Saha was in touch with Nehru from the late thirties on matters relating to science and technology planning. But after Independence, it was Bhabha who got ahead and made most of the opportunities offered to him, leaving Saha to retreat into opposition politics. Perhaps, having all along grown up in a revolutionary atmosphere, this was the natural inclination of Saha. Bhabha too started as a socialist and all that but when the time came, he left rhetoric behind and transformed himself into a corporate executive in the mould of the Tata clan. How his father would have delighted to see the son in this role! Until the end, Bhabha was second to none in his love for physics and mathematics but he also knew that a country becomes stronger through modern technology having native roots. And he knew how to push technology, as well as fight for the right administrative set-up for the growth of science and technology. In a nutshell, Bhabha brought "big science" to India.

Bhabha was a perfectionist. I recall a paper written by some of my colleagues which Bhabha was to communicate to the *Proceedings of the Indian Academy* for publication. Bhabha went through the manuscript carefully, scrutinising not only the scientific content but also catching spelling and grammatical errors. He also made suggestions for polishing up the text here and there. As Leyden remarks,

> Anything that was haphazard, casual, shoddy, would make him passionately angry ...

Here one sees some parallels with Chandra. The parallel also extends to matters of refined taste, liberal outlook and so forth. But whereas Chandra has been content to remain a connoisseur of art and music, Bhabha went so far as to design sets, make sketches and dabble in painting; certainly Bhabha moved much more with the art crowd than Chandra appears to have done. And when it came to architecture and landscaping, Bhabha seized the opportunities given to him to dream big. Altogether, he was as someone said, "one of the few 'universal men' of our age".

Bhabha was drawn to all the arts but music held a special place. And yet, music did not stand in isolation because, for him it was a reflection not only of the philosophy of the composer but indeed a commentary on the ethos of the times. Thus, about the power of Beethoven's music he writes:

> Mozart came at the end of an epoch; Beethoven at the beginning of another. It is Beethoven's birth after the French Revolution that

> explains the new force in his music and the new spirit of faith in human progress. In Mozart's time, the inequalities that were so strong had always existed and, in the mentality of those times, might have gone on always existing. In Beethoven's time, the French Revolution had shown that the inequalities of opportunity and class could be overcome and that the oppressed classes could be raised to a higher position. This eliminated the hopelessness of the spiritual atmosphere before the Revolution. This is one of the main reasons for the great power of the music of Beethoven and his heroic themes.

The marvellous fullness of Homi Bhabha's life and the extraordinary range of his achievements are neatly echoed in a letter he wrote to a friend in 1934. In it he said:

> I know quite clearly what I want out of life. Life and my emotions are the only things I am conscious of. I love the consciousness of life and I want as much of it as I can get. But the span of one's life is limited. What comes after death no one knows. Nor do I care. Since, therefore, I cannot increase the content of life by increasing its duration, I will increase it by increasing its intensity. Art, music, poetry and everything else that I do have this one purpose – increasing the intensity of my consciousness of life.

There is no better way I can end this book than by quoting the moving tribute paid by Lord Redcliffe-Maud (see Box 8.3 for other tributes). He said:

> Affectionate and sensitive, elegant and humorous, dynamic, one of the very few people who enhance life whatever the content of their living – fantastically talented but so fastidious about standards that he was never a dilettante. Whatever he set himself to do, he did as a professional – but one who worked for love; restlessly creative, enhancing life because he loved all forms of it. So he became a living proof that scientific excellence can go with excellence in art, and racial differences need be no bar to friendship. He stood out as a world citizen qualified in all three subjects – education, science and culture.

Box 8.2 Professor Sreekantan has this story.

> In January 1965, Dr. Bhabha spent a few weeks in Nilgiris on a holiday. He was staying at the Hampton Hotel at Coonoor ... On the last day of this holiday, he had left Coonoor by car, to

his home in Ooty when an important message came to his hotel on telephone from the DAE office at Bombay. Dr. Bhabha's P.A. who was still at the hotel received the message and immediately passed on the same to me over the phone. As soon as Dr. Bhabha arrived in Ooty, I got into his car and gave him the piece of paper in which I had written the message. He read it and gave the paper back to me saying, "it is still a confidential matter. So make sure you destroy this paper". To comply with his instructions I tore the paper into bits and put them out of the window. Immediately Dr. Bhabha reacted, "While you did well in tearing the paper into bits, you should not have thrown the bits out of the window of the car. You have cluttered the streets of Ooty".

Box 8.3 Collected together here are a few of the many tributes that have been paid to Bhabha, as also comments about his personality.

Sir John Cockroft F.R.S., N.L.

Shortly after the Geneva Conference the International Atomic Energy Agency (IAEA) was created and Homi Bhabha became a Governor. The choice of Vienna for its location was pressed by Homi Bhabha for obvious political reasons and perhaps also because he would be able to combine attendance at the Governor's meetings with the enjoyment of the opera and concerts in the evenings ...

One of Homi's characteristics was his apparent unawareness of the passage of time. He was meticulously punctual at the meetings of the U.N. Scientific Advisory Committee meetings chaired by Dag Hammerskjold [the Secretary General]; indeed if he had been half an hour late he might have found the meeting finished. The IAEA/SAC, however, was more discursive, and Homi Bhabha would often appear very late – so much so that the Secretary began to advertise the official time of the meeting half an hour before the real time. Homi would then appear in time for the beginning of the discussion – to the amusement of all.

C.F. Powell F.R.S., N.L.
Professor of Physics, Bristol University

Homi was surely, in a sense, a man out of his own time. He had the wide breadth of interests, the penetrating intellect, the abounding personal confidence in the ability of the human understanding, by observation and experiment, to unravel the secrets of Nature, which are characteristic of the great figures of the Renaissance. But perhaps such figures have an essential role to play in all ages.

Jerome B. Wiesner
Scientific Adviser to U.S.President John F. Kennedy

An eminent theoretical physicist, he [Bhabha] was also an artist of rare skill and feeling. A creative and effective administrator and a scientific leader, he was also an intensely sensitive and warm human being. Intent upon bringing India into the twentieth century, he was at the same time jealous of her cultural and religious heritage. He was a thoroughly modern man who kept a spiritual as well as a rational self and detected no incongruity in doing so.

Homi Bhabha was among the most broadly informed people I have ever known. He was as versed in Western culture as he was in that of his native land, and he derived joy and guidance from both. His own considerable talent as an artist made him especially sensitive to the beauty of his surroundings and the two institutions which he guided have a rare beauty reflecting this facet of his life.

J.R.D. Tata

The most outstanding of the distinguished men I have known was, undoubtedly, Homi Bhabha. In addition to the unique intellectual gifts Nature had bestowed on him, he was, in the mould of Jamsetji Tata, a visionary with the boldness, relentless energy and drive to convert his vision into reality. Homi was one of those who made me believe that some men in human history are born with the stamp of predestination on them which leads them to accomplishments beyond ordinary human capabilites. Some of them – and Homi, alas, was one – are also predestined to die young, an unconscious premonition which drives them to superhuman effort to complete their task in the short time allowed to them ...

Scientist, engineer, master-builder and administrator, steeped in humanities, in art and music, Homi was a truly complete man.

Indira Gandhi

He was a scientist of great originality. He was an artist endowed with unusual sensitivity. His interest in music was as serious as it was deep. The flower beds, the landscaping, the architecture of the buildings in Trombay, all bear witness to the keenness of Homi Bhabha's perception of colour, form and design.

India will long cherish Homi Bhabha's memory, for he was deeply involved in her destiny and in the process of changing the texture and quality of her society.

Index

Note: Page numbers in brackets refer to illustrations